GT
2420
.R57
2005

**Rituals and patterns
in children's
lives.**

$45.00

DATE			
	WITHDRAWN		

BAKER & TAYLOR

RITUALS AND PATTERNS IN
CHILDREN'S LIVES

A RAY AND PAT BROWNE BOOK

Series Editors
Ray B. Browne and Pat Browne

Rituals and Patterns in Children's Lives

EDITED BY

KATHY MERLOCK JACKSON

THE UNIVERSITY OF WISCONSIN PRESS
POPULAR PRESS

The University of Wisconsin Press
1930 Monroe Street
Madison, Wisconsin 53711

www.wisc.edu/wisconsinpress/

3 Henrietta Street
London WC2E 8LU, England

1   3   5   4   2

Printed in the United States of America

Library of Congress Cataloging-in-Publication Data
Rituals and patterns in children's lives /
edited by Kathy Merlock Jackson.
          p.   cm.
"A Ray and Pat Browne book."
Includes bibliographical references and index.
ISBN 0-299-20830-3 (hardcover: alk. paper)
        1. Family—United States.
      2. Rites and ceremonies—United States.
   3. Children—United States—Family relationships.
        4. United States—Social life and customs.
          I. Jackson, Kathy Merlock, 1955–
            GT2420.R57   2005
        306.4—dc22   2004025632

TO NICK WITH LOVE

AND THE HOPE

THAT YOU NEVER UNDERESTIMATE

THE IMPORTANCE OF RITUAL

CONTENTS

PREFACE AND ACKNOWLEDGMENTS

I began thinking about rituals when I was a child growing up in an Italian-Polish neighborhood on the outskirts of Pittsburgh. Every Sunday, members of my extended family would arrive at one for a dinner consisting, always, of pasta (though we never called it that), two meats, two vegetables, salad with vinegar and oil dressing, Italian bread, and a dessert to die for, usually a homemade pie or cake with ice cream, and freshly baked cookies on the side. My widowed great-uncle, who had lost his leg in the war and wore a prosthetic limb, always came, but every Sunday morning, my mother had to spend about fifteen minutes coaxing him to do so. After he ate, he promptly went into the living room and fell asleep. That, too, was part of the ritual. Holidays called for even more elaborate celebrations, such as the preparation of *fritelle,* orange-flavored dough, deep fried and rolled in sugar, for St. Joseph's Day and a neighborhood trick-or-treat each Halloween. On family occasions, such as a birthday, first communion, wedding, or funeral, there was always a clear blueprint of the way things were to be done and a story to go along with it. Ritual prevailed, establishing for me a rhythm no calendar could provide and a sense of who I was and what was important.

All children in America experience ritualized patterns, and this book addresses them—their history, function, and permutations in contemporary culture. Although many have lamented the loss of rituals, they have continued to flourish in both traditional and new ways, forming the glue that holds families, groups, and communities together and assuring children a place and a voice.

This project has been long in the making, and I thank those who helped me along the way. I can trace its beginning to a two-week January term course in wedding rituals that I team-taught with my colleague Eve Blachman. As the course progressed and we read and talked more about rituals, we began to see the possibilities in a book that collected essays on children's connections to rituals. Eve not only encouraged this work but also shaped it, acting as a sounding board and a consummate editor. It would not have reached completion without her.

I also appreciate the work of Barbara Hodges and Catherine Hartman, who prepared the manuscript at various stages and worked out the many graphic details. I will always appreciate their commitment to this volume.

The contributors to this book were a joy to work with, and I thank them not only for their thoughts and careful writing on childhood ritual but also for their patience and enthusiasm.

Finally, my colleagues at Virginia Wesleyan College offered their support, as did my family. Dad, Ray, Joe, and Nick have taught me much about the importance of rituals and of family, and they, along with the memory of my mother, will always be my inspiration for everything.

RITUALS AND PATTERNS IN
CHILDREN'S LIVES

Introduction

KATHY MERLOCK JACKSON

In any culture, rituals serve important functions. They bind together members of a family or community, transmit social values, contribute to one's sense of belonging and identity, provide for the continuity of traditions, acknowledge initiation, and celebrate the movement from one stage of life to another. At perhaps no time in one's life are rituals more prevalent, or more meaningful, than during childhood. Children in America participate in many rituals and from them receive influential first lessons regarding society's expectations, values, and roles. These experiences, met at times with anticipation or apprehension, serve as markers in a child's life, setting the stage for future perceptions, attitudes, and social connections.

The significance of rituals and patterns can perhaps be tied to a child's first experiences. Children are creatures of habit, and as early as infancy, they find comfort and pleasure in the familiar, especially the parent's face, voice, smell, and touch. Babies initially bond with their mothers, forming an important attachment that provides the foundation for a child's capacity for building later social relationships (Miller 151).

3

As Ainsworth and Mahler have shown, the attached parent functions as a "secure base" for exploration, establishing a home port from which the child ventures out to investigate the new, only to return occasionally for "emotional refueling" (quoted in Miller 363).

Later, as children grow older and begin the process of individuation, or differentiation of themselves from their mothers, they adopt "security objects," which serve to ease separation (Miller 151). As any parent or caregiver can attest, it is not unusual for a child to carry his or her favorite blanket or stuffed toy everywhere, until it is tattered beyond recognition; to insist on having the same picture book read night after night; or to prefer wearing a favorite sweater or hat. These familiar objects imbue a child with a sense of well-being; they inject order and regularity into the child's world.

Rituals function for children in very much the same way, providing patterns of meaningful, predictable events. Anna Quindlen captures this essence when she writes in *Living Out Loud,*

> tradition is the mainstay of my life. It keeps me whole. It is the centrifu-gal force that stops the pieces from shooting wildly into the void. The only way I can bear the changes that grind on inexorably around me is to pepper the year with those things that never change. Bath and books for the boys before bedtime. Homemade cakes on their birthdays. The beach in August. Chestnuts roasting on an open fire. (272–273)

Such patterns anchor the child. Thus, children, by forming attachments to people, things, and events, fulfill a necessary step in the developmental process and establish a security that prepares the groundwork for their future undertakings.

For the purposes of this book, a ritual can be described as an event in the life of a child that has cultural meaning and is experienced, in the same or variant forms, by other children. It can be regularly occurring or rendered by a special occasion. Rituals impose order on the chaotic existence of childhood. Certainly, traditional rituals have been defined and studied in different ways by many groups, especially sociologists, anthropologists, folklorists, and literary and religious studies scholars. As Eric W. Rothenbuhler writes in *Ritual Communication: From Everyday Conversation to Mediated Ceremony,* "There are, in the literature of ritual studies, almost as many definitions as authors" (7). Traditionally, rituals are linked to religion and myth. W. Robertson Smith, for example, regards ritual as "the core of religion, fixed and sacred, obligatory and meritorious" (quoted in de Waal Malefijt 187). In *The Elementary Forms of the Religious Life,* social theorist Emile Durkheim argues that rituals help to maintain social order through sentiment and solidarity. Among folklorists, ritual fits into the category of custom, which Jan Harold Brunvand defines as

> a traditional *practice*—a mode of individual behavior or a habit of social life—transmitted by word of mouth or imitation, then ingrained by social pressure, common usage, and parental or other authority. When customs are associated with holidays, they become *calendar customs;* and when such events are celebrated annually by a whole community, and especially over a period of several days, they become *festivals.* (406)

Brunvand observes that many rituals are associated with changes of status, or rites of passage (408). Ray Browne, in *Rituals and Ceremonies in Popular Culture,* comments on the evolution of ritual: "At first deeply based in and strengthened by the religious and quasi-religious attitudes, rituals and ceremonies in America have gradually changed through the years, as America, for various reasons, has changed its lifestyle in many ways and become more secularized" (1).

While definitions of ritual vary, they tend to share one commonality: whether religious or secular, rituals are powerful manifestations of a society's values. Childhood rituals, in particular, fit this description, but whose values do they manifest? Because many childhood rituals are engineered by adults, they fulfill an important purpose: to transmit cultural norms and expectations from one generation to the next, enabling elders to exert a subtle control over children's developing psyches. These patterns, then, can maintain social boundaries, reinforce social mores, and promulgate social taboos. For this reason, they have been criticized as leading to mindless adherence and stereotypical thinking. Robert Merton, for example, regards rituals as "meaningless routines, as unthinking habituated activities, or as . . . overly elaborated ceremonies" (quoted in Bird 19).

Despite conflicting views regarding their value, rituals and patterns of behavior in the history of childhood have remained central, undergoing continual evolution and reflecting changing views toward children. As childhood historians have noted, during the Middle Ages there were no children, only small adults, because no concept of childhood existed. Philippe Aries, a French historian whose *Centuries of Childhood: A Social History of Family Life* became a seminal work in the field, notes that at the beginning of modern times, and for a long time after that in the lower classes, children were mixed with adults as soon as they were considered capable of doing [so]. . . . They immediately went straight into the great community of men, sharing in the work and play of their companions, old and young alike. (411)

The arrival of the printing press in the fifteenth century slowly introduced a concept of childhood, defined as a necessary period of education during which the child learns to read (Postman 36). Still, by the time of the Puritans in the American colonies, parents remained intent on molding their children into pious, responsible little adults and punished them, sometimes harshly, if they failed to live up to expectations (Grylls 42). Due to the high child mortality rate, parents reasoned that children needed an adult sense of morality to guide them. This stance was reflected in a popular children's book of the period, James Janeway's *A Token for Children: Being an Exact Account of the Conversion, Holy and Exemplary Lives, and Joyful Deaths of Several Young Children* (1672), which warned that children "are not too little to die, they are not too little to go to Hell" (quoted in Grylls 42). It was not until the late eighteenth and early nineteenth centuries that this idea of childhood began to change.

The Romantic era brought with it a realization that every life was important and that the child, the embodiment of goodness and innocence, represents humanity in its most perfect state. As this concept took hold in America, childhood emerged as a special period of development, children were treated with greater tenderness, and the importance of family was espoused. In *A World of Their Own Making: Myth, Ritual, and the Quest for Family Values,* John R. Gillis expresses this new notion: "that every natural family deserves its own rituals and myths, its own history, its own roots" (13–14).

By the twentieth century, as Neil Postman notes, the concept of childhood in America hit a high watermark, and children were accorded

their own clothing their own furniture, their own literature, their own games, their own social world. In a hundred laws children were classified as qualitatively different from adults; in a hundred customs, assigned a preferred status and offered protection from the vagaries of adult life. (67)

As children became more valued and families became more child-centered, rituals were enacted for the sake of the child; thus, along with the establishment of childhood came many of its distinctive rites of passage and celebrations. Not surprisingly, children's parties, such as birthday parties and tea parties, were first established and popularized during this historical period (Day, Edens, and Poltarnees 72).

As the history of childhood emphasizes, children have never lived in isolation, neither practically nor ideologically; hence, although they are not powerful figures, they have nevertheless influenced, as well as been influenced by, adults (Hiner and Hawes xxi). Given this reciprocal relationship, investigation into childhood rituals and patterns helps to explain the child's role in many social groups, especially family, community, church, school, and peers. The family, of course, controls the child's first rituals, designed to enhance the child's sense of family identity and belonging and his or her knowledge of traditional texts, customs, lore, and artifacts (Brunvand 56). In America's many ethnic communities, the same function is at work, as neighborhoods provide arenas for learning old traditions and assimilating new ones (62). Finally, as members of a religious group, children may participate in rites of passage that solidify their inclusion in the family's chosen faith (such as a baptism or first communion in Christian denominations). By partaking in these rituals, children are taken into the fold, made participants of the life and lore of the family, community, or religious group, where they, too, influence events.

It is important to note that children, sometimes operating in a preliterate state, learn these patterns through observation and imitation, and their desire for order and predictability may necessitate almost obsessive convention. Folklorist Jan Brunvand recalls collecting materials from children "in which some items are transmitted completely by word of mouth in an atmosphere of great textual conservationism—as any adult who has changed the wording of a bedtime story or tried to instruct a child in the 'right way' to play a game like kick the can knows" (54–55). Thus, even if an adult chooses to modify a ritual, the child may insist on the familiar.

As children grow older and connect with their neighborhood and school peers, however, their rituals and patterns of behavior often change, becoming more child-initiated and sometimes clashing with family norms. This phenomenon is apparent in Jack Santino's childhood recollections of Halloween:

> As a young child, I was escorted on my trick-or-treating adventures by members of my immediate family, either a parent or an older sister. As

I got older, perhaps about ten years of age, I began to trick-or-treat with a group of friends from my street. When I reached early adolescence, about the age of twelve or thirteen, I continued to go out with a group of friends on Halloween, but the friends were from school, the territory we walked was larger, and we no longer rang doorbells to ask for (or demand) treats. Instead we made mischief, soaping the occasional car window or throwing the occasional egg. (xxv)

As Santino shows, the Halloween ritual functions as a rite of passage for older children, offering them opportunities to break away from the family, connect with their peers, and commit pranks on one day of the year that such subversive behavior is expected and, generally, socially sanctioned.

Is this ritual adult-initiated or child-initiated or, perhaps, both? Certainly, children act without adult supervision when running amok each Halloween; however, by doing so they are imitating behavior practiced by many youths who preceded them, possibly their own parents, who may condone the behavior because they did it, too. Rituals, then, suggest a continuum of influence as traditions are passed down; however, successive generations may respond to and interpret them in new ways.

Childhood peer group and play rituals, such as Santino's mischief making, are often gender-specific, establishing a child's gender identity and, at the same time, perpetuating stereotypical roles. Little girls' ritualistic play with Barbie dolls (centering on finding the right products to achieve the right look) and boys' with G.I. Joe, wrestlers or other action figures (emphasizing the need to be strong and powerful) also support this.

The study of childhood rituals also sheds light on the passage of time in a child's life, how one's day and year are structured, how predictable patterns and events shape the totality of childhood experience. Welleran Poltarnees suggests this in his introduction to *Children from the Golden Age, 1830–1930,* a collection of illustrations from children's books built around the theme of a child's day:

All existence is rhythmical, but this civilization, more than most, is aware of an underlying rhythm, and arranges matters in obedience to it. The seasons are embraced, their influences ritualized. Clothing exaggerates the changes, and holidays emphasize pattern and return. The days are performed to a metronome's pulse. Mornings are emphatic beginnings, celebrating the reawakening of the world. Afternoons are long and quiet. Buzzing insects or falling rain are their music. Clocks tick in every home. Nights are the time for the pulse of life to show—whispers, spluttering lamps, reading, drowsiness, sleep. (Day, Edens, and Poltarnees 6)

Such is the routine of childhood, at least sentimentalized in memory. Young children have no grasp of time; they structure their lives by events, both routine and special, predictable and mundane—going to bed, losing a tooth, telling a story.

In particular, child-centered rituals, often associated with holidays and celebrations, give children something to look forward to; they acknowledge the child's importance as well as his or her milestones. As Simon J. Bronner writes in *American Children's Folklore,*

> Children have great expectations of birthdays, Halloween, and Christmas in America, for they are filled with the exuberance of youth and the thrill of consumption. They are times when the child is at the center of attention among other children, and gets to act out cultural priorities of her or his world. The small circles of children's culture also are acted out in private rituals unrelated to national holidays. Being stuck in the back seat of a car looking out into traffic, listening at dinner to two persons saying the same thing simultaneously, breaking the wishbone of a turkey—all of these occasions offer children a chance to express themselves. (168)

Rituals offer children a continuum of predictable experiences; thus, it can be said that when a child has progressed through the requisite rituals, childhood is over.

Of all childhood occasional rituals, one of the most repeated and anticipated is the birthday, celebrated in the midst of both family and friends and accompanied by behaviors that do not occur on any other day. As Brunvand writes,

> Children's birthdays almost invariably are the occasion for spanking, one spank for each year, with extras "to grow on" or "for good measure." Children in some regions maintain a fairly rigid schedule of extra-punishment days before and after the birthday anniversary— "pinch day," "hit day," "kiss day," and so forth. Blowing out birthday-cake candles and wishing are standard customs, sometimes varied by naming the candles for possible marriage partners and assuming that the last candle smoking marks the mate. Birthday gifts at a party may be held over the head of the celebrating child for him or her to guess the donor or to announce the use to which that gift is to be put. For each correct guess, the child is granted a wish. (408–409)

The many patterns associated with children's birthdays in America and the costs that accompany lavish parties reinforce the value that our culture places on children and the celebrations that signal each stage in their development.

Exploring these rituals of childhood helps us to understand cultural change. While some speculate that ritualized patterns in American society are waning, nothing could be further from the truth. However, they are in flux, reflecting the rise of single-parent and blended families, changing trends in careers and lifestyles, the digital explosion, and the power of American mass culture.

Today, especially, it is fitting that we study childhood and the rituals associated with it. As the *Chronicle of Higher Education* reported in its August 7, 1998, cover story on the "booming interest" in children's culture studies, in the late twentieth century "scholars, like everyone else, seem to be obsessed with children" (Heller A14). This movement, characterized by a proliferation of new texts in the field, reflects several current research trends. First is scholarly inquiry into the future, triggered by millennial anxiety (A5). Because children function as symbols of the future at a time when we are obsessed with it, they have moved to the forefront of research. Second is a need to study the less powerful in society. Just as women, minorities, and gays have often been marginalized or ignored in mainstream research, so too have children, who are often difficult subjects for study because they lack sophisticated verbal ability (Hiner and Hawes xv). Revisionists seek to correct this omission by telling their story. Third is the growing interest in psychohistory and emotional history, both of which acknowledge the influence of children's early experiences and feelings. Fourth is a regard among folklorists for the work of Peter and Iona Opie, Herbert Knapp, Jack and Olivia Solomon, Brian Sutton-Smith, and Simon Bronner, whose many volumes chronicle the folklore and traditions of the child's world. Finally is a growing awareness, in our highly technical and consumerist society, of both the effects of media on children and the increased media attention given to sensational crimes in which children are the perpetrators or victims. Such exposure places greater attention on children and the issues that dominate their lives.

Another reason children's culture studies have attained prominence corresponds to two related demographic trends: the baby boom and the "baby boom echo" (Russakoff A4). As Landon Y. Jones reports in *Great Expectations*, between 1946 and 1964 over 76 million babies were born in

America, creating one of the greatest postwar baby booms the world has ever known (2). These baby boomers, today in their thirties, forties, and fifties, are reaching the higher echelons of academe, while at the same time confronting the demands and often guilts associated with juggling parenthood and careers. They are also reliving, through their offspring, their own childhoods. As professional and personal lives dovetail, the result is a certain self-absorption and more research geared to issues of childhood (Heller A14–15).

At the same time that baby boomers comprise the bulk of the scholarly community, more children are entering the picture. As Dale Russakoff of the *Washington Post* reported in July 1998,

> Nobody knows precisely which child deserves the credit, but within the past year, the population of children in the United States rose beyond the peak of the baby boom. The generation of children younger than 18 has grown from 69.5 million in mid-1997 to 70.2 million today, according to the Census Bureau, surpassing the high of 69.9 million set in 1996. And unlike the baby boom that began in 1946, this one shows no sign of ending. (A4)

Dubbed the Millennium Generation, these children may well look different from their predecessors: according to the Census Bureau, 88 percent of the under-eighteen population between 2000 and 2050 will be children of immigrants (A4), a group likely to practice rich ethnic rituals as a way of maintaining connections to their cultural heritage. As the number of children in America increases and more immigrant children are assimilated, additional research into childhood, and the traditions associated with it, is warranted.

This volume addresses that need. Although no book could be so comprehensive as to cover all rituals and patterns of childhood, the fourteen essays collected here are divided into seven categories, with two complementary essays in each, exploring a wide range of children's experiences. They highlight behaviors that may be historic or current, daily or once in a lifetime, gender-specific or gender-neutral, and common to all children or limited to a small religious or ethnic group. Although some of the childhood rituals and patterns profiled are more rare than mainstream, all have been practiced at one time or another by children in America and, as such, demonstrate the rich texture of American culture. Interdisciplinary in nature, the collection represents several different styles of scholarship and methods of inquiry, including autobiographical reminiscence, literary criticism, image deconstruction, historiography, audience analysis, and social science methodology.

At the center of each essay lies the same question: What is the function of rituals and patterns in the lives of American children? Perhaps, by studying the events that structure children's lives, we can better understand how personal sensibilities, social connections, and cultural values develop over time. We can also ascertain how childhood experiences establish character. Rituals and patterns defy easy definition or explanation. They are always changing, in response to shifting paradigms in family, community, and national cultures; nevertheless, they remain powerful agents of self-identity. Childhood remains a universal life experience. And when all is said and done, what we remember most about childhood are its rituals.

WORKS CITED

Aires, Philippe. *Centuries of Childhood: A Social History of Family Life*. Trans. Robert Baldick. New York: Vintage Books, 1962.

Bird, Richard. "The Contemporary Ritual Milieu." In *Rituals and Ceremonies in Popular Culture*, ed. Ray B. Browne. Bowling Green, OH: Bowling Green State University Popular Press, 1980.

Bronner, Simon J., ed. *American Children's Folklore*. Little Rock, AR: August House, 1988.

Browne, Ray B. "Ritual One." In *Rituals and Ceremonies in Popular Culture*, ed. Ray B. Browne. Bowling Green, OH: Bowling Green State University Popular Press, 1980.

Brunvand, Jan Harold. *The Study of American Folklore*. New York: Norton, 1998.

Day, Alexandra, Cooper Edens, and Welleran Poltarnees . *Children from the Golden Age, 1880–1930*. San Diego: Green Tiger Press, 1987.

de Waal Malefijt, Annemarie. *Religion and Culture*. London: Macmillan, 1968.

Durkheim, Emile. *The Elementary Forms of Religious Life*. Trans. J. W. Swain. New York: Free Press, 1965; first published 1912.

Gillis, John R. *A World of Their Own Making: Myth, Ritual, and the Quest for Family Values*. New York: Basic Books, 1996.

Grylls, David. *Guardians and Angels: Parents and Children in Nineteenth-Century Literature*. Boston: Faber & Faber, 1978.

Heller, Scott. "The Meaning of Children in Culture Becomes a Focal Point for Scholars." *Chronicle of Higher Education*, 7 August 1998, A14–15.

Hiner, N. Ray, and Joseph M. Hawes, eds. Introduction to *Growing Up in America*. Urbana: University of Illinois Press, 1985.

Jones, Landon Y. *Great Expectations: America and the Baby-Boom Generation*. New York: Ballentine, 1980.

Miller, Patricia H. *Theories of Developmental Psychology*. New York: W. H. Freeman, 1983.

Postman, Neil. *The Disappearance of Childhood*. New York: Vintage Books, 1994.

Quindlen, Anna. *Living Out Loud*. New York: Random House, 1988.

Rothenbuhler, Eric W. *Ritual Communication: From Everyday Conversation to Mediated Ceremony*. Thousand Oaks, CA: Sage, 1998.

Russakoff, Dale. "Focus: The Millennium Generation." *Virginian-Pilot*, 7 July 1998, A4. Reprinted from the *Washington Post*.

Santino, Jack. *Halloween and Other Festivals of Death and Life*. Knoxville: University of Tennessee Press, 1994.

PART I

FAMILY

Children learn patterns of behavior in the context of family. From parents, siblings, grandparents, and other members of the extended family, children learn to be a part of an intimate group. Children's birthday celebrations, which begin at age one and typically last through elementary school, involve family members in often lavish events and highlight the emphasis that America places on its youth. Children gain a sense of their own importance and niche within the family structure.

Each family's rituals vary, reflecting a particular system of values. For example, a family that celebrates scholastic achievement may mark various events in the school year: home-baked cookies on the first day of school, dinners at a favorite restaurant to reward children for good report cards, and a last-day-of-school party to signify the need to relax after an intensive year of work. Other families may center their events around children's or professional sporting events, holiday or seasonal activities, or vacations and leisure-time ventures. Sometimes childhood rituals link only certain members of a family, such as a father taking his son on a hunting trip each autumn, thereby transmitting lessons about the father-son bond, nature and survival, and guns and violence.

The two essays in this section demonstrate the diversity of this volume. The first, Anne Tuominen's "The Endurance of Ethnic Family Rituals," takes a sociological approach and speaks to the melting pot that is American culture, emphasizing how ethnic foods, holiday celebrations, and traditional gender expectations shape a child's sense of identity and belonging. Mark I. West's reminiscence, "Stories My Father Told Me," shows how a ritualistic reading of literature helps a child to better understand his father as well as develop his own aesthetic sense. In both cases, patterns initiated by family members provide children's earliest and most indelible patterns.

I

The Endurance of
Ethnic Family Rituals

ANNE TUOMINEN

As children, many of us participated in family rituals that connected us not only to our immediate families but also to broader ethnic, cultural, or religious communities.[1] Irish-style corned beef and cabbage dinners or Hanukkah celebrations have been as much a part of American childhoods as camping trips and Fourth of July fireworks. In fact, ethnic family rituals are as important as ever, especially among children whose generations are far removed from the immigrant experience and whose ethnic ties are weakest. In contrast, immigrant children and children of immigrants have often been more resistant to family rituals that distinguish them ethnically. What explains the endurance of ethnic family rituals among descendants of immigrants, especially in late-twentieth-century American society? How and why do we establish ethnic family rituals? What makes rituals that connote ethnicity so important?

The ethnic nature of family rituals *is* an especially American tradition. When the first immigrants arrived in North America, all they had in terms of ritual experiences was what they knew from their childhoods.[2] Some of their family rituals were modified to fit their new environment

and the availability of appropriate supplies, but these rituals nevertheless reflected the British and, later, Irish or German ethnic backgrounds
of the immigrants. Had these immigrants stayed in their homelands,
they would have practiced similar rituals, but the ethnic connotations
would not have been so notable since everyone else would have been of
the same ethnicity and would have practiced similar rituals. The ethnic
content of their family rituals only stands out because they were in an
environment in which other ethnicities were present.

Although ethnic family rituals are especially common in immigrant
societies such as the United States, family rituals in general are typical in
young families with children across all societies. Often, having children
is the reason that parents establish family rituals in the first place, and
they do so because they want to transfer family and other identities to
their children. Childless families and adult families do practice rituals,
but the rituals occurring in families with young children, especially
when these family rituals connote ethnicity, are quite powerful. Ethnic
family rituals link children to their family's origins and values, and give
children a sense of family continuity.[3]

How immigrant families establish ethnic family rituals reveals a
great deal about the salience of such rituals in both immigrant societies
and young families. Immigration is, after all, one source of changing ritual forms,[4] and thus it impacts how ethnic family rituals come about and
how they look. In addition, immigrant families often have special rituals
connecting them not only to particular ethnic identities but also to linguistic ones. Language is an important marker of ethnicity, and rituals
associated with language use may also say something about the importance of ethnic rituals. Finally, immigrant family rituals transmit ethnic
or cultural values about gendered norms and roles. Research on immigrant and multilingual families allows an exploration of these issues.

Family Rituals in General

Ritual can be defined generally as "a pattern of prescribed formal behavior, pertaining to some specific event, occasion, or situation, which
tends to be repeated over and over again."[5] As such, rituals are not natural, but social. Societies—that is, people—construct rituals of all kinds
in order to create stability and solidarity in their institutions. Family rituals are just one category of rituals created by all societies.[6] Many of

these family rituals follow the same form, too, of celebrations, traditions, or patterned interactions.[7] It is the content of family rituals and the commitment to them that vary, from society to society, family to family. In other words, family rituals serve common functions across all cultures, even if the content of these rituals differs. In fact, the content is what provides information about families' distinct ethnic or cultural backgrounds and values.

Many family rituals come about in the presence of children, just like many childhood rituals occur within the context of family.[8] The birth of a couple's first child is usually the catalyst for establishing deliberate family rituals, such as reading bedtime stories on a nightly basis. Actually, the process of family ritual establishment often precedes childbearing, because adults usually go through negotiations over rituals when they first form couples, when they leave behind their families-of-origin and join households. These negotiations intensify when the couples become parents; then, family rituals get more clearly defined, enacted, and even disputed.[9] These new parents strive to establish family rituals with their children that identify and symbolize the meanings of family with which they themselves are familiar or at least comfortable. Usually these rituals are an amalgam of rituals from families-of-origin and families-of-procreation.

Family rituals, especially those established in families with young children, have many functions. They socialize children about what family means. They set boundaries around the family and teach children about the roles they are to play in their family. Formal rituals associated with rites of passage, such as christenings or first communions, also give meaning to children's lives by teaching them about the human life cycle of birth, maturity, and death. Simple, mundane, and spontaneously created rituals such as taking regular family walks or enjoying a weekly Sunday dinner help children identify with the meaning of family and enhance their sense of belonging and solidarity.

Additionally, some research suggests that family rituals can be potentially important indicators of marital satisfaction and successful transitions to adulthood.[10] Other findings point to family rituals as important stabilizers in times of family trauma, whether such trauma is caused by divorce, death, or pathological behaviors such as alcohol abuse.[11] Family rituals, such as gift giving, allow us to bolster vulnerable familial relationships by reaffirming these relationships periodically.[12] Family rituals also seem to transmit family and culture-specific norms of gender, such as when mothers cook the daily meals but fathers barbecue on special occasions; indeed, rituals and ceremonial occasions often create and reinforce our identities as gendered individuals.[13] And, as will become clear, family rituals can be the means by which ethnic identity and heritage are passed down from parents to children.

Finally, family rituals also reflect the importance of families to society. In fact, the importance of the institution of family in the United States is reflected by the relative newness of the concepts of "family ritual" and "family time," both of which became popular and significant only in the twentieth century.[14] Even the "family rituals" of the late twentieth century are relatively new, such as Thanksgiving celebrations or birthday celebrations, and don't represent historical continuity as thoroughly as participants believe. Celebrating Thanksgiving or the Fourth of July might have brought families together in the past, but the focus of these rituals was on civic solidarity, not individual family solidarity. Rituals have often helped establish political situations and alliances, and in the case of these "American" rituals, they helped create a civic awareness and solidarity about what it means to be an American. Only when American society modernized, fertility rates dropped, and the boundaries defining family became less clear due to new working and coupling arrangements did "family rituals" become popular. As family forms and identities change with corresponding societal changes, it becomes important to clearly delineate what society means by "family." One way to do this is to mark certain practices as family practices and to establish family routines that signify the boundaries of family units.[15] Clearly, given all their various functions, family rituals, especially as they occur in young families, are quite "loaded" with meaning and purpose.

How Do Ethnic Rituals Come About in Families?

To understand and explore the ethnic roots of family rituals, the experiences of eighteen multilingual families in Seattle, Washington, are considered. These families were part of an original study about language choices and were all multilingual, with one or both parents also being immigrants to the United States.[16] The immigrant parents' ethnic and linguistic backgrounds were Chinese, Filipino, French, German, Japanese, Korean, Norwegian, Russian, Swedish, Swiss, and Turkish. For these parents, language choice was an important issue because their native languages were so closely tied to their ethnic identities. Not surprisingly, many wanted to pass down their language to their children. However, these immigrant parents were also actively involved with establishing what might be called "ethnic" family rituals—celebrations, traditions, and patterned interactions that reflect a cultural or ethnic background and language different from that of the mainstream society in which the families lived. Many parents used culture-specific family rituals with their children. For example, a Swedish mother and her American-bred son baked Swedish cookies together to share at the son's school, while a Chinese couple with an American-born daughter celebrated Chinese New Year. However, ritual establishment was a far more complicated process for these parents and their families than it is for American-born-and-raised parents.

Like all parents, immigrant parents go through periods of ritual negotiations when they first become parents. They borrow from their own childhood rituals because these are what they know, and on another level, these connect them to their original home and kin. However, setting up family or childhood rituals is more challenging for immigrant parents because their family rituals may have little in common with those of mainstream society and thus may not be well supported outside the family home. Whether the parents are establishing these rituals deliberately or serendipitously, the rituals are taking place in a cultural context that is different from the one in which they themselves were raised. The stories that immigrant parents tell their children, the foods they prepare together, the songs they sing—all may be completely foreign to the society in which they live.

Because the meanings and enactment of immigrant family rituals may not be supported by the existing societal and cultural framework, immigrant parents are often challenged when they try to establish their own rituals. How can they set up and perpetuate rituals that are so foreign in their new society? How do they get the supplies or materials they need to celebrate certain holidays? Where do they get the support for their cultural values? A Korean mother in my study voiced the challenges that she faced from "liberal" American culture and the fears she had about disciplining her children according to Korean norms:

KOREAN MOTHER: Sometimes I have problems . . .
INTERVIEWER: How do you mean?

KOREAN MOTHER: . . . I want to raise my children in Korean culture, to
    respect elders and . . . I think American culture is too liberal. But it's very
    difficult. That's why I send her to the [Korean] church.
INTERVIEWER: I understand. It is impossible not to have American culture
    though . . . how does your husband feel about this, raising in Korean
    culture?
KOREAN MOTHER: He likes it more than I do [she smiles]. He doesn't
    approve of how American children are raised. They're too free.
INTERVIEWER: Yes. But for children, it is difficult to be different . . .
KOREAN MOTHER: For American children, you can't discipline them. If
    you hit, it's child abuse, they can call the police. You can hit (it's not like
    beating), in Korea. Here, when you're 18, you're on your own.

Some of the challenges from the new culture come by way of the
children in these immigrant families, many of whom are American-
born and all of whom are being raised in American society. These children experience peer pressure to conform and may prefer to participate
in the rituals that represent American family life. So the family negotiations about rituals become intergenerational; children introduce their
parents to "American" rituals that they have learned about in school or
from their peers. For example, many immigrant children or children of
immigrants learn about North American–style Christmas with its Santa
Claus, decorated fir tree, and gift giving. In fact, Christmas seems to be
a big favorite in many immigrant families, often regardless of the
families' religious backgrounds,[17] as a Turkish mother explained:

INTERVIEWER: Do you celebrate Christmas now?
TURKISH MOTHER: I have a friend in Canada who's an authentic, traditional
    Moslem. I consider myself very liberal, on the fringe. They [the friend's
    family] had refused to celebrate Christmas, but their son came home
    from school one day in tears. He said he was a bad boy, because Santa
    didn't come to his house. They changed after this. I give her credit for
    doing this. It's an occasion I enjoy. I never thought of holding it back to
    be culturally pure.

Other children force negotiations over rituals by refusing to participate in certain rituals that differ too much from "American" rituals.
The Korean mother mentioned earlier who felt challenged by the dis-
parities between her cultural norms and those of America was challenged by her daughter as well.

KOREAN mother: When she's [the daughter] doing something with her friends we don't allow, she knows it. We can't tell her in English she shouldn't do it. We say it in Korean and she knows but says she can't understand. She turns off her ears. She knows she's doing something wrong, but she pretends she can't understand, if she doesn't want to hear. Sometimes it's frustrating . . .

Thus, not only was the mother worried about the possibility of being reported for child abuse because the "Korean" way of disciplining doesn't correspond to what is appropriate in the United States, but she was also frustrated because her daughter sometimes refused to follow and listen to the parents' rules.

The mainstream culture and the accompanying rituals might also infiltrate the immigrant home through one of the parents. When both parents are immigrants of the same nationality (or share the same religion or language, for that matter), establishing the family rituals will be easier because of similar cultural understandings. The Korean wife and husband who both agreed that American culture is too permissive are a case in point. However, many immigrant parents have native American spouses, and in the original study the non-immigrant spouses varied greatly in their understanding and connection with their immigrant spouses' cultural and linguistic backgrounds. Some spouses were very interested in maintaining the familial and culturally distinctive traditions of their immigrant spouse and even knew about many of their traditions, whereas others were more passive in their support. The American husband described below participated in and understood some of the finer points of his wife's traditional Japanese rituals and celebrations, but he was less involved in some of the mundane daily rituals she wanted, such as eating Japanese food or reading Japanese books to their daughter:

INTERVIEWER: When I look around I see some things that are very Japanese. This looks like a Japanese home. How do you make it Japanese? Do you prepare Japanese foods? I noticed you were eating Miso soup, weren't you?

JAPANESE MOTHER: Yes, but Tim doesn't like fish and so much of Japanese food is fish. So dinner is not really Japanese. I'll share lunch with the [Japanese] neighbors next door.

INTERVIEWER: Well, do you take your shoes off at the door?

JAPANESE MOTHER: Yes. *[She thought for awhile and then pointed to this large*

ornamental stage that had two Japanese dolls on it as if on an altar.] We have
this. Those are like bride and groom. After March 3 we have to put it
back. It's a Japanese tradition, like a festival. Before March 3 you open
it and after, you close it. If it's not closed, then the person won't get
married soon. Tim wants [our daughter] to stay home always and
doesn't want to close it yet!

When the parents are of two very different cultural backgrounds, the
negotiations over family rituals are between rituals originating in two
different families-of-origin that existed in entirely different cultural
frameworks.

Clearly, immigrant parents experience a host of challenges to their
efforts to set up family rituals that are meaningful to them. How do they
cope? Most have to adjust and often do so by creating a hybrid set of
family rituals for their children that combine not only rituals from two
families-of-origin but also rituals from two cultures. Examples of such
rituals might include celebrations combining elements of American
Christmas and Chinese New Year. Even mundane rituals such as what
to eat for dinner and what books to read with one's children often require adjustment. For example, many immigrant parents reported that
they read to their children in both English and their native tongue. The
members of one Russian family explained how they ate Russian foods
often but also enjoyed "American" cuisine and were buying their food
supplies from an especially American source—the ubiquitous bulk-
food warehouse!

INTERVIEWER: Do you eat Russian food at home?
BOTH RUSSSIAN PARENTS: Yes . . .
INTERVIEWER: Like what?
RUSSSIAN MOTHER: . . . potatoes . . . what I cooked in Russia I cook here.
RUSSSIAN FATHER: She started to cook other . . .
RUSSSIAN MOTHER: I do lasagna . . .
RUSSSIAN FATHER: . . . some Italian and some Chinese foods at home.
RUSSSIAN DAUGHTER: Borscht.
INTERVIEWER: [That's] a Russian food, okay!
RUSSSIAN FATHER: We get most [food] from Costco warehouse.

Other adjustments to rituals are also in response to pressures from
outside the family. One mother pointed out that some of the ritualistic
adaptations her family had made were purely economic; she had to
work to support her family whereas other Korean mothers generally
would not work outside the home. Indeed, some families must adjust

economically while others adjust to environmental conditions and the availability of certain foods or other supplies; all of these adjustments change the look of family rituals and practices.[18]

How Do Language Rituals Foster a Sense of Family?

Childhood and family rituals do often connect us to an ethnicity or ethnic community, and this implies also a connection to a linguistic community. For example, taking part in Halloween festivities connects us to American culture and gives us a vocabulary of "witches, goblins, ghosts" that ties us to an American-English language community. However, in most assimilated American families, family language rituals are seldom deliberately organized because family members all speak English more or less automatically at home and outside the home. In contrast, immigrant or non-native English-speaking parents who wish to give their children an ethnic connection may seek to establish particular language rituals in the home.

In fact, some immigrant family rituals do involve the conscious use of the parents' native languages, and this is related to the parents' quest to make some connection to their ethnic heritage. One such ritual involves speaking the parents' native language during family interactions or within the family home. Many parents in the study indicated that they had firm rules about what languages were to be spoken at home and in which circumstances. A bilingual American father whose wife is Korean was very specific about his family's language ritual in the home:

INTERVIEWER: What language do you two speak to each other?
AMERICAN FATHER: Korean. *[Korean wife nods head in agreement.]*
INTERVIEWER: When you're all together here at home, which language do you speak?
AMERICAN FATHER: Korean. Always Korean at home.

When this family was outside the home, the language rituals changed:

INTERVIEWER: What about if you are out somewhere and you need to say something to [your daughter]—do you say it in Korean or English?
AMERICAN FATHER: In English. I find it rude when people are speaking a foreign language around others. They think someone is talking about them. I do it for their benefit, not [for my daughter's].

Despite the well-articulated language "rules" of many families, the actual enactment of these rules or rituals was weak. Instead, the more commonly enacted rituals in these families were those that actually emphasized cultural traditions or values, rather than everyday language use. For example, some children participated in Saturday language schools, others visited relatives in the parents' native countries, and still others occasionally watched special videos or television broadcasts in their parents' native languages. They also participated in rituals involving traditional "ethnic" food or holiday preparations. Indeed, the cultural emphasis seems to have been more important than the language, as a Korean mother suggested in her rationale for using a Korean nanny: "The reason to have a Korean baby-sitter is, culturally, I feel better. She knows how I'm raising my children; I don't have to give instructions."

On the whole, at the time of the original study, many parents were not particularly successful in passing down their language to their children.[19] This is partly due to the social traits of many immigrant parents and to the ability of their children to gain an upper hand in power within the family because of their burgeoning English language skills and knowledge of the American lifestyle.[20] Because of these sociological forces, many parents cannot employ the language maintenance strategies that would likely yield the most positive results, such as staying at home to expose their children to the language as much as possible, or having a large supply of appropriate and attractive reading materials and videos, or spending significant amounts of time visiting family in the "old country."

However, immigrant parents may be relieved to know that even if they are unsuccessful at establishing language rituals with their children, the ethnic rituals are still quite important. After all, studies of immigrant children show that "immigrant students who retained strong cultural and family identity tended to outpace others in school," and this finding is probably as true for children of immigrants as it is for immigrant children.[21] Second, ethnic rituals might contribute in a small way to children's language learning because they provide children with a context in which their parent's native language is usable or salient. Helping a Filipino mom prepare chicken adobo provides opportunities to use Tagalog, just as playing children's games at a Japanese Saturday School allows Japanese conversation.

Third, rituals that emphasize ethnicity rather than language often do stay with children, even as they grow to adulthood. Mothers who sang songs from their own childhood or recited rhymes in their native tongues may find that their adult children continue to remember these "ethnic" rituals fondly and may continue them yet in the following generation:

SWEDISH MOTHER: You know, to this day, the children only relate to Swedish nursery rhymes. I didn't know any others. They are so deprived. Even now I'll recite one to Leonard and he'll smile.

Even in families where parents had decided to stop celebrating the holidays to the extent they had in earlier years, the grown children were often not ready to abandon their childhood rituals. This same Swedish mother who taught her children nursery rhymes pointed out how her grown children were actually loath to give up other Swedish rituals:

SWEDISH MOTHER: The kids are very interested in ham and having a Christmas tree. I am ready to stop that, but the children won't give let me give it up. . . . We had the Christmas tree with lights and a whole pig for Swedish Christmas dinner! Now when I try to get rid of this, the family refuses. It is their heritage. [My daughter] was not going to give this up. . . . Swedish Christmas is very important to them; it is part of their heritage.

So, while it is disappointing for many parents that their children do not have a good command of the parents' native language, at least the ethnic content of the childhood or family rituals may benefit their children. Also, ethnically tinged family rituals are often remembered nostalgically and passed down in some form to successive generations. In cyclical fashion, then, family rituals are the fodder young adults and new parents use to establish new rituals. Immigrant parents, like all parents, may be gratified to see that their efforts to instill meaningful rituals are reproduced in the next generation.

How Does Gender Play into Ethnic Family Rituals?

Gender is a component of many family rituals because many such rituals are organized around gender-specific scripts. For example, Coltrane suggests that the American Thanksgiving ritual is highly gendered: women do the background work, preparing the food, while the men have the turkey-carving honors and then retire to watch football.[22] Additionally, women—mothers and wives—tend to be the kin keepers and tradition setters in families, so the establishment of rituals is primarily a feminine task.[23]

How is gender reproduced in specifically *ethnic* family rituals? Among the multilingual families in the study, when the mother/wife was the immigrant, she had a better chance of bringing in her childhood family rituals than did an immigrant father. Even if the immigrant mother was married to a non-immigrant or someone of a different ethnic background, her childhood family rituals were more strongly represented in the family's rituals. Why is this the case? Simply, mothers are more likely to be more involved in their children's upbringing and will likely spend more time with the children. In the case of a Chinese-German family living in the United States, the Chinese mother was more successful in establishing Chinese rituals with her child than was her German husband in establishing German rituals. Consistent with other cases, she spent more time with the child, and time spent with the child strongly influences which parents' ethnic rituals prevail.

Indeed, when fathers are the immigrant parents, they often have a harder time establishing ethnic rituals, primarily because of their breadwinner status. One Norwegian father pointed out that his American wife had helped set up some Norwegian rituals, but that he had often been too busy even to speak Norwegian to his children:

INTERVIEWER: When they were younger, did you speak Norwegian to them?
NORWEGIAN FATHER: I didn't; I didn't spend enough time at home. You know, children, they get up at seven in the morning and go to bed at seven at night. I didn't see them very much. In the first couple years, I needed to speak English, so my wife and I spoke English. I have been terribly busy the past 21 years. I was very busy and stressed. There wasn't much time.

Clearly, when fathers, immigrants or non-immigrants, spend much time away from their families, they have fewer opportunities to establish rituals from their own background. For absentee immigrant fathers, however, the cost of lost parenting opportunities may be higher. Often, the only way children can connect to their father's ethnic family rituals is by personal initiative or perhaps by visiting the father's native country.

Not only is the transmission process gendered, but the content of ethnic family rituals is also relevant from a gender perspective. Many rituals send messages to children about the gender norms and roles of a particular culture. For example, during the interview of the Chinese-German family mentioned above, the family's young son became increasingly fussy and was taken to bed by the German father. The Chinese mother explained that the father always took the boy upstairs to change him and put him to sleep for the night because she took the baby up the stairs so often during the day that she felt the baby would not realize when it was really bedtime. She said, "When Father takes him up, he knows it's final." So the young son was learning early that his dad's word is final, and perhaps that he too, given his male gender, may someday occupy a father role in which he has similar authority. The bedtime ritual may also suggest that such a role is typical of fathers and men in both China and Germany. Thus, the nighttime ritual gives the child a perception and expectation about ethnically determined gender roles.

Gender thus often affects the success of parents in establishing ethnic family rituals,[24] and the content of these ethnic rituals identifies gender roles. For example, because mothers play a central role in the establishment and preparations for ethnic family rituals, this in itself teaches children that ritual preparations are women's work. The specific content of the family rituals then further reinforces the gender distinctions, such as in the example above where a child learned that in the case of bedtime, his father's word and behavior were final. Of course, ethnic family rituals are not the only rituals that reflect gender values and norms; all family rituals do this, but they do so in different ways.

Why Is It That Our Childhood Rituals Continue to Have Ethnic Content?

Many family rituals from our childhoods are indeed laden with ethnic meanings, even though we often have had to make adjustments to and have negotiations over the nature of these rituals. What is so salient about ethnicity?

Despite the depiction of ethnic family rituals as a novel and uniquely American tradition, the ethnic roots of family rituals are actually much deeper and older than American history. Anthropologically speaking, the need to pass down traditions and heritage is rooted in kinship, and both ethnicity and family are forms of kinship. Our closest kin are our immediate family members, but we also share kinship with our ethnic compatriots. In early times, all members of one particular tribe or "ethnicity" were somehow related, like an extended family. The difference today is that the "tribes" have grown, which has weakened the ties but not eliminated their importance. For example, an Italian American may not see consider herself related to each Italian person she meets, but from an anthropological standpoint, they do share kinship. And despite not consciously realizing this shared kinship, we do establish ethnic family rituals that connect us in some way with our fellow ethnics.

Immigrant parents, of course, may be much more aware of their ties to a broader kinship group than non-immigrant parents. For them, ethnic ties may be particularly salient and more obviously represented in family rituals, because acknowledging these ties gives immigrant parents an immediate sense of belonging to a group. A feeling of belonging may be especially important to them because they are, after all, living in a completely foreign place. People like to belong to something, and when people are isolated in a new place, the search for belonging can emerge through the rituals and practices related to ethnic and family heritage. The process by which immigrant parents establish rituals does in fact provide an understanding of how and why family and childhood rituals are initially so "ethnic."

Thus, some family rituals reflect parents' kinship ties to "ethnic" kin. Other rituals, though, also begin to tie these same parents and their children to a new culture. Establishing family rituals in immigrant families is challenging because of the balancing act that takes place between the parents' and children's desires to be connected to different "tribes" or ethnic groups or cultures. Both generations want their ties represented in the families' rituals. Effectively, the establishment and enactment of family rituals does not always require a "natural" kinship tie to a particular ethnicity. We do not need to be Americans to adopt American holidays, but ultimately some of our most meaningful family rituals do reflect out "natural" ethnic origins.

The experiences of immigrant families give us a good sense of how ethnic family rituals come to be and why they endure. These experiences also highlight the challenges of establishing ethnic and language rituals and the role of gender in such rituals. Clearly, ethnicity is connected to our sense of family, even in modern society where we often focus only on our immediate, nuclear families. Our most cherished and remembered childhood rituals reflect our ties to past generations of family members as well as to a larger "family" or nation of people, one that is often difficult for us to conceptualize. As a Swedish immigrant mother put it, "I've heard this one thing—'if you don't know where you're coming from, you won't know where you're going.'" By connecting us to our private families as well as to larger kinship groups, ethnic rituals give meaning and direction to our lives.

NOTES

1. See Linda A. Bennett, Steven J. Wolin, and Katharine J. McAvity, "Family Identity, Ritual and Myth: A Cultural Perspective on Life Cycle Transitions," *Family Transitions*, ed. Celia Jaes Falicov (New York: Guilford Press, 1988), 211–243.

2. Some settlers had contact with Native Americans who undoubtedly influenced some of the settlers' rituals, such as Thanksgiving.

3. The "power" of ethnic childhood rituals has been pointed out by several scholars: Barbara G. Myerhoff, "A Symbol Perfected in Death: Continuity and Ritual in the Life and Death of an Elderly Jew," in *Life's Career—Aging: Cultural Variations on Growing Old*, ed. B. G. Myerhoff and A. Simic (Beverly Hills, CA: Sage, 1978), 163–205; Carolyn J. Rosenthal and Victor W. Marshall, "Generational Transmission of Family Ritual," *American Behavioral Scientist* 31.6 (1988): 669–684.

4. This point is made by Rosenthal and Marshall, "Generational Transmission of Family Ritual" (674), who are careful to point out that ethnic rituals are not just manifestations of immigrant culture but may be the result of other changes in society. Societal change as a catalyst for rituals is an old theme, dating back to Durkheim and discussed more recently by the following: Guenther Lueschen, "Family Interaction with Kin and the Function of Ritual," *Journal of Comparative Family Studies* 3.1 (1972): 84–98; David Cheal, "The Ritualization of Family Ties," *American Behavioral Scientist* 31.6 (1988): 532–643.

5. James H. Bossard and Eleanor S. Boll, *Ritual in Family Living* (Philadelphia: University of Pennsylvania Press, 1950), quoted at 9.

6. Other categories include religious, civic, and economic rituals.

7. Steven J. Wolin and Linda A. Bennett, "Family Rituals," *Family Process* 23 (1984): 401–420, quoted at 403.

8. As pointed out by Rosenthal and Marshall, "Generational Transmission of Family Ritual," 670.

9. Family rituals are actively established in young families especially when children reach preschool age, as pointed out by Barbara H. Fiese, Karen A.

Hooker, Lisa Kotary, and Janet Schwagler, "Family Rituals in the Early Stages of Parenthood," *Journal of Marriage and Family* 55 (1993): 633–642. See also Bennett et al., "Family Identity, Ritual and Myth," for a discussion of the process of ritual development in families, especially 214–215; Lillian E. Troll, "Rituals and Reunions," *American Behavioral Scientist* 31.6 (1988): 621–631.

10. Fiese et al., "Family Rituals in the Early Stages of Parenthood," 633–642.

11. See Bennett et al., "Family Identity, Ritual and Myth"; Evan Imber-Black and Janine Roberts, "Family Change: Don't Cancel Holidays," *Psychology Today* 26.2 (March/April 1993): 62 ff; Marjorie A. Pett, Nancy Lang, and Anita Gander, "Late-Life Divorce: Its Impact on Family Rituals," *Journal of Family Issues* 13.4 (1992): 526–552; Wolin and Bennett, "Family Rituals," 401–420.

12. Theodore Caplow, "Christmas Gifts and Kin Networks," *American Sociological Review* 47 (1982): 383–392.

13. Scott Coltrane, *Gender and Families* (Thousand Oaks, CA: Pine Forge Press, 1998).

14. John Gillis, "Making Time for Family: The Invention of Family Time[s] and the Reinvention of Family History," *Journal of Family History* 21.1 (1996): 4–21.

15. See discussion of family rituals and how they have evolved as societies have evolved in Coltrane, *Gender and Families*, 13–19.

16. See Anne Tuominen, "Who Decides the Home Language: A Look at Multilingual Families," *International Journal of the Sociology of Language* 140 (1999): 59–76.

17. For a study in which religious background did matter for the celebration of Christmas, see Rosenthal and Marshall, "Generational Transmission of Family Ritual."

18. Rosenthal and Marshall, "Generational Transmission of Family Ritual," 675.

19. The children were not tested for fluency, nor were all the children living at home at the time of the interviews. However, through the course of my interviews, the children's language abilities were assessed, either through the parents' assessments or through observations made by the interviewer of the younger children.

20. See Tuominen, "Who Decides the Home Language," 71–73.

21. Min Zhou, "Growing Up American: The Challenge Confronting Immigrant Children and Children of Immigrants," *Annual Review of Sociology* 23 (1997): 63–95, quoted at 80.

22. See characterization of Thanksgiving as gendered holiday in Coltrane, *Gender and Families* 13–19.

23. For the importance of rituals to women and for women's prominence in ritual maintenance, see William H. Meredith, Douglas A. Abbott, Mary Ann Lamanna, and Gregory Sanders, "Rituals and Family Strengths: A Three Generational Study," *Family Perspective* 23.2 (1989): 75–83; Pett et al., "Late-Life Divorce."

24. For an example of gender not being correlated with the transmission of ritual, see Rosenthal and Marshall, "Generational Transmission of Family Ritual."

2

Stories My Father Told Me

MARK I. WEST

It was about eight o'clock in the evening, and my brother, sister, and I congregated in the living room, waiting for my father to begin reading to us. He picked up *David Copperfield*, asked us to name the author, and after we all called out "Charles Dickens" for what seemed like the hundredth time, he began reading aloud. About a minute into the story, Dad stopped. His bushy eyebrows knitted together, his nostrils slightly flared, and he said, "Mark, put Callie out." Callie, one of the family cats, had a bit of a problem with flatulence, which always annoyed Dad. After I took Callie outside, Dad resumed reading, but his eyebrows still had that disapproving look.

I paid a lot of attention to Dad's eyebrows during my childhood. His forehead always looked fierce and furrowed when he disapproved of something, and there were a number of things that fell into this category. He disapproved of professional sports, especially the contact sports of football and boxing. He disapproved of hunting and posted "No Hunting" signs all over the mountain that he and my mother bought when they moved to Colorado in the mid-1950s. He disapproved of the land developers who carved up the mountain next to our property. And he adamantly disapproved of television, which is one of the reasons why he read to us nearly every night. He did not want us to "waste" our evenings watching television, so he took it upon himself to provide us with an alternative form of entertainment.

While Dad was reading *David Copperfield,* I closely monitored his eyebrows, like a weather forecaster watching a barometer. As the lingering odor that Callie left behind gradually faded away, Dad's facial muscles relaxed, his voice changed, and I soon forgot about flatulent cats and furrowed brows. Through the magic combination of Dickens's words and Dad's voice, my siblings and I left the decade of the 1960s and the mountains of Colorado and took up residence for a few hours in nineteenth-century London.

None of my friends had fathers who read to them. In fact, some of my friends thought it odd that I was still being read to when I could easily read complex books by myself. They didn't realize, however, that this nightly ritual involved much more than the sharing of books. Through this experience, I began to form a sort of bond with my father. My friends may have bonded with their fathers during camping trips or sporting events, but for me, the countless evenings I spent listening to Dad read helped me better understand him and appreciate his unique approach to life.

The books that Dad selected to read aloud provided me with glimpses into his interests and values. He grew up in a Jewish neighborhood in Brooklyn during the Great Depression, but even as a child he had a fascination with the American West. This interest not only contributed to his desire to move to the Rocky Mountains long before it was a fashionable place to live, but it also predisposed him to select books about the settling of the West. Over the years, he read dozens of books to us that dealt with this topic, including Robert Lewis Taylor's *The Travels of Jamie McPheeters,* Emerson Hough's *The Covered Wagon,* Ralph Moody's *Little Britches,* and Charles Portis's *True Grit.* The obvious zeal with which Dad read these stories helped me understand the depth of his feelings toward his adopted state of Colorado and more specifically toward the mountain that served as my backyard.

Dad also selected stories that had direct connections to his childhood. In some cases, they were stories that he had enjoyed as a child, such as Robert Louis Stevenson's *Treasure Island,* Mark Twain's *Adventures of Tom Sawyer* and *Adventures of Huckleberry Finn,* Rudyard Kipling's *Jungle Book,* and several of Dickens's novels. When Dad first picked up one of these books to read aloud, he would tell us how much he liked it when he read it during his school years, and this aroused my curiosity. Thinking of my father as a boy made me feel somehow closer to him.

Sometimes he read us stories set in the New York City of his youth, including Gerald Green's *To Brooklyn with Love* and Leo Rosten's *The Education of Hyman Kaplan*. For a boy who spent his whole life living on the side of a mountain, I found these books rather exotic. I sometimes wondered what it would be like to live in a big city, and these books answered some of my questions about the nature of urban life. Once, for example, when Dad was reading *To Brooklyn with Love*, he came across a reference to stick ball. This passage jarred his memory. He put the book down and told us about his experiences playing stick ball with his boyhood friends. His little anecdote revealed a side of Dad that I had never known before, and for a moment I wanted to travel back in time and play stick ball with this new boy version of Dad. I also sometimes wondered about the Jewish side of my family history, and these books gave me an inkling of an idea about this remote part of my heritage.

Dad seldom talked about his Jewish background, but it always influenced his reactions to the extravagant Christmases my Mom organized. Throughout the month of December, Mom, my siblings, and I decorated two Christmas trees, one of which was about twelve feet high, baked Christmas cookies, and decked our front hall with an elaborate display of Christmas cards. Dad had a hard time getting into the rest of the family's Christmas spirit, but through his love of Dickens, he found a way to participate. Every year, just before we opened our presents, he read Dickens's *A Christmas Carol*. Usually Mom didn't listen to Dad reading aloud, but when he read *A Christmas Carol*, she would join us. I still cherish the memory of our entire family sitting in the living room, gazing at our giant Christmas tree and listening to Dad once again relate the story of Scrooge's reformation. This Christmas ritual reflected the high value that both Dad and Mom placed on family traditions.

Occasionally, Dad would read us autobiographies of people whom he admired. The two examples that come immediately to mind are William O. Douglas's *Men and Mountains* and Willie Morris's *North toward Home*. When Dad read these books, he often expressed his positive feelings toward these men. In a sense, Dad used these books to share some of his values with us. I came to understand that these books were about real people, and I began to view them as potential role models. I absorbed Dad's admiration of Douglas's commitment to protecting civil liberties. Now that I am an adult, I have become an anti-censorship activist, and I suspect that hearing Dad read Douglas's autobiography had something to do with this development. Morris's autobiography also left a mark on me. As I listened to Dad read about Morris's efforts to become an author, I began toying with the idea of becoming an author myself. The fact that Dad admired authors such as Morris led me to speculate that perhaps this would be a way to make him proud of me. I'm embarrassed to admit it, but a vestige of this thought still surfaces each time I send my parents an autographed copy of one of my books.

In addition to learning about Dad through his book selections, I also gained some insights into his personality by observing his reactions to the material he was reading aloud or, in one instance, his lack of a reaction. When I was around seven, Dad often took time out on Sunday mornings to read us the comic strips published in the *Denver Post*. One Sunday, I decided to play a trick on him. I dug through the stack of old newspapers next to the fireplace, found the comics from the previous Sunday, and slipped them inside the current week's comics. Then, after Dad woke up, I handed him the double dose of comics to read aloud. He began by reading *Blondie,* which always ran on the first page of the comics section, and then he turned the page and found another *Blondie.* To my glee, he also read the second one. He went on to read both weeks' worth of every strip, never letting on that something was not quite right. I came away from the whole experience elated. The thought that I had actually tricked Dad made him seem more approachable, more like an ordinary human and not the stern man whom I sometimes imagined him to be.

When Dad reacted emotionally to the stories he read aloud, it further altered my image of him. I always liked it when Dad laughed at the funny passages in books. I remember, for example, feeling especially close to Dad while we were all sharing a good laugh over some of Tom Sawyer's ridiculous predicaments or Penrod's antics. What left the deepest impression on me, however, was Dad's emotional responses to the sad books he read to us. I've only seen Dad cry twice in my life, and both times it was while he was reading aloud. The first time came at the end of Marjorie Kinnan Rawlings's *The Yearling* when the young hero is forced to shoot his pet deer. The second time occurred while he was reading about the hardships facing the Scandinavian immigrants in Ole Edvart Rolvaag's *Giants in the Earth.* On both occasions, I was astounded to see tears in Dad's eyes, and my brother and sister had the same reaction. We certainly did not think of Dad as being any weaker because we saw him cry, but we began to realize that he was not quite as invulnerable as we had always assumed him to be.

I am sorry to say that a few years later my siblings and I unknowingly hurt Dad in one of his few vulnerable spots. As we become more involved in the activities that swallow up teenagers' time, we found it difficult to spend two hours every evening listening to Dad read. When it became impossible for all of us kids to assemble in the living room on a regular basis, Dad reluctantly stopped reading to us. The last book he read aloud was James Dickey's *Deliverance*. Mom later told me that it deeply saddened Dad when this family tradition finally came to an end.

I don't know if it's any consolation to Dad, but scarcely a day goes by that I don't flash back on one of the stories that he read to us or remember an incident that happened while we were together in the living room listening to him read. As I see it now, Dad was not only sharing stories with us; he was also sharing a part of himself, and that's the sort of gift one tends not to forget.

PART 2

RELIGION

Every religion has its rituals, and participation in them renders a child a member of the fold. These rituals may be small and intimate, such as a nightly recitation of prayers on bended knees beside one's bed, or large and elaborate, such as baptismal ceremonies in the presence of an entire congregation. Designed and perpetuated by adults, religious rituals convey to children what followers of a particular faith deem important. In America, the dominant religious rituals in which children participate are Christian. Roman Catholics, for example, generally baptize children during the first few months of life and offer first communion at age seven and confirmation during adolescence. Each ceremony, accompanied by distinctive clothing, invocations, and practices, signifies a rite of passage as children move toward a more mature acceptance of their religious beliefs and community. Other religious patterns are associated with holidays, especially Christmas and Easter, and often involve the lighting of candles, singing, and processions.

Many immigrants ventured to America in search of religious freedom, and as a result, the nation's religious tapestry displays a rich and varied texture. This is reflected in the two essays that follow, both addressing non-Christian rituals. In "Hindu Samskāras: Milestones of Child Development," Jyotsna M. Kalavar details an intricate progression of rituals celebrating the child that begin even before birth, thereby demonstrating the child's importance at each stage in the evolution to adulthood. Ellen J. Narotzky Kennedy takes a different approach in "Bar Mitzvah and Bat Mitzvah: Rites of Affirmation and Integration," focusing on the single most significant ritual in the life of a Jewish child and its connections to Judaism's emphases on learning and community.

Part of growing up is developing a belief system. Rituals provide a physical manifestation of the child's coming of age in a particular faith.

3

Hindu Samskāras

Milestones of Child Development

JYOTSNA M. KALAVAR

Every culture consecrates periods of life or developmental milestones with rituals, traditions, or festivities. Among Hindus, *samskāras* (pronounced "sums-kaara") are rites of passage that extend across the lifespan and mark our spiritual journey on earth. *Samskāras* have been arranged to produce suitable impressions from the very beginning of one's life (conception) and to direct one's energies into a well-guarded and purposive channel.

Each *samskāra* is an important milestone that marks major biological, emotional, intellectual, or social influences. When properly observed, *samskāras* are believed to empower the individual's spiritual life. As a marker for various milestones of child development, Hindu *samskāras* fulfill an integrative role. Although each *samskāra* is described in the traditional context, the practice of childhood *samskāras* in the United States is also examined. In contemporary society, many Hindus within and outside India fail to perform all of the prescribed *samskāras*. Instead, many Hindus selectively perform what they consider "important *samskāras*."

Rooted in Vedic tradition, this Sanskrit word *samskāra* defies accurate translation into English. However, literally speaking, *samskāra* means "betterment of a thing." According to Raj Pandey, the word *samskāra* is used in a very wide sense, to describe refinement, training, embellishment, impression on memory, a purificatory rite, sanctification, merit of action, and the like (16). Designed for the welfare of the individual, the practice of *samskāras* is believed to develop eight auspicious *gunās* (pronounced "goo-nas"), or attributes that can impact the soul. Acquisition of these eight *gunās* will help the person move toward the state of *mokshā* (pronounced "mokh-shaa"), or ultimate liberation. The eight *gunās* are compassion, forbearance, freedom from envy, purity, calmness, righteousness, generosity, and dispassion (Sadagopan 8). The cleansing process that is set in motion by the observance of *samskāras* is believed to inspire the individual to move toward greater spiritual attainment (Sarma 26). In other words, this is a purificatory ritual that sanctifies the whole individual.

Samskāras, or sacramental rites, can be traced back to the Vedas and have also found expression in a few *Brāhmanas* (pronounced "braa-manahs"), the *Grhyasūtras* (pronounced "gruhya-sootras"), the *Dharmasūtras* (pronounced "dharma-sootras"), the *Smrtis* (pronounced "smru-thi"), and the later treatises. Although references to *samskāras* have been made in the above works, they are primarily described in the following *Grhyasūtras* (Asha 15). These primarily include those authored by Āpastamba, Āśvalāyana, Baudhāyana, Bhāradvājā, and Pāraskara. The most commonly cited number of lifespan *samskāras* is sixteen, though *Āśvalāyana Grhyasūtra* enumerated eleven *samskāras* while *Gautama-Dharmasūtra* suggested forty *samskāras* (Pandey 17).

Characteristics of *Samskāras*

Most childhood *samskāras* are brief and may be performed at home, in the temple, or in community locations. *Samskāras* are age-specific, for there is a prescribed age for the performance of each of these rituals. However, there are substitute *kālas* (pronounced "kaalas"), or periods, mentioned, if a person misses the prescribed time period. If none of the childhood *samskāras* have been performed, Hindu priests often conduct a highly abbreviated version at the Hindu wedding ceremony.

Since some *samskāras* are considered gender-specific, the *samskāras* to be observed for boys and girls may vary. For instance, consider one of the educational *samskāras* called *upanayana* (pronounced "upah-naya-na") that serves as a platform for commencement of Vedic instruction. The contemporary practice of *upanayana* is strongly restricted to boys, though centuries earlier this *samskāra* was performed for girls also. Similarly, in earlier periods the ear-piercing ritual called *karnavedha* (pronounced "kar-na-ved-ha") was performed for boys and girls, though now it is largely observed for girls.

Despite the different types of childhood *samskāras,* several constituents of *samskāras* are common to many of them. They typically share certain elements, including fire, prayer/offering, orientation, lustration (or sprinkling of water), and symbolism. *Agni* (pronounced "ug-nee"), or fire, is an indispensable part of the performance of *samskāras* and is usually invoked by priests in the presence of family, elders, and community members. Most rituals begin with offerings to the sacred fire along with the chanting of Vedic hymns and prayers/offerings to divine beings, ruling stars, and ancestors. The offering of prayers to Lord Ganeśa (remover of obstacles) is seen in all Hindu *sanskāras* and undertakings. During the performance of *samskāras,* the priest or family elders express blessings that convey good feelings toward others. When performing *sanskāras,* the recipient is oriented to face the eastern direction, as this is suggestive of light, warmth, glory, and life. Lustration and ceremonial sipping of water are features of most *samskāras.* Symbolic of bathing, these elements are regarded as washing off physical or spiritual impurities. Symobls are used in *samskāras* to convey different characteristics that are salient for the ceremony. For instance, gold represents solar radiance and the ability to purify (Stork 98) and is used in the newborn ritual called *jātakarma* (pronounced "jaa-ta-karma"; Dange 25), while a stone represents steadfastness in character and is used in the educational *samskāra upanayana* (Paramanthananda 17).

While *samskāras* are prescribed Hindu rituals, there are tremendous regional and sectarian influences in their practice. For instance, within South India, the prenatal *sanskāra* termed *sīmantonayana* (pronounced "see-manto-unayana") is typically performed in the seventh month of gestation in the state of Karnataka, while this same ritual is customarily conducted in the eighth month of gestation in the neighboring state of Tamil Nadu. Further, *kulā cāra* (pronounced "koola-chaara"), or family custom, may dictate which *Grhyasūtra* may be consulted. Since there are slight variations in the different *Grhyasūtras* that are authored by different individuals, the practice and timing of certain *sanskāras* may vary. The *upanayana samskāra* is restricted to Brahmin, Kshatriya, and Vaishya castes, with different time periods suggested for each of the above castes (Pandian 5). No such restrictions are evident for any of the other childhood *samskāras*.

Childhood *Samskāras*

The purpose of this essay is twofold: (a) to describe Hindu *samskāras* that span the period from conception through childhood and (b) to understand the significance of these childhood *samskāras* for Hindu families residing in the United States. The following description of childhood *samskāras* is largely based on interviews held with six Hindu priests from South India (representing the *Vaiṣṇava* tradition and *Smārta* tradition) presiding at Hindu temples in the northeastern and midwestern regions of the United States. Based on the *Grhyasūtra* followed, there were differences in the timing of *samskāras* that were cited by the Hindu priests of both traditions. Presented below is the modal response that was used to describe the suggested timetable for performance of childhood *samskāras*. Further, this essay explains how the priests elucidated the significance of each *samskāra*, what they considered the three most salient childhood *samskāras*, and which *samskāras* they frequently conducted in the United States.

Sri Venkateśwara Temple, established in 1976 and located in Monroeville, Pennsylvania, is the oldest consecrated Hindu temple in the United States. With the cooperation of Sri Venkateśwara Temple, the author interviewed ten Hindu families who sought to perform various childhood *samskāras* within the temple premises. Besides sociodemographic information, respondents were asked three open-ended questions, a) "What *samskāra* are you performing today?" b) "Why?" and c) "What benefit do you foresee from performing this *samskāra*?"

Prenatal *Samskāras*

Garbhādhāna

The prenatal *samskāras* begin with the rite of conception of *garbhādhāna* (pronounced "gar-bhaa-dhaana"), where physical union is privately consecrated through prayer and invocation with the purpose of bringing a worthy soul into physical life. Unlike earlier times, this ceremony is now rarely conducted as an independent ceremony. Instead, it is frequently performed at the conclusion of the wedding ceremony.

Pumsavana

Pumsavana (pronounced "pum-sa-vana"), or the third-month blessing, sanctifies pregnancy's critical trimester of development. In this ceremony, which is also called *prājāpatya*, special prayers are offered for the healthy development of the fetus, and special blessings for a male child are invoked at this rite. This ritual is prescribed when the moon is in conjunction with a male star, as this is believed to be conducive to the birth of a son. Evident in this *samskāra* is the Hindu obsession with a male child, by whose birth it is believed one can pay off ancestral debt and maintain the family lineage. When regarded as a *kshetra* (pronounced "shay-tra") *samskāra* (purification of the womb), this ceremony is performed only for the first pregnancy. In contemporary Hindu society, this *samskāra* is often overlooked or combined with the most popular prenatal *samskāra, sīmantonayana.*

Sīmantonayana

Sīmantonayana, the hair-parting ceremony of the expectant mother, is usually performed in the last trimester of the first pregnancy. This ceremony is named *sīmantonayana* because the hair *(símanta)* of the expectant mother is parted upward *(unayana).* There is also symbolic representation of the body being divided into two parts, preparing for the fetus to begin independent living. As alluded to earlier, regional variations dictate whether the seventh or eighth month of gestation is considered more auspicious for this ceremony. This rite is usually performed when the moon is in conjunction with a star regarded as male. The significance of this *samskāra* is multifaceted—to seek divine blessings for the physical and mental well being of the expectant mother and child, to ward off evil influences through prayers (Asha 55), and to provide an opportunity for the expectant mother to feel special. Prayers are offered, blessings are sought, and the expectant mother is showered with gifts, affection, and support.

Samskāras of Infancy

Jātakarma

The post-natal *samskāras* begin with *jātakarma*. The birth of a baby is a joyous occasion, and this ritual was primarily focused on bonding between the father and child. The original time prescription for performing *jātakarma* was immediately after birth, before the mother nurses the child. Over time, this *samskāra* has been routinely combined with the subsequent *nāmakarna* ceremony.

Through *jātakarma*, the father welcomes the newborn shortly after birth. Using an object made of gold, the newborn's tongue is touched three times with *ghee* (clarified butter) and honey to the accompaniment of Vedic hymns that ask for intelligence for the baby. This is the *Medhā-janana* (pronounced "may-dha-janana"), or production of intelligence part of the *jātakarma* ceremony, and it signifies the Hindu emphasis on the intellectual development of the baby. The father recites the *Gāyatri mantra* that contains a prayer for stimulating talent.[1] The second part of the *jātakarma* focuses on ensuring longevity for the newborn. The father leans over the right ear or the navel of the newborn while chanting mantras that seek to bestow a long life. These mantras usually refer to long-lived elements such as fire, ocean, etc., with the belief that the baby's life will also be similarly lengthened. For permitting a safe delivery, the father thanks the earth where the child was born. The concluding part of the *jātakarma* ceremony emphasizes the character or personality of the child. The father recites the mantra that requests that the child "Be a stone, be an axe, be like indestructible gold. Thou art indeed the Veda. So, live a hundred autumns" (Gopalakrishnan 59). This is believed to be symbolic of the desire that the child should be strong like stone, sharp like an axe, and worthy like gold. Following this part of the ceremony, the child is washed and given to the mother for nursing. A pot of water is placed near the mother's head as a protection from evil influences. For the same reason, a fire offering of white mustard seeds with rice grains is made for the next ten days, during the morning and evening.

Nāmakarna

The *nāmakarna* (pronounced "naa-ma-kar-na"), or naming ceremony, commonly occurs on the eleventh day after the birth of the baby. Based on the health and convenience of the family, it may be postponed till the hundredth day or a year after birth. The first ten days after the birth of a baby are considered a time of impurity, and therefore this ceremony is popularly conducted on the eleventh day after birth. From a practical standpoint, this ceremony acknowledges the value of a name in social interactions since name and fame are so intricately interwoven. Meticulous care is taken by the parents to choose a name that reflects religious, familial, or secular considerations, and it is chosen as a life-long reminder of an ideal. At least three names are given for a child at the *nāmakarna* ceremony: the *nakṣatra nāma* (pronounced "nuk-shat-ra naama"), the name derived from the star under which the child was born; the *māas nāma* (pronounced "maa-sa naama"), the name after the month deity; and the *vyavahārika nāma* (pronounced "vya-va-haarika naama"), the name of day-to-day or popular usage). It is prescribed that the chosen name hold an even number of syllables for boys and odd number of syllables for girls.

The *nāmakarna* ceremony begins with offerings to the sacred fire, the chanting of hymns, and offerings to divine beings, ancestors, and ruling stars. The freshly bathed mother and child, clad in new clothes, are brought into the midst of family members. The father touches the nose of the child, representing the breath or awakening of life force. He leans over to the right ear of the child and addresses the baby by the *māsa nāma*, *nakṣatra nāma*, and *vyavahārika nāma*. At the conclusion of this ceremony, the family elders are invited to bless the newborn. This postpartum ceremony gives the mother an opportunity to socialize with everyone and allows family members an occasion to interact with the newborn.

Niṣkramana

The newborn's introduction to the grandeur of the outside world is heralded by the *niṣkramana* (pronounced "nish-kra-mana"), or first outing, ceremony. The baby has been confined to the inner quarters of a home since birth because of the dangers of the outside environment, so a ceremonial introduction is seen as necessary. Recognizing each step in the infant's development, this ceremony acknowledges the need for widening sensory stimulation for the baby.

The time for performing the *niṣkramana* ceremony varies from the twelfth day after birth to the fourth month after birth (Raja 62). On the chosen day, innovations are offered to the family deity, the guardian of eight directions, the sun, moon, sky, and Lord Krishna before the ceremonial exiting of the home. Then, the freshly bathed infant is carried out of the home to the sounds of a conch shell and recital of Vedic hymns. The *śakunta* hymn—"Whether the child is conscious or unconscious, whether it is day or night, let all the Gods led by Indra, protect the child"—is repeated by the father (Raja 62). The ceremony concludes with a visit to a temple, where blessings are sought for the welfare of the baby. While the interviewed priests did not consider this a major *samskāra*, they acknowledged that this ceremony features in some *Grhyasūtras*. According to these priests, the first outing to a Hindu temple is frequently the only aspect of this *samskāra* that is adhered to by Hindus in the United States. They also pointed out that this practice is intricately linked with the issue of easy accessibility to a Hindu temple.

Annaprāśana

There comes a time in the infant's life when weaning from the mother's milk must take place. As the quantity of mother's milk declines, the infant's body growth demands greater amounts and different types of food. Addressing the physical development of the child, *annaprāśana* (pronounced "un-na-praa-sh-na") celebrates the child's first intake of solid food. Giving solid food before the fourth month is strictly prohibited in the scriptures (Pandey 91). Divine blessings for improved digestive capacity in the infant are invoked for this *samskāra*, which is typically performed in the sixth month of a child's life.

The first food is usually sweetened rice gruel prepared with milk that is fed to the infant by parents and elders of the family. Offerings of food to the sacred fire are followed by offerings to Vākdevi (pronounced "vaak-devi"), the goddess of speech, and Shakti (pronounced "shuk-thi"), the goddess of energy. The final prayers are offered for the satisfactory functioning of the sensory systems in the infant and the complete welfare of the child.

Chūdākarma

Chūdākarma (pronounced "choo-daa-karma"), or tonsure, is the ritual prescribed for the removal of the postnatal virgin hair of the child. The time recommended for this *samskāra* is the tenth month after birth or, if delayed, the third year of the child's life. The tenth month after birth is believed to correspond to the period when teething troubles begin and is often associated with digestive problems. In earlier periods, ringworms were a common problem that led to skin rashes on the scalp. To address the issue of cleanliness and hygiene, shaving off the hair was seen as a viable option. A sharp razor coming into contact with an infant's head evoked apprehension in family members. These sentiments led to prayers for the welfare of the child, which eventually came to be instituted as the *chūdākarma* ceremony. This practice is considered essential for the educational progress, health, vigor, purity, and beauty of the child.

The ceremony begins with the infant seated on the mother's lap while the father moistens the child's head with water in preparation for the barber's work. After invoking divine blessings, the cut hair is often offered to the *kūla devatā* (pronounced "koola dey-va-taa"), meaning family deity, or *iśta devatā* (pronounced "ish-ta dey-va-taa"), meaning favored deity. Or, alternatively, the cut hair is disposed off in a ball of cow dung that is tossed into a small pond. Traditionally, a *śīkhā* (pronounced "she-khaa"), or tuft, is created for the boy. The purpose of the *śīkhā* is to protect the most sensitive nerve center on top of the head (known as the *Brahma Rāndra*) from any abnormal vibrations (Sadagopan 13).

According to the Hindu priests interviewed, *chūdākarma* has been reduced to a token ceremony these days. They indicated that most families in the United States seek to remove a clump of hair rather than have the entire mass of hair removed. They also indicated that a *śīkhā* is rarely maintained by Hindu infants in the United States. Further, for economic reasons and convenience, *chūdākarma* is frequently combined with *karnavedha* (Stork 97).

Karnavedha

Karnavedha, or ear piercing, was originally prescribed for boys and girls during the first, third, or fifth year. This was believed to be a useful way of protecting the child from disease (Stork 97). Mentioned only in the *Kātyāyana Sūtra*, this *samskāra* is neither widely prescribed nor practiced. Today, this traditional practice, if followed, is usually limited to young girls. It was considered essential to pierce the ear lobes when the child was young so that they could be adorned with earrings. Sometimes this practice is coupled with nose piercing for ornamentation. Since the procedure involved physical discomfort, it became customary to invoke divine blessings. According to one of the *Vaiśnava* priests at Sri Venkateśwara Temple, "Hindus in America hardly come to the temple for *karnavedha*. Instead, they just go to the mall these days."

This ceremony is usually performed in the first half of the day, when natural lighting is optimal. After the preliminary prayers and offerings, the child is placed on the mother's lap. A goldsmith or craftsman is usually invited to the home, and according to the status of the family, a gold, silver, copper, or iron needle may be used. While no explanation was available from any of the priests, it is suggested that the right ear of the boy and the left ear of the girl be pierced first. With the ears now sanctified, the child may be ready to receive formal education.

Educational *Samskāras*

Aksarabhyāsa

Formal education is initiated with two *samskāras*. The first, *aksarabhyāsa* (pronounced "uk-shar-abh-yaasa"), signifies the child is prepared to learn and receive education. As Sanskrit was primarily a spoken language, the use of alphabets came about much later. Consequently, *aksarabhyāsa*, or the learning of alphabets, was a ceremony that was instituted later, and therefore it is ignored in the earlier texts. Known variously as *aksarārambha*, *aksarasvīkarana*, or *aksarālekhana*, this ritual is not mentioned in the *Grhyasūtras* but reportedly is featured in other treatises, such as *Vīramitrodaya* and *Samskāra ratnamālā* (Pandey 106).

Prescribed in the fifth year of life, when the sun is in the northern hemisphere, this *samskāra* is performed on an auspicious date. After prayers to Lord Ganeśa, the remover of obstacles, and Goddess Saraswati (pronounced "saras-wa-tee"), the goddess of learning), the family deity is duly worshiped. On a tray of uncooked rice, the father guides the child's fingers to form letters that salute various deities. Then, the child is asked to repeat aloud what is written. The ceremony concludes with prayers, blessings, and gifts for the teacher.

Upanayana

Upanayana, or the sacred thread ceremony, is the second educational *samskāra* prescribed for boys between the fifth and eighth year after birth and is an initiation into Vedic knowledge. This important rite of passage emphasizes that the childlike days are over, and the student is being introduced to a life of discipline, responsibility, and acquisition of knowledge. The word *upanayana,* derived from *upa* (near) and *nayana* (leading to), signifies the child being led to the teacher for acquiring Vedic knowledge. Through *upanayana,* a child is introduced into *Brahmachāryāśramā* (pronounced "brah-machaarya-ash-ramaa"), or the first stage of life (Parthasarthy 91), and is ranked a *dvija* (pronounced "dveeja"), or twice-born. As the child is now qualified to enter the teacher's home as a resident learner (which is being compared to a womb, where tremendous growth occurs), he earns the status of a twice-born. This ritual symbolizes the purification of the child's personality that takes place through initiation into the *Gāyatri mantra.*

This is an elaborate *samskāra* that includes several rites. First, prayers and blessings are sought from various deities and familial ancestors. In earlier times, this was the eve of departure to the teacher's home. Therefore, the child consumed a meal with the mother because a long period of separation was anticipated. After the feast, the boy's hair was shaved off and a *śikhā* maintained. The hair shaving is symbolic of the removal of material and sensual desires, while the *śikhā* represents the few spiritual aspirations that the student brings to the teacher (Parthasarathy 92). Today, usually just a clump of hair is removed. Bathing, which symbolizes purification of the mind and body of the recipient, follows the hair cutting. A specific set of new clothes is given to the child to highlight his social consciousness regarding expected social decorum and dignity. He is then invested with the *yagnopavīta* (pronounced "yug-no-pa-veeta"), or sacred thread, that is hung over the left shoulder. The three folds of the thread carry many symbolic representations. Interpretations include representations of the three Vedas, a reminder of the three debts (debts to sages, ancestors, and gods), and a reminder of the three qualities (reality, passion, and darkness) that prevail in the universe. This is followed by a series of actions that indicate the teacher accepts the student into his fold and asks him to be steadfast in character. These include actions such as water being dropped from the joined palms of the teacher into the joined palms of the student, touching the pupil's heart, and mounting a stone. As they face the sun, the sacred *Gāyatri mantra,* believed to stimulate the mind, is secretly conveyed to the student by the teacher. After the student learns the mantra, enkindling and offerings to the sacred fire are performed. Commitments regarding a disciplined life, implicit faith in the Vedas, and avoidance of indiscriminate ways of behavior are made. *Vedārambha* (pronounced "veda-ar-amba"), or commencement of Vedic study, follows *upanayana*.

Upanayana was ranked unanimously by the Hindu priests as the most significant ritual of childhood for boys. One of the priests described it as "acquiring a passport to see the sublime beauty of the Vedas." However, with the advent of educational institutions, there has been a corresponding decline in the learning of Vedas. According to Kanitkar, there has been a changing emphasis of the ritual "from a request for the privilege of education to a purely bodily *samskāra* in which the performance of ritual is sufficient for a boy to move to a new status" (110). It was pointed out by the priests who were interviewed that if none of the earlier childhood *samskāras* had been performed for boys, a condensed version preceded the *upanayana*. In instances where the *upanayana* was not performed in childhood or adolescence, this was consolidated before the wedding ceremony. Regretting the loss of the earlier purpose and significance, Pandey described the delayed arrangement "a ceremonial farce" (152).

Samāvartana

Akin to a graduation ceremony, the conclusion of Vedic instruction or end of studentship is marked by *samāvartana* (pronounced "samaa-vartana"). This ritual is sometimes called *snāna* (pronounced "snaa-na"), meaning bathing, because bathing is a prominent feature of this *samskāra*. In the Sanskrit literature, learning is compared to an ocean. A student who completes his course of studies was considered a *Vidyāsnātaka* (pronounced "vid-yaa-snaa-taka"), or one who has bathed in learning. This ceremonial bath at the end of the student career symbolizes the crossing of the ocean of learning by the student. With the conclusion of Vedic learning, during which celibacy must be adhered to, the individual has completed the first *aśramā* (pronounced "ash-ra-maa"), meaning stage of life, and is ready to move to the second stage of life as a householder, *Grihasthaśrama* (pronounced "gru-hastha-ash-ra-maa").

With the loss of the original significance of *upanayana*, the salience of *samāvartana* has eroded. Rather than maintaining the interval of studentship (approximately twelve years) between the *upanayana* ceremony and the *samāvartana* ceremony, the latter is being merged with the former ceremony. As Pandey indicates, the *samāvartana* has been "reduced to an absurd simplicity . . . performed either with the *upanayana* or the *vivāha* [marriage] in a hurry" (125).

Hindus in the United States

The United States Census 2000 (United States Census Bureau, 2002) showed that Asian Indians formed the third largest group of Asians in the United States. The Asian Indian population nationwide was 1,678,765 in 2000, up 105.9 percent from 1990 (Sundaram, 2001). And this trend is expected to continue. Demographics suggest that Asian Indians reside primarily in the northeastern part of the United States and are an affluent community. Their median family income is higher than the national averages (Xenos 10–18). They are proficient in English, and their occupational and income profiles reflect their high educational attainments. Although census information does not offer a breakdown by religious affiliation, it is estimated that there are two million Hindus in the United States (Subramaniyaswami xxii). Despite changing demographics, very little is known about the Hindu community relative to other immigrant/religious groups.

During the 1960s and 1970s, it was very difficult to perform Hindu *samskāras* in the United States. Most Hindu families elected to return to India to perform what they considered "salient *samskāras*." With the rapid increase in the number of Hindu families in the United States, the past two decades have seen a rapid proliferation of Hindu temples throughout the country. Apart from multiple Hindu temples in major metropolitan areas, Hindu temples are appearing in smaller towns from Canton, Michigan, to Stroudsburg, Pennsylvania. These temples offer religious services through scripturally well-trained Hindu priests and, thereby, facilitate performance of Hindu *samskāras*.

The interviews with six Hindu priests yielded a rich description of childhood *samskāras*, including the rationale, symbolism, and timetable for performing them. When asked to rank order the three most important childhood *samskāras*, the majority of the priests interviewed indicated *upanayana* followed by *annaprāśana* and *nāmakarna*. The rationale provided was that having a name allows one to be established in a social milieu, good digestive capacity promotes health, and the investiture of the sacred thread to commence learning is a significant milestone. When asked to rank order the most commonly conducted childhood *samskāras*, nearly all the priests indicated *nāmakarna*, *chūdākarma*, and *annaprāśana*. They also quickly pointed out that many families choose to perform the *upanayana* ceremony amid extended family in India. Of the prenatal *samskāras*, all the priests prioritized *sīmantonayana* and indicated that this was the most frequently performed prenatal *samskāra*.

Those parents who consented to being interviewed after performance of a childhood *samskāra* at Sri Venkateśwara Temple provided the basis for the following description. At this temple, most childhood *samskāras* may be performed on a drop-in basis at pre-advertised times over the weekend. On weekends over a onemonth period, ten families that came in to perform *samskāras* were randomly invited to participate. Of those interviewed, six families were performing *annaprāśana* (for four girls and two boys) and the remaining four families (all male children) came in for *chūdākarma*. Over this one-month period (weekends), none of the other childhood *samskāras* were conducted at the temple on a drop-in basis. All ten families invited some kinship and or nonkinship networks when performing *samskāras*.

Listed below are three themes that emerged in response to the following questions: a) "What *samskāra* are you performing today?" b) "Why?" and c) "What benefit do you foresee from performing this *samskāra*?"

a) A typical response was "It is performed for the child's welfare," a global rather than specific understanding. The intrinsic merit of the performed *sanskāra* was not fully evident. While some participants could not appreciate why this was beneficial, their response suggested no harm could come of it.

b) Respondents expressed a desire to seek Hindu expression within the Western context. This is an opportunity to retain facets of Hinduism or affirm one's Hindu background. The aspired outcome was that the child would maintain his or her Hindu identity.

c) Families saw a value in maintenance of long-standing familial traditions of performing *samskāras*. Participants indicated they would have performed these *samskāras* regardless of whether they resided in the United States or India. The benefits of "cherishing tradition" and aiding the "well-being of the child" were frequently mentioned.

Clearly, those who sought to perform *samskāras* saw some merit in doing so; however, a generalization to entire populations of Hindus in the United States is rather limited.

As the original interviews reflected the parental perspective on *samskāras* (because the children were too young to articulate effectively), the author followed up by talking to three young male children whose parents has recently conducted the *upanayana* ceremony in the United States. The children's responses suggested an affirmation of being a Hindu and an ascent to another developmental status. According to one of the respondents, who was fourteen years old, "In America we have so many rituals that we hardly think of them as such. For instance, the sweet 16 party, graduation party, Presidential inaugural ceremony, and so on. Each is meant to create an impression or suggest some responsibility being assumed. I really don't think the *upanayana* is any different. It is a ceremony for Hindus. And it means you are growing older." A nine-year-old respondent said, "I got great gifts. We had a major family reunion. Everyone made such a big deal of it. My Uncle kept saying that I was not a child anymore. I should treat this seriously as a Hindu. I just had a good time even though I was doing things the priest wanted me to that I never understood."

Conclusion

Samskāras were intended as a gradual training in spiritualism, not as an end in themselves. The purpose was to purify the whole individual (body, mind, and intellect) to facilitate acquisition of spiritual knowledge. This essay focuses on Hindu childhood *samskāras:* their prescribed practice, symbolic meanings, and expression in contemporary American society.

With rising numbers of Hindus and Hindu temples in the United States, demographics suggest that *samskāras* will play a pivotal role in retaining Hinduism within these families. The very fact that they are perpetuated in the United States may reflect the Hindu community's need to preserve their religious and cultural heritage. However, if performance of *samskāras* is expected to be maintained with future generations of Hindus in the United States, it is important that the significance of *samskāras* be clearly understood, or they face the risk of being dismissed off as irrational and irrelevant.

The historical rationale and salience of each Hindu *samskāra* must be examined by Hindus. Hindu priests who are able to communicate fluently in English with youngsters have the advantage of directly disseminating the value of performing *samskāras*. Parents must seek to fully appreciate the explanation behind each *samskāra* and convey the richness of this tradition to their children. It is significant in contemporary society for parents to be able to relate to dynamic social processes and to changing social structures. Do certain *samskāras* hold relevance when blended with other *samskāras* as a matter of convenience? Should *jātakarma* be routinely performed with *nāmakarma*? Similarly, should *samāvartana* be appended at the conclusion of *upanayana*? By doing so, the twelve-year period of studentship is being reduced to a few minutes. Is the original significance lost? What is the relevance of doing this? Is it better to combine these rituals than to forsake them forever? Not only will such an examination uphold a religious heritage, but it will also promote the ethno-religious identity of the children, so that Hindu children raised in America do not miss out on an opportunity to celebrate and sanctify important milestones of child development.

The author wishes to acknowledge the assistance of Dr. Beverly Peterson for her review of the earlier version of this manuscript and for her suggestions and comments.

NOTES

1. The *Gāyatri mantra* is the famous Vedic mantra used in prayer and personal chanting to the Sun God, written in the Gayatri meter, hence the name (Rig Veda). This sacred verse is considered a universal mystic formula so significant that it is called *Vedamatri*, "mother of the Vedas."

WORKS CITED

Asha, R. "Simantonayana." *Tattvaloka* 27 (1994): 14–16, 55–58.

Dange, Sindhu. *Ritual Symbolism in the Grihyasutras*. Delhi: Ajanta, 1985.

Gopalakrishnan, P. "Jatakarma." *Tattvaloka* 27 (1994): 59–60.

Kanitkar, Helen, ed. *Religion and Ethnicity: Minorities and Social Change in the Metropolis*. Netherlands: Kok Pharos, 1993.

Pandey, Raj. *Hindu Samskāras*. Delhi: Motilal Banarasidas, 1969.

Pandian, V. *Upanayana in Social Perspective*. Madras: Vijayavanamahadevi, 1980.

Paramarthananda, Swami. "Upanayana." *Tattvaloka* 27 (1994): 17–22.

Parthasarathy, A. *The Symbolism of Hindu Gods and Rituals.* Bombay: Vedanta Life Institute, 1989.

Raja, Hareesh. "Postnatal Samskaras." *Tattvaloka* 27 (1994): 61–64.

Sadagopan, Varadachari. "Hindu Samskaras." *Tattvaloka* 27 (1994): 8–13.

Sarma, D. *A Primer of Hinduism.* Madras: Sri Ramakrishna Math Printing Press, 1981.

Stork, Helene. *Roles and Rituals for Hindu Women.* London: Pinter Press, 1991.

Subramaniyaswami, Satguru Sivaya. Introduction to *Dancing with Siva.* Kapaa: Himalayan Academy, 1997.

Sundaram, V. "The travails of Ageing in America." *India West* 26 (30), A1 and A36, 2001.

U.S. Bureau of the Census. "We the Americans: We, the Asians and Pacific Islanders." *Current Population Reports.* Washington, D.C., 1989.

U.S. Bureau of the Census. "The Asian Population: 2000." *Census 2000 Brief.* Washington, D.C., 2002.

Xenos, Peter, at al. *Pacific Bridges: The New Immigration from Asia and the Pacific Islands.* New York: Center for Migration Studies, 1993.

4

Bar Mitzvah and Bat Mitzvah

Rites of Affirmation and Integration

ELLEN J. NAROTZKY KENNEDY

Jewish boys and girls throughout the world study and prepare from age eight or nine until thirteen to have a bar or bat mitzvah celebration.[1] The child studies biblical Hebrew intensively during this time. At the synagogue ceremony itself, standing alone in front of perhaps several hundred friends, relatives, and the members of the synagogue, the child chants a passage in Hebrew directly from the Torah (the first five books of the Bible), chants a second Hebrew passage from another part of the Bible called the Haftarah, reads his original translation of the Torah portion, and delivers a small sermon, called a d'var Torah, on the meaning of the Torah passage. This ritual of bar mitzvah has been an essential part of Jewish life for a long time. As Byron Sherwin asserts, "Bar mitzvah claims a place in Jewish social and religious life that is unparalleled in Jewish history. Already in 1887, a commentator records that in America, bar mitzvah is the most important religious occasion amongst our Jewish brethren" (53). This essay focuses primarily on the celebration of bar mitzvah in America, the country with the world's greatest number of Jews, and in particular on bar mitzvah among Reform Jews, the dominant group in American Jewry today.[2]

The bar mitzvah is a centuries-old tradition that is known primarily as a rite of both physiological and religious passage. Although the origins of this ritual certainly reflect these "coming-of-age" moments, current Reform Jewish practice indicates an increasing emphasis on affirming the potential of the child academically and socially as well as integrating the child into the family, the synagogue community, and the child's peer group. The function of religion to socialize a child in these important ways is particularly crucial during early adolescence, a time of emotional turbulence and change. This childhood ritual can exert a positive and stabilizing effect in an otherwise difficult transitional stage to maturity.

In order to understand this ritual and its significance, three major areas are addressed in this essay. The first is the history of the bar mitzvah ritual and ceremony. Second is the significance of the bar mitzvah rite in developing strong educational goals and skills in the young person. The academic demands and educational rigor of the bar mitzvah celebration are likely influences on American Jews' success in academically rigorous professions. The final topic is social integration, the way in which the child becomes part of the group as well as the community's role in coming together to support and encourage the child's efforts. The essay closes with memoirs of two recent ceremonies as exemplars of the issues that have been discussed.

History of the Bar Mitzvah Ritual

The term *bar mitzvah* occurs as far back as in the Talmud, a book of ancient Hebrew writing canonized between 200 and 500 CE.[3] The term was used to denote a person who was subject to the religious laws of Judaism (*Encyclopaedia Judaica Jerusalem* 243). Ancient Midrashic literature gives many references for age thirteen as a turning point in a young person's life, such as Abraham smashing the idols and Jacob and Esau going their separate ways at that age.[4] According to Sherwin, there were reports of calling the thirteen-year-old boy to the Torah in the eighth century. By the time of the fifteenth century, bar mitzvah became the occasion to mark one's assumption of religious and legal obligations at age thirteen.

In nineteenth-century Eastern Europe the thirteen-year-old boy was called to the Torah to read in Hebrew on the Monday or Thursday following his birthday.[5] An additional tradition among some Eastern and Central European Jews included the boy giving a discourse during the banquet that followed the ceremony, in which he thanked his parents for their love and care and thanked the guests for participating in the celebration. In Western Europe the occasion had more ceremonial importance; the boy read on the first Sabbath after his birthday and spent considerable time in preparation for the event. In the seventeenth and eighteenth centuries in parts of Germany, those boys with ability conducted all or part of the service itself in addition to reading from the Torah (*Encyclopaedia Judaica Jerusalem* 243).

Most Jewish rituals have shown a decline from one generation to the next, but bar mitzvah remains universal. In addition, bat mitzvah has become much more common as gender-free religious rituals and the ordination of women rabbis have spread through Reform Judaism (Schoenfeld). The next section examines the functions of this ritual for Reform Jews.

The Foundations of the Bar Mitzvah and Bat Mitzvah Ritual

Early Purposes of the Ritual

The age of thirteen appears to have been chosen as the age of physical puberty and was determined by specific signs of maturation (Fishbane 157). The young man was able to procreate, and given that maturation, the father was no longer bound for the son's debts or transgressions. Physiological maturity thus was the signpost for the consequent legal maturity. In addition, the son as a physical and legal adult could participate in the rites of the synagogue that required a *minyan*, a minimum of ten adult males.[6] Today, of course, we do not recognize thirteen as the age of adulthood by any standard: physiological, legal, or religious. Physiologically, puberty begins at a wide range of ages; legally, responsibility occurs in different domains at different ages (e.g., the right to vote occurs at age eighteen and the right to drive typically at age sixteen); and religiously, in most congregations, a child who has completed a bar or bat mitzvah is counted in a *minyan* but is unlikely to have a vote on congregational matters. The young boys and girls themselves realize that adulthood is not the meaningful issue of bar and bat mitzvah in our society. One student says quite eloquently, "We're not kids and we're not adults—except that we can get an aliyah" (Sager 206).[7] The child realizes that the bar mitzvah does not bestow adult status within the congregation, and certainly not within the secular would. However, it does carry with it some special privileges that act as stepping-stones on the pathway to adulthood. For today's children, then, like children of centuries ago, bar mitzvah signifies an end to childhood and the taking on of some special privileges, although not all of those that accrue with adulthood.

Function and Bar Mitzvah

Rituals serve many important functions for individuals, families, and various groups: allowing people to express strong feelings; providing ways for families to acknowledge and affirm basic expectations; allowing families to represent who they are to themselves and to others and to celebrate; and developing group identity and solidarity. Although these functions are all found in the bar mitzvah ritual, it is important to understand the foundation upon which these functions rest.

Bar Mitzvah and Education

The foundational element of this ritual has been described as a "compressed form of education" (Spiro, "Educational" 383). This ceremony, which seems to be unique and different when compared to children's ritual ceremonies in other religions, is actually a reflection of the ethos of the Jewish community and culture. In other words, "the uniqueness [of the bar mitzvah] is also a characteristic of commonality in the ceremonies practiced by every group or culture and are indigenous to its ethos and character" (384). The boy is on trial, "perhaps not the kind of trial involved in walking over hot coals. But [bar mitzvah] is an intellectual trial, no less traumatizing as he stands before relatives and authorities to demonstrate his skill, ability, and the knowledge of Torah and Jewish law" (396). This high degree of emphasis on learning may be unique within the Jewish culture. Because learning is at the heart of the Jewish culture, is the very ethos, the trial is one of demonstrating one's readiness to become part of that culture.

Educational Preparation for the Ritual

There are several ways in which children prepare for bar mitzvah. Children who attend private Jewish day schools, which combine religious and secular studies, find that bar mitzvah preparation is integrated into the general course of studies (Jacob 599). Children in secular schools, however, prepare by studying for at least four years in after-school Hebrew classes. This training begins when the child is about nine years old. Children learn to read the Hebrew alphabet, learn rudimentary Hebrew conversation, and begin the study of biblical Hebrew. This mixture of linguistic goals presents difficulties. The grammar and vocabulary of these two forms of Hebrew, biblical and conversational, are significantly different; yet most religious schools make an effort to move in this direction—that of teaching both biblical and conversational Hebrew. Biblical Hebrew is taught because it is used for ritual purposes, and conversational Hebrew is taught because Hebrew is the language of the Jewish state of Israel. These language skills are clearly formidable educational objectives for American children, most of whom have no previous instruction in a foreign language, let alone one with a different alphabet and a right-to-left reading pattern. In addition, for those children who must rely on after-school Hebrew education, this training represents direct competition with the secular activities that are important for many children of this age, such as sports and music.

In virtually all synagogues the children are also required to attend religious school classes on either a Saturday or Sunday morning. For most children this is a commitment that begins at age five with the ritual of consecration and continues weekly until the child reaches confirmation at the age of sixteen or seventeen.[8] The religious school curriculum for the early adolescents relates to bar mitzvah and to the study of the ceremony itself with a focus on ethics, the ritual liturgy, and Jewish history.

A third educational component begins approximately six months prior to the bar mitzvah date. The children meet individually with a special tutor to study the prayers and Hebrew passages from the Torah and the Haftarah that they will read and translate.[9]

This focus on education, beginning for children at such a young age, illustrates that the bar mitzvah is a ritualized expression of the centrality of learning in Judaism. The Hebrew language itself embodies this value: the word for *parent* means "teacher" in Hebrew.

Beginning at least as far back as the eighth century, a time when literacy was a rare accomplishment, learning was placed at the forefront of the definition of what it meant to be a Jew. In most of Europe Jews were forbidden to own land and were required to live in densely populated ghettoes (Stark 46). The professions that were open to European Jews in past centuries were restricted and required more learning than was necessary for non-Jews, who typically were farmers. Jews therefore became concentrated in occupations such as commerce, manufacturing, or highly skilled trades (Steinberg), occupations in which a certain level of literacy and learning was important. The bar mitzvah thus embodies the value of education both as a normative expression of the importance of scholarly religious study and as a link toward occupational attainment within the scope of available professions. Jews developed strong norms regarding schooling to the extent that males who showed the greatest academic aptitude were expected to adopt the role of scholar and to devote their lives to study and learning. Wealthy merchants sought scholars as sons-in-law because of the prestige that surrounded the scholarly life. In fact, the scholar would be supported by the wife's family so he could devote himself to full-time study. Scholarship, then, probably had its origins to some extent in financial survival for Jews beginning several centuries ago, and to ensure that learning would occur, study became a highly valued and integral part of both social and religious life beginning at an extremely young age (Zborowski and Herzog).

Educational Ritual as Affirmation

Ritual as "a compressed form of education" suggests that so much is taking place intensively through the peak experience of the ceremony itself that "it makes an indelible impact on the celebrant as to his roles and responsibilities" (Spiro, "Educational" 383). The young boy receives a sense of achievement from this ritual akin to nothing he has ever experienced in any other context. As one parent from our congregation said following his son's bar mitzvah,

> I was glad for Jacob in that he got a tremendous sense of accomplishment out of it, out of doing a good job . . . kids can benefit tremendously in so many ways, growing their self-confidence, sense of accomplishment—these are very valuable things that you don't get many times going through school. You don't experience that in school. Here's something they can work at and accomplish and come away with lasting experiences that they can look back on their whole lives and benefit from.

The children all do remarkably well with highly challenging material due to the long preparation period for language learning, time spent with the rabbi in study, and the intense and personal relationship in the

Hebrew tutoring process. As a result, "b'nai mitzvot,[10] virtually without exception, credibly enact their roles" (Schoenfeld 599); the boys and girls all complete the ritual successfully. This enactment, often in front of hundreds of family, friends, and congregants, provides a powerful affirmation for the Jewish youngsters of the importance of education and, indeed, of the rewards that one can achieve through learning.

The children receive the intrinsic gift of an enormous accomplishment. They also receive extrinsic gifts as well, not only from their families and friends, but also from the congregational board and from the rabbi. Many of the gifts are items used in Jewish ritual celebration, such as a Kiddish cup, Sabbath candlesticks, a *yad*, or special prayer books.[11] In addition, children often receive popular books, particularly those with some special Jewish content, such as *The Diary of Anne Frank*. In some communities the children also receive certificates entitling them to partial scholarships on youth study trips to Israel as recognition for completing the bar mitzvah. This acknowledgment of the ongoing nature of Jewish study and education emphasizes that the bar mitzvah ritual is only part of the development of one's Jewish learning.

This highly cognitive and difficult ritual, occurring as it does in early adolescence, motivates the Jewish child for academic success in the important school years ahead. The ability to complete the bar or bat mitzvah rite successfully makes the ordinary school trials seem almost trivial. As Aaron B. Seidman states,

> [bar mitzvah] is a portent and a promise . . . it . . . insure[s] him of eventual advancement and self-definition. For a young person to have less is to deprive him of a sense of continuum and to cause him to thrash about in generalized rebellion. Bar mitzvah can help the Jewish youth maintain his equilibrium and perspective. (89)

Family and Education

The educational element of bar mitzvah and bat mitzvah is not reserved only for children. Indeed, as Elliot Schoenberg claims, "a child's forthcoming bar-bat mitzvah can be the greatest inspiration for our own adult Jewish education" (259). Many parents begin attending regular services with their children, for whom attendance often is a bar mitzvah requirement. This creates a bond between the child and the parent; they spend time together on a Friday evening or Saturday morning for

Shabbat services at a time when, following bar mitzvah, the child is often with his peers instead. Parents find that their own preparation for their child's ceremony is to prepare by "growing Jewishly" themselves. One mother from our synagogue whose two sons each had a bar mitzvah recently said,

> I think going through this with my children and for myself has made me know that I am a Jew. . . . A friend and I were arguing about ritual, and is ritual dead in you, and you just accept things without thinking about it. And I said, it isn't; for me the ritual just makes it deeper.

The mother went on to speak about actually being able to learn from her son: "I do look to Alex for interpretation of things, because he knows more."

Often the parents of b'nai mitzvot enroll in adult education programs at their synagogues, study for their own adult b'nai mitzvot if they had not participated as children, and revitalize Jewish rituals in their own lives and the lives of their families. The affirmation of "growing Jewishly" extends not only into the lives of the children but also throughout the entire family. This has a positive influence on the child as well, who sees the parent continuing with Jewish education even as an adult.

Jews and Scholarship in the United States

Most of the Jews in the United States came from Eastern Europe in significant numbers at the beginning of the twentieth century. They carried this tradition of scholarly achievement with them, and early Jewish involvement in American higher education far outpaced that of any other immigrant group. Thomas Sowell reports that, in New York in 1916, Jews comprised 44% of students at Hunter College, 73% at City College, and 20% at Catholic Fordham University, far outstripping their proportion of the population. By the mid-twentieth century, more than 25% of Jewish males had four or more years of college, compared to less than 10% of the American population as a whole. In 1953, one in twenty Americans completed college, while one in six of all Jews (male and female) did so.

These educational achievements are reflected in occupational choices. Sowell's figures show that although only 8% of the population of Cleveland was Jewish in 1938, Jews comprised 18% of the dentists, 21% of the doctors, and 23% of the lawyers. At that same time, Jews constituted 25% of New York City's population but made up 64% of the dentists, 55% of the doctors, and 65% of the lawyers. More recently, Krefetz notes that in a national population that is only about 2.5% Jewish, over 20% of the country's lawyers are Jews and fully 60% of New York City's lawyers are Jews.

Law is something of a Jewish calling, because Jews had to deal with a diversity of societies and a multitude of economic systems in the Diaspora.[12] Gerald Krefetz noted, "Law appealed to the Jewish predilection for scholarly reflection" (187). Indeed, this reflection is something that the child learns during the bar mitzvah preparation. He must translate the Torah portion into his own words, struggling with meanings and shades of meanings of Hebrew words, and then provide his own commentary and reflection on that portion, usually guided by the rabbi's thoughtful and challenging questions. A Jewish friend relates attending Shabbat services with a friend of hers. They had listened to the Torah portion for that week. She said,

> We asked a lot of questions, and what does this Torah reading mean, and I was questioning back and forth. And I realized, we're working on this critical thinking paradigm. . . . And this is what we do, we do question everything, and that is part of being a Jew. This constant questioning and not accepting is a ritual.

The famous criminal lawyer and professor Alan Dershowitz says in public appearances that his early Torah and Talmudic training and argumentation taught him the skills necessary to be successful in the field of law.[13]

Jews have constituted significant proportions of the nation's physicians as well. At one point, roughly half of all the articles in American medical journals were authored by Jews (Krefetz 176). However, no trade, business, or profession is so exclusively Jewish as the fields of psychology and psychiatry. Estimates suggest that 30% of all psychiatrists are Jews. Krefetz writes, "So disproportionate is their representation that it apparently lends truth to the observation that the development of the mind is not only a Jewish avocation, but a vocation as well" (180). The development of the mind is a value that has both strong normative merit as well as professional benefit for Jews, as we have seen.

There can be no doubt that Jews play a large role in American intellectual life. In 1975, nearly half of the Jewish professors were teaching at the top-ranked institutions, and Jews made up 24% of the academic elite—those who have published twenty or more articles. Silberman's data on American Nobel Laureates indicate that in the last fifteen or twenty years, the Jewish proportion of Nobel Prize winners has been about 40%, and this is from a group that comprises less than 3% of the national population.

The culture of learning, therefore, is remarkably strong. The Jewish tradition is a literate one, and it is a tradition that engages young people in scholarly study at an early age. The outcome is the ability to be highly successful in areas that are based on rigorous intellectual inquiry. The seeds are sown in the public exhibition of the youths' ability with Torah, translation, and commentary. The young people learn to study, to prepare difficult material, to speak and to present arguments publicly, and to write critical material. All of the components are part of the bar mitzvah preparation, and all happen by age thirteen.

The Integration Function of Bar Mitzvah and Bat Mitzvah

We have looked at the role of bar mitzvah to reinforce the traditional Jewish importance of learning, both as a value in itself that is strongly held by the group and for occupational purposes. An equally important function of bar mitzvah is a social one.

Integration through Education

One of the many functions of rituals is providing for social integration. As Spiro explains, "Rituals serve an integrative function, keeping the society together and integrating the individual into the society in order to secure the perpetuation of the culture's life forces" ("Educational" 386). Childhood rituals are carried out in order to bring the child into the culture and into the group. This is accomplished by the bar mitzvah ritual in numerous ways, beginning with the educational training.

The Reform Jewish child most likely attends a secular day school with mostly non-Jewish children. At age five, when Jewish children begin attending religious school, they associate with other Jewish children in a formal and regular way. This once-weekly Jewish setting is supplemented by the additional four years of Hebrew schooling with Jewish children of the same age. Friendship formation among Jewish peers is strongly encouraged, and the Jewish child develops a series of relationships with Jewish teachers. The training with the tutor, usually an adult but occasionally a senior high school student, creates yet another opportunity for the child to develop attachments to Jews who are highly trained in Hebrew language and culture. Finally, several times during the bar mitzvah process, the child meets with the rabbi and the cantor to review and plan the order of the service.[14] Thus the child learns to participate in the religious ritual through a series of interactions with several groups of Jewish peers and adults.

Integration with the Parents

The bar mitzvah student is also deepening connections with the parents during late childhood and early adolescence at the very point that most children are separating from their parents. Much of the modern Reform Jewish preparation may involve time when the parent is alone with the child driving to lessons or to the synagogue, selecting ritual objects for the ceremony, planning the celebratory banquet, or selecting the invitations. This is a time between early childhood, when important conversations are not possible, and later adolescence, when the child often does not spend a great deal of time with the parents. This hiatus provides an opportunity that many parents speak of warmly, a time when the parent and child can communicate about a wide range of topics over a period of weeks and years. In this process, the parents' values and beliefs can be transmitted to the child as part of the ritual of membership and belonging.

Integration into the Community

The child is becoming integrated into his or her peer group of Jewish youngsters and into the family through the mechanism of Jewish education and bar mitzvah preparation. The rite provides integration into the community. The bar mitzvah as a religious "rite of passage" is perhaps less important than the coming-into-membership in the Jewish community. A moving example of this is Kenez's memoirs about life in Szekesfehervar, a small Hungarian town, shortly after the Holocaust. He speaks of his sense of belongingness as a Jew:

> Believing in God and being Jewish were two separate matters. My Jewishness was obviously not a matter of choice. It was a given, as my

awkward, gangly body was a given. What fool would have chosen it
given the times in which I lived? I knew that being Jewish was a burden,
but I am not sure that I recognized that it was also a small blessing, for
it gave me a sense of belonging that I overtly rejected but also unconsciously wanted. But you did not have to believe in God to be Jewish.
God really had nothing to do with it. . . . Jansci and I had our birthdays
only three weeks apart. . . . Our bar-mitzvah would belong not only to
Jansci and me, but to the entire little Jewish community of Szekesfehervar. For the community we represented the next generation. . . . About
a hundred fifty people came, almost the entire Jewish community. Most
of them I hardly knew, yet they wanted to come. I . . . was immensely
moved. (113–114)

The bar mitzvah belonged to the entire congregation. They came to
share and to participate in the sense of continuity and tradition. The
mother of a recent bar mitzvah boy said, "This [the people at the syn-
agogue] was our community. . . . All the people that I care about were
there . . . this was something that we were sharing with so many other
people."

Within the Reform ceremony, which takes about two hours and has
many moments of rich ritual significance, there is a single custom that,
for me, affirms Torah, education, religion, family, and history in one
moment. A "chain of tradition" is created with grandparents, parents,
and the bar mitzvah child standing together in front of the congregation. The heavy Torah scroll, representing Jews' commitment to a spiritual life exemplified by good deeds, ethical laws, and a love of learning,
is slowly handed down from one generation to the next, moving from
the arms of the grandparents to the arms of the parents and finally coming to rest in the arms of the child. The child then leaves the family in
a symbolic act of separation and marches with the Torah around the
entire congregation. This act represents the child's participation in that
community in a new status, alone without the parents. The Torah is
quite heavy, and this walk is sometimes a struggle for many children
who are still quite small. As the child makes this traditional walk, congregants reach to the aisles to touch the Torah with their prayer books
and then touch the books to their lips, symbolizing the love and sweet-
ness of learning Torah. The child is often greeted warmly by family and
friends during this brief but symbolic walk. The child concludes the
walk by going up to the bimah, the platform at the front of the synagogue, and then begins reading the Hebrew passages diligently studied

for so long and at so young an age. The child has literally "received the wisdom" of the older generations.

Following the child's Hebrew readings, in many congregations the parents are called to the bimah to address their child. The parents speak unabashedly about their love for their child and the strengths that the child has exhibited in reaching this momentous occasion. These speeches are often very powerful and highly intimate affirmations of parental love. The bar mitzvah ceremony represents the only time in a child's life when the parents are likely to proclaim the child's goodness, intelligence, and talents in front of virtually every person who is important in that child's life. These moments of highly charged emotion between the parents and their child, shared so publicly, create deep feelings in the ceremony's guests as well. There is tremendous affection for the child as all of the guests share in the parents' pride. This portion of the service embodies the ritualistic elements noted by Frederick Bird: the expression of strong feelings, and the representation and affirmation by the family of who they are to themselves and to others, usually including a strong value for education.

Near the conclusion of the service, the bar mitzvah child receives a blessing giving thanks for bringing him to this most special day. To symbolize the ongoing nature of this educational and integrative process, this brief blessing for the thirteen-year-old is given by a younger relative or younger family friend. Often a very young child, perhaps only three or four years old, is chosen to give this blessing. Typically even very young children are able to recite Hebrew prayers; there usually is considerable emphasis on teaching short Hebrew prayers to young children in home rituals such as lighting Sabbath candles. The young child has usually learned this prayer in Hebrew through diligent rehearsal and delivers it with a great deal of pride and occasional help from whispered parental coaching. This participation of the very young child represents the continuing process of Jewish tradition. We see the future in front of us: in a decade or less, that child will be on the bimah chanting a Torah portion and continuing the cycle of learning.

The family usually hosts a party after the service for relatives and friends to commemorate the child's achievement. This is a very emotional time; grandparents are often still alive who may not survive to see the wedding ceremony. The party often includes traditional foods, Israeli or Jewish music, and folk dancing.

A final celebratory event in a weekend filled with attention, praise, love, and ritual is a party for the child to which he or she invites school friends. For many Reform Jewish children, this party often includes non-Jewish friends. This is the first time that many Jewish children celebrate religious rituals with their mixed-religion friends. The opportunity to have a special party that honors the bar mitzvah's accomplishments in a group of non-Jewish children serves to reinforce peer relationships within the Jewish framework. For Reform Jewish children who usually live in predominantly non-Jewish environments, the bar mitzvah thus integrates them into their wider community.

Because of the familial, historical, and community importance of bar mitzvah, the celebrations are often quite elaborate and expensive. However, each synagogue and each Jewish community creates its own specific way of marking this event, with an increasing trend toward simplification.

Bar Mitzvah and Bat Mitzvah Memories

Our synagogue, Congregation Shir Tikvah, anticipates children's b'nai mitzvot well in advance of the actual ceremonies. Each Shabbat the children who are not yet of bar mitzvah age gather together on the bimah to recite the Kiddish, the blessing for a ceremonial cup of wine. The child who is next in line for the ceremony gets to hold the special silver Kiddish cup and to take a sip of wine at the end of the blessing. The congregation thus gets a "preview," a chance to see which child is going to be celebrating soon. My children participated in these recitations for several years leading up to their bar and bat mitzvot.

In addition, a month before a bar mitzvah, the child's picture is in the synagogue newsletter along with an article about his interests, his school activities and academic accomplishments, and a general announcement about the service and the luncheon to which all congregants are invited. Everyone in the congregational community thus gets to "know" the child, to recognize him on sight and by name, and to acknowledge his membership in the religious group. The child's abilities and hobbies are therefore publicly acclaimed even before the ceremony itself.

My daughter Louisa celebrated her bat mitzvah a year after my mother's death. Louisa was also the first Jewish grandchild in the family, although not the first grandchild, which made the occasion extremely rich with significance. She had once asked my mother, "Grandma, are you Jewish?" Grandma had laughed and replied, "Honey, if it weren't for me, *you* wouldn't be Jewish!" Louisa's bat mitzvah was truly a tribute to her grandmother's memory and provided all of us with a sense of intergenerational Jewish continuity.

Although bat mitzvah ceremonies are becoming quite common among Reform Jews, this is a fairly new phenomenon; as recently as the 1960s it was still rather unusual. One of the fathers of a bat mitzvah commented that his wife, who was not Jewish (but has since converted), recognized what a

> tremendous achievement this was for a 13-year-old girl to do, and what a tremendous ego-booster for a girl, and all that. And she didn't understand that it was unusual for a girl to do. She just assumed you were supposed to do that. *[Laughs]* You know? "Isn't that great, all Jewish girls get to do that?" Well, actually, all Jewish girls don't get to do that. *[Laughs]* So Shir Tikvah was very good in that it's so egalitarian that when you've got daughters, you're expected to do it, and that's it!

For girls to have this opportunity at the beginning of their teen years is indeed special, and for many of them, it opens the door to strong Jewish identity and leadership in their synagogue community. This has been the case with many young women in our synagogue.

Louisa's Torah portion was particularly meaningful: Lech Lecha, the covenant between Abraham and God. The passage reflected Louisa's familiar role in carrying on Jewish tradition and belief. Louisa is deeply committed to Judaism, and this selection was especially appropriate for her. A poignant moment occurred immediately before she entered the sanctuary with the rabbi. Louisa had enjoyed her preparation and study, and she asked the rabbi when she could read from the Torah again in front of the congregation. She and the rabbi chose the date of my mother's yahrzeit for her Torah reading, thereby continuing the tradition of Torah study with the added dimension of honoring the memory of the past generation through that study.[15]

My son Jonathan's bar mitzvah three years later marked not only his thirteenth birthday but also my father's eighty-fifth birthday. At the beginning of the service Grandpa draped Jonathan in his tallit, or prayer shawl. The richness of the moment of passing along the tradition, of giving the learning and wisdom of the old man to the young man, was almost palpable and set the tone for the rest of the highly emotion-laden and beautiful service.

Jonathan had worked very hard to reach his big day. He had been quite ill and had undergone surgery a month before the bar mitzvah. When I addressed him on the bimah, I spoke of his commitment and dedication to the ceremony. He had rehearsed his Torah portion daily as he convalesced at home, looking weak and wan but struggling diligently until he perfected his Hebrew, his translation, and his d'var Torah. This was an effort of almost Herculean proportions for a young man not quite thirteen studying under very adverse conditions. I was so proud of him and spoke publicly about the love that I felt for him.

Everyone had tears as we realized the joy and magnitude of his accomplishments, tears that Rabbi Salkin calls "immortal tears" (17). He says that the River of Tears flows because of a sense of immortality. Personal immortality is the unspoken, unarticulated prayer at every lifecycle event. It is in all our thoughts: "At a bar or bat mitzvah, a parent thinks not so much of the future as of the past, especially if a grandparent or a parent is deceased; the entire family one has known has assembled, and that is as much the past as the future" (17). Rabbi Salkin writes of a particularly unemotional man who wept profusely at his daughter's bat mitzvah. The man explained much later why he wept:

> My father and my brother are both deceased. My kids are named for both of them.[16] And now my daughters are both mature Jewish adults. I felt that the cycle was complete. Certain things touch you that persuade you of a Higher Power. For me, it was the memory of people who had died. . . . I could hear them taking pleasure in my daughter reading the Torah. (18)

We all had feelings that day of the cycle, of Jonathan beginning his adult life as his grandfather was approaching his own life's end. These same emotions had flooded over me as my daughter brought back so many memories of my mother.

Both children invited many non-Jewish friends and their parents to the ceremony. This was an opportunity to share their Jewish tradition and to introduce their friends to rituals that were quite different from their friends' Christian practices. Their friends saw them excel in an environment filled with love and support. Louisa and Jonathan also were able to demonstrate their knowledge and training before a very large group of people. As Jonathan said to me while he was preparing for the service, "Everybody I know in my life who's important to me will be there." At no other time do children demonstrate their academic prowess so extensively and in so visible a setting. For non-Jews seeing this ceremony for the first time, it is quite awesome that thirteen-year-olds are so skilled in a difficult language and so poised in front of "everybody they know in their lives."

Louise and Jonathan each had parties with their friends. Most of their friends are not Jewish, since we live in a midwestern city with a fairly small proportion of Jews. The friends acknowledged the tremendous effort that went into the bar mitzvah and also learned about the ritual itself. Louisa and Jonathan experienced a special and privileged status at these parties: they were being recognized in positive and public ways by their friends for being Jews, with gifts, cards, and an enormous amount of praise. They were particularly touched when friends gave them gifts with Jewish content that obviously represented a great deal of thought and effort to purchase.

The outcome for Louisa and Jonathan at this point is continued academic excellence, broad extracurricular involvement in their secular schools, and an ongoing involvement with Judaism. Louisa works as a teacher's aide in the religious school, is president of the synagogue's youth group, and has received awards for her work in the Jewish community. She tutors a young girl who is preparing for bat mitzvah. Jonathan read Hebrew prayers at Rosh Hashanah services that autumn after his bar mitzvah, and he continued his studies on the way to confirmation. They were asked to read Torah together at one Shabbat service and enjoyed the opportunity to share in the study, preparation, and event. This shared reading represents the siblings coming together in the sacred event of Torah study, taking their places as scholarly adults in the synagogue community and carrying on the family involvement as Jews.

Conclusion

The bar mitzvah ritual is a complex one. Elliot Schoenberg writes, "For many families, the bar mitzvah stands out as an exceptional event, to be confronted in its exceptionality" (594). The ceremony requires years of study, interaction with many adults, and a level of commitment that most thirteen-year-olds would not be able to achieve. That young Jews throughout the world continue to celebrate this centuries-old rite is a testament to its power. Bar mitzvah represents the "ethos" of Judaism: learning and community. The religion has survived for several thousand years in part because of the power of this ritual in affirming Jewish learning as well as the child's role in the life of the family, the synagogue, and the general community. This ritual occurs at a crucial point in a child's development, the threshold between childhood and adolescence, a time of vulnerability. The bar or bat mitzvah ceremony in its richness and complexity makes an indelible impression and, for most young people, creates a lifelong commitment to education and to Jewish life.

The methodological perspective for this essay is based not only on research but also on extensive personal participation and involvement during the bat and bar mitzvah celebrations of my own children: Louisa in 1993 and Jonathan in 1997. In addition, I have been an active member of Reform Jewish synagogues my entire life. I have served on the board of trustees, have taught in the religious schools of several congregations, have chaired various committees, and have participated in many synagogue educational and social activities. Although some scholars argue that such an "insider" role precludes objectivity, this role also "provides information about dimensions of inner life not readily available to pure researchers" (Fishbane 156). I have tried to write with both objectivity and with a sense of sharing some of those "dimensions of inner life."

I would like to thank Rabbi Stacy Offner of Congregation Shir Tikvah, Minneapolis, for help with many resources for this essay. I also thank Elise Sicard, Carrie Milbrett, and Joy Anderson, students at the University of St. Thomas, for their bibliographic assistance.

NOTES

1. A *bat mitzvah* refers to the ceremony for Jewish girls. The bat mitzvah was officially introduced in France and Italy and was widely adopted in other countries during the twentieth century (*Encyclopedia Judaica Jerusalem* 1972). In both Reform and Conservative synagogues, the girls' participation is the same as that of the boys; however, in Orthodox ceremonies, the girls' participation is much more limited (Unterman 125). For the purposes of simplicity in this essay, the terms *bar mitzvah* and *his* will be used in most statements; the reader is asked to understand that *bat mitzvah* and *hers* are also implied.

2. The various streams of Judaism include Orthodox (those who adhere quite strictly to traditional ritual practice and belief), Conservative (a branch formed in reaction to the nineteenth-century Reform movement), Reform (a liberal and progressive movement), and Reconstructionist.

3. Jews typically use BCE (before the common era) and CE (of the common era), rather than the designators BC (before Christ) and AD (*anno Domini*, in the year of the Lord).

4. The writing of Midrash, commentaries on religious laws, took place largely between the years 400 and 1200 CE (Holtz 178).

5. Readings from the Torah (the first five books of the Bible: Genesis, Exodus, Leviticus, Numbers, and Deuteronomy) occur in synagogues on Mondays, Thursdays, and Saturdays; Saturday is the Jewish Sabbath, called Shabbat, which begins Friday at sundown and concludes Saturday at sundown. The readings on Shabbat are of more import than those on the other days, and in most Reform synagogues, Torah is read only on Shabbat.

6. A *minyan*, a group of ten adult males (this can include females in Reform and Conservative Judaism), is required for conducting ritual prayers in the synagogue.

7. *Aliyah* refers to being called to the front of the synagogue to recite a benediction prior to and following the reading of the Torah.

8. *Consecration* is a ceremony marking the beginning of a child's formal Jewish training. In most synagogues the child is called to the front of the congregation and receives a miniature Torah that represents the study of the biblical laws and the Hebrew language that begins at that time.

9. The Haftarah includes the biblical books of the Prophets. Each week a prescribed section of the Torah and its thematically related portion of the Haftarah are read; these readings are fixed and are repeated annually in the same order in all synagogues throughout the world.

10. *B'nai mitzvot* is a plural for either *bar* or *bat mitzvah*.

11. A *Kiddish cup* is a special wine glass used in various synagogue and home rituals; Sabbath candlesticks are used for lighting candles on Friday evening to usher in the Sabbath; a *yad* is a pointer, usually made of silver, to guide one's place in reading from the Torah instead of touching one's finger to the parchment.

12. *Diaspora* refers to all Jews living outside of Israel.

13. Dershowitz made this point at Temple Beth El, Minneapolis, MN, October 1997.

14. The *cantor* is the man or woman who leads the congregation in music during the service.

15. A *yahrzeit* is the anniversary of a person's death. It is marked in the synagogue with special prayers and in the home with the lighting of a long-burning candle and the recitation of prayers.

16. In the Eastern European Jewish tradition, called *Ashkenazic*, Jews typically name children after a loved one who has passed away. In the *Sefardic*, or Southern European tradition, children are named after a living relative.

WORKS CITED

Bird, Frederick B. "Family Rituals and Religion: A Functional Analysis of Jewish and Christian Family Ritual Practices." In *Ritual and Ethnic Identity: A Comparative Study of the Social Meaning of Liturgical Ritual in Synagogues*, ed. Jack N. Lightstone and Frederick B. Bird, 185–195. Waterloo, ON: Wilfrid Laurier University Press, 1995.

Encyclopaedia Judaica Jerusalem. Vol. 4, "Bar mitzvah," 243–247. Jerusalem, Israel: Keter, 1972.

Fishbane, Simcha. "Contemporary Bar Mitzvah Rituals in Modern Orthodoxy." In *Ritual and Ethnic Identity: A Comparative Study of the Social Meaning of Liturgical Ritual in Synagogues*, ed. Jack N. Lightstone and Frederick B. Bird, 155–167. Waterloo, ON: Wilfrid Laurier University Press, 1995.

Holtz, Barry, ed. *Back to the Sources*. New York: Summit Books, 1984.

Jacob, Walter. "Initiation into Judaism." *Religious Education* 74:6 (November–December 1979): 597–602.

Kenez, Peter. "Bar Mitzvah in Szekesfehervar: Remembrance of Life in Hungary," *Judaism* 44 (Winter 1995): 104–114.

Krefetz, Gerald. *Jews and Money: The Myths and the Reality*. New Haven, CT: Ticknor and Fields, 1992.

Sager, Steven R. "The Jewish Identity of Confirmation: Problem and Proposal." *Religious Education* 78:2 (Spring 1983): 201–209.

Salkin, Rabbi Jeffrey K. *Putting God on the Guest List: How to Reclaim the Spiritual Meaning of Your Child's Bar or Bat Mitzvah*. Woodstock, VT: Jewish Lights, 1992.

Schoenberg, Elliot Salo. "Conservative Judaism and Adolescence." *Religious Education* 81:2 (Spring 1986): 251–266.

Schoenfeld, Stuart. "Recent Publications on Bar/Bat Mitzvah: Their Implications for Jewish Education Research and Practice." *Religious Education* 89 (1994): 594–609.

Seidman, Aaron B. "Bar Mitzvah—An Approach to Social Maturity." *Tradition* 13 (Winter 1973): 85–89.

Sherwin, Byron L. "Bar Mitzvah." *Judaism* 22 (Winter 1973): 53–65.

Silberman, Charles E. *A Certain People: American Jews and Their Lives Today*. New York: Summit Books, 1985.

Sowell, Thomas. *Ethnic America: A History*. New York: Basic Books, 1981.

Spiro, Jack. "The Educational Significance of the Bar Mitzvah Initiation." *Religious Education* 72:4 (July–August 1977): 383–399.

Stark, Rodney. *Sociology.* 7th ed. Belmont, CA: Wadsworth/Thomson Learning, 1997.

Steinberg, Stephen. *The Academic Melting Pot.* New York: McGraw-Hill, 1974.

Unterman, Alan. "Judaism." In *Rites of Passage,* ed. Jean Holm with John Bowker, 113–137. London: Pinter, 1994.

Zborowski, Mark, and Elizabeth Herzog. *Life Is with People: The Culture of the Shtetl.* New York: Schocken Books, 1962.

PART 3

EDUCATION

C hildren learn through repetition, a careful plan of lessons reinforcing and building upon the ones before. This pattern is
built into American education and manifests itself in many
ways. How and what children learn reflect the values of a culture. For
example, a classroom arranged with desks in neat, straight rows emphasizes independent learning and structure, whereas fluid groupings of
tables and chairs suggest collaboration and informality. The decisions
to use same-gender or mixed-gender classes and traditional or revision-
ist texts also contribute to the educational experience. Most research
into the rituals of learning takes a positive approach, focusing on the
diversity of methods used to create educated individuals; however, not
all learning and school practices end happily. The rituals of bullying
among older schoolchildren and classroom experiences that lead to
lower expectations for success among females and the less privileged
classes shed light on the darker side of familiar school-time rituals.

Two essays follow, each addressing the ritualistic quality of education in America. Taking a historical and literary approach, Luise van
Keuren in "The American Girl at Her Sampler, ca. 1633–1850: Inspir-
ing a Feminine Ideal" argues that both the physical practice of constructing samplers and the messages inscribed on them provided powerful lessons in behavior for colonial girls. Barbara Martinson, in "The
Journey to School: Illustrations from Popular American Magazines,
1900–1962," explores twentieth-century school rituals as derived from
an analysis of familiar Rockwellian images presented in the *Saturday
Evening Post* and other mainstream publications. Both articles show how
lessons regarding gender roles are embedded and inescapable in

Americans' educational experiences. Further, if children's learning takes place not only at home and at school but also through friends, media, and other sources, these lessons take on greater importance.

5

The American Girl at Her Sampler, ca. 1633–1850

Inspiring a Feminine Ideal

LUISE VAN KEUREN

America's First Sampler

Lord guide my Heart that I may do thy will
And fill my hands with such convenient skill
As will conduce to Virtue void of shame
and I will give the Glory to thy Name
(From a sampler by Loara Standish, ca. 1633)

This reverent little verse appears on the earliest surviving sampler created by an American girl. Miles Standish's daughter Loara (sometimes spelled "Lora") was probably about ten years old at the time she embroidered her sampler, and we know she was born in 1623. On display now at Pilgrim Hall in Plymouth, Massachusetts, this sampler is characteristic of the earlier American type. Its embroidery ornaments a long, narrow strip of linen, the shape reflecting the narrow looms in use then. Though the fabric is browned with age, one can see the varied colors of the silken embroidery threads, in pastel hues popular in that era (Edmonds 14). Loara's work represents a ritual that was already a well-established practice in several countries in Europe when her parents emigrated with the Plymouth Pilgrims, and the custom may date as far back as the Middle Ages. In the New World, after Loara's time, American samplers evolved, growing squarer as looms changed, the embroidery colors becoming brighter and richer, the designs moving away from English models to New World innovations. Certainly this young Pilgrim's sampler was preserved because of its connections to a historically prominent family, but Loara's is one of thousands of samplers preserved in institutional and private collections. These artifacts betoken thousands more, lost to time, that were created abundantly by American girls until the mid-nineteenth century, providing through this enduring ritual an insight into the ideal of girlhood in an earlier era.

A Ritual of Girlhood Education

Today we think of sampler making and similar needlework as a pastime—producing a charming decorative handicraft. But to these young girls from the prime period of sampler making, this was no pastime. It was important business—a requisite task of girlhood education. Elias Howe received his first American patent for a sewing machine in 1846, and some years passed before his and other machine models were widely available. Before that time women made many, if not all, of the family's garments and hemmed the linen in the household, sewing everything by hand. Sewing was a staple of feminine skills. Naturally, it was also a staple of girlhood education. As Joan Edwards has written:

> It is probably correct to say that behind every sampler is a girl who, before she began it, already knew how to cut out small garments and sew them together with infinitesimal stitches, and to perform such tricky feats as inserting gores and gussets, stroking gathers, making darts and fine pintucks, inserting lace, sewing on buttons and working strong buttonholes, matching up patches and doing invisible mending. (17)

A knowledge of embroidery stitches—which sampler making trained a girl to acquire—was something she could expect to use in adulthood. Her sewing skills made her a more attractive prospective spouse and capable homemaker. As one sampler verse put it:

> Of female arts in usefulness
> The needle far exceeds the rest.
> In ornament there's no device,

Affords adorning half so nice.
(Shelburne Museum, Shelburne, VT)

The word *sampler* suggests the custom's function. As Joan Edwards points out, the earliest embroidery pattern books were called Books of Exampla (18). The term *"sampler* denotes the "examples" of stitches displayed. In fact, the earliest samplers, before the seventeenth century, were merely strips of cloth embroidered with rows or blocks of varied stitches; there were no alphabets or pictures or verses. A girl kept this collection of stitch models through adulthood, added and referred to it through the years. By the time sampler making came to America, however, the familiar additional sampler features were common—and are shown on Loara Standish's sampler.

At the height of the American sampler era—throughout the colonial period to the mid-nineteenth century—embroidery ornamented many kinds of garments. It also was used to mark each piece of the household's valuable linen with identifying marks. This custom is referred to in Louisa May Alcott's *Little Women* when Aunt March enlists a neighbor to "buy, have made, and marked, a generous supply of house and table linen" as a wedding present for Meg (Alcott 271).

Sampler making became an educational task at the point in a girl's life when her education diverged into a particularly feminine curriculum. In her earliest years, a girl at this time might be taught by her mother or by local women who operated in their homes what was variously called a "cent school," "penny school," or "dame school." In such schools both girls and boys studied the rudiments of reading, writing, and ciphering. After that point, while the boys went their way to study a more academic curriculum, the girls received an education focused on "the accomplishments" or "graces." This might be in privately arranged education with a teacher or, as they became available, in a public school. In the eighteenth century the private academy for girls became popular, and girls' boarding schools were numerous by the early 1800s. The "graces" taught in these circumstances included not only French, psalm singing, playing musical instruments, and drawing, but also such handiwork as filigree work, featherwork, quill work, turkey work, painting on fans and glass, embroidering pictures, japanning (resembling decoupage), and making objects or pictures from shells, hair, or wax (Harbeson 51). Other "accomplishments" included the more practical skills of quilting and sampler making.

The Girlhood Sewing Circle

Since sampler making was a task of schoolgirl life, the activity also provided occasions for girls to work together, each on her own handiwork. This opportunity for companionship might last for years. As she grew older, a girl typically progressed toward more elaborate samplers. She might begin when as young as six years old with a "marking" sampler that practiced the letters and numbers used for marking and identifying linen and clothing. The sampler might be quite small—sometimes as small as a modern potholder. As she gained skill, a girl moved on to a larger, more complex sampler depicting, with her thread and needle, animals, flowers, trees, and people, and including borders and a motto or verse—sometimes verses of multiple stanzas. Other kinds of "fancy" samplers, as these were called, included map samplers, genealogical samplers listing family names and life dates, and wedding and mourning samplers. In their American heyday, samplers frequently included the girl's name and the completion date of the sampler, sometimes her birth date or her town, and occasionally the name of her teacher. Throughout her girlhood a child often completed a series of samplers, documenting her increasing skill. Historical collections show that pupils, sometimes sisters, often worked side by side with the same teacher—as we see by the verses and patterns they all used and the inclusions of their common town and their instructor's name in the text.

Did these girls enjoy the companionship of the sampler-making circle? In Shakespeare's *A Midsummer Night's Dream,* the bard alludes to the bonding this childhood activity brought the participants. His Helena appeals to her friend Hermia to remember these precious childhood hours:

> HELENA: (to Hermia)
> . . . O, is it all forgot?
> All schooldays friendship, childhood innocence?
> We, Hermia, like two artificial gods,
> Have with our needles created both one flower,
> Both on one sampler, sitting on one cushion,
> Both warbling of one song, both in one key;
> As if our hands, our sides, voices, and minds
> Had been incorporate.
>
> (III, ii)

Certainly this opportunity for friendship came to America with the sampler-making tradition. An elaborate sampler required several months of work and, thus, many hours with a child's companions. We can imagine the quiet conversation shared, the mutual encouragement as each child's work developed.

The practice of signing one's name to a sampler became increasingly common from the seventeenth century onward. Some of the verses also included the child's name proudly marking her creation with her own identity:

> Lydia Hart is my name
> And with my needle I wrought the same
> But if my skill had been better
> I would have mended every letter.
> > (New Hampshire Historical Society,
> > Concord, NH)

> Tamson Evans is my name
> New England is my nation
> Barrington is my dwelling place
> And Christ is my salvation
> > (Sturbridge Village, Sturbridge, MA)

Some sampler verse clearly celebrates a girl's accomplishment:

> In the pleasant season of youth
> When cares are small and few,
> I'll show to others of my age,
> What busy hands can do.
> > (Sturbridge Village, Sturbridge, MA)

Undoubtedly, there were girls who did not ply a needle with any joy. A delightful proof of this is the comment sewn on a sampler by one spirited young seamstress:

> Patty Poke did this and she hated every stitch she
> did in it. She loves to read much more.
> > (Bolton and Coe 96)

While there must have been moments of weariness or annoyance, most of our evidence shows that girls—and the adult women they became—were proud of their accomplishments, as were their families. As a popular sampler verse reflects:

> How blest the maid whom circling years improve
> Her God the object of her warmest love

Whose useful hours successive as they glide
Her book, her needle, and her pen divide.
(Society for the Preservation of
New England Antiquities)

In the eighteenth century some samplers began to be framed and displayed in the home. Numerous samplers were passed on to heirs in women's wills as precious heirlooms (Ring 24). Many samplers in institutional collections have been donated with archives of letters, journal pages, and other documents, testifying to the appreciation of the maker's affection for her childhood accomplishments and to her descendants' pride in them.

Apt Emblem of a Virtuous Maid

Sweet stream that winds through yonder glade
Apt emblem of a virtuous maid
Silent and chaste she steals along
Far from the world's gay, busy throng
Intent upon her destined course
Blessing and blessed wherever she goes.
(Strong DAR Museum, Addison, VT)

The ritual of sampler making was more than a practical exercise. It was also an early form of values education for young girls. The sewing expertise this ritual developed implied that a child's goal was to prepare herself for the duties of a homemaker—a useful, skilled, moral guardian of the household. As young girls worked together in a solely female activity, strengthening the bonds among friends, they also prepared themselves to provide a feminine influence in the community as well, since women often provided nursing, midwifery, neighborly care, early childhood education—not only for their own families but also for their communities. Beyond this, these girls could expect that their circle of support in adulthood would come from other women. Their confidantes, advisers, and role models would be women. Childhood education, as they worked their samplers, helped girls cultivate this feminine community.

Sampler making also developed qualities of character a girl would need in a difficult, demanding, and uncertain world. Patience, perseverance, fastidiousness, and an aesthetic appreciation were nourished by the careful, precise nature of the sampler-making task.

However, it is in the sampler verses a girl inscribed with her stitches that the activity took on its most blatantly edifying function. The verse chosen for a girl's sampler—by her teacher, her parents, or herself—was unquestionably chosen to express the ideals to which American girlhood should aspire, according to her contemporary society. As a child worked painstakingly at her sampler, she certainly committed her embroidered verse to memory and probably retained its lines in her mind throughout her life.

As a representation of the feminine ideal of the period, the hundreds of sampler verses that have survived create a consistent picture of what a girl should strive to be. The ethics of these verses were clearly intended to help a child successfully confront the expectations and blunt realities of a woman's world.

Of all the sampler verse themes, virtue is the most prominent:

> Here is this green and shady bower
> Delicious fruits and fragrant flowers
> Virtue shall dwell within this seat
> Virtue alone can make it sweet.
> > (Society for the Preservation of
> > New England Antiquities)

Sampler verse speaks of a world fraught with threats to feminine purity and of a feminine sphere in which women were kept sequestered from the world's corruption. A sampler from Boston in 1800 compares the female to a "fair violet" whose "mild fragrance" blooms modestly out of public view, "unknown to flourish and unseen be great."

Feminine purity remained the ideal when Alexis de Tocqueville and Harriet Martineau visited America in the 1830s. Martineau observed of the American woman, "her morals are guarded by the strictest observance of propriety in her presence" (292). Tocqueville wrote that "religious peoples . . . consider the regularity of a woman's life the best guarantee and surest sign of the purity of her morals," and stated that marriage provided that regularity, a woman's home being "almost a cloister" (Tocqueville 568).

A common sampler verse theme on virtue was to warn a child against the dangers that lurk in the world, ready to corrupt the young mind:

> See here the Youth by Wisdom led
> The paths of life securely tread

> The dangerous lures of folly shun
> and virtue's course serenely run.
> > (Vermont Historical Society,
> > Montpelier, VT)

The "dangerous lures" most commonly mentioned are vanity and pride. Spurning the superficial vanities is constantly recommended by sampler verse. "Beauty may fade and empires fall," a common refrain warns, "but Virtue triumphs over all." The virtuous "sigh not for beauty nor languish for wealth." "The Glowing Gem" is to be scorned in favor of "truth and innocence." It is "Spotless Innocence," in fact, that guards "inexperienced youth / from Vanity and Pride."

Such temptations are not only in the external world but also within the child, in her own emotional self. Suspicion of emotions is a recurrent motif:

> Virtue's the chiefest beauty of the mind
> The noblest ornament of Humankind.
> Virtue's our safeguard and our shining star
> That stirs up reason when our senses err.
> > (Society for the Preservation of
> > New England Antiquities)

The "fair violet" of womanhood thrived with "her passions all corrected or subdu'd."

> May I govern my passions
> with absolute sway
> and grow wiser & better
> As life wears away.
> > (Sandwich Glass Museum, Sandwich, MA)

The mind, as well as the senses and the passions, was vulnerable to temptations. "The joys of earth" are the "tempters of the mind," and the prudent child learns to know them as "false as the smooth deceitful sea / And empty as the whistling wind."

Duty and obedience were the right path for the growing child. Tocqueville observed that "public opinion carefully keeps woman within the little sphere of domestic interests and duties and will not let her go beyond them" (568). Some sampler verses allude to these restrictions and admonish girls to "live contented in that state you own." Alexander Pope's advice is sometimes quoted, to "act well your part / There all the honor lies."

In its most pragmatic context, a girl needed to acknowledge the restraints in her world on such things as legal status, marriage choices, voice in community affairs, and a social position compared to fathers, husbands, and—as a widow—even to sons (Hoffman and Albert 68). In its least complimentary tone, this restricted feminine sphere is grounded on the concept of the female nature. As one of the most submissive sampler verses declares:

> Plain as this canvas was, as plain we find
> Unlettered, unadorned the female mind.
> No fine ideas fill the vacant soul
> No graceful colouring animates the whole.
> (Trayser Museum, Barnstable, MA)

Thus it was natural that a child would be encouraged to revere those who offered her guidance. It was their role to lead the child to virtuous conduct, to "pluck out the weed / And cultivate the flower." To her parents she pledged to "strive to mend and to be obedient ever." On this theme this common sampler verse extolls parental care:

> Next unto God, Dear Parents, I address
> Myself to you in Humble Thankfulness
> For all the Care you have on me Bestow'd
> The means of Learning Unto me Allowed.
> Go on, I pray, and let me still pursue
> Those Golden Arts the vulgar never knew.
> (Colonel Jeremiah Lee House,
> Marblehead, MA)

A child's "green unpractis'd years" were molded by parents who pruned "every fault and every worth improves."

Duty also extended beyond the home in the form of the obligation to serve the community's less fortunate. One emotion a girl was encouraged to have was sympathy. "The virtuous thrift of doing good / This great ambition still she calls her own." The young sampler maker was urged to offer charity to poor neighbors, to care for widows and orphans, and to nurse the sick. Such lines promoted mercy for the "naked wanderer" and the "cold and destitute," that "thine own soul may live."

It was the link between the feminine and social duty that eventually brought criticism of sympathetic women in the nineteenth century who became active in reform movements. Martineau made note of the reproaches in American society against women who spoke in public arenas and attended public meetings. The offense of such women was not in their sympathies but that they "chose their duty for themselves" (293–294).

Of course, above duty to parents, teachers, and friends—all subjects of sampler verses—came duty to God. "First to my God my gratitude I owe," a popular verse begins. Here again, virtue is the key sign of reverence. "May I repay the care on me bestow'd," the verse concludes, "by aiming to be virtuous, pious, good."

Religious faith served to guard a child against temptations and also to strengthen her against her own weak nature. When we consider the transience of life in this era, we must appreciate that this theme of religious faith was also intended to prepare a girl for the abundant reminders of mortality all around her. In early America about four out of every ten children died before age six, and many childhood diseases, such as measles, mumps, whooping cough, and chicken pox, were often fatal (Swan 30). Even by the end of the nineteenth century, the death rate for children under one year old was 145 per thousand, about ten times our modern rate *(Historical Statistics)*. As women, these girls would face the threat of death in childbirth. In her role as nurse and midwife, a woman could expect to sit at many a deathbed. So it is not surprising that a girl would be encouraged to inscribe verses such as these on her sampler:

> When I am dead and in my grave
> And all my bones are rotten
> Look at this and think of me
> When I am quite forgotten.
> (Woodstock Historical Society, Woodstock, VT)

> The rising morn can't assure
> That we shall end the day
> For death stands ready at the door
> To snatch our lives away.
>   (Sturbridge Village, Sturbridge, MA)

The transience of life was all the more reason to cling to virtue and faith. Religious devotion helped the growing child to accept mortality as a natural part of life, rising "with willing minds and ardent feet / To yonder happy skies." Fleeting time pressed the obedient child to use her time well, pursuing the ideals of industry and virtue:

> Behold, alas, our days we spend.
> How vain they are, how soon they end.

May useful arts employ my youth
In love of virtue and of truth
So when these fleeting moments end
A crown immortal I may find.
> (Colonel Jeremiah Lee House,
> Marblehead, MA)

Remember Me When I Am Dead

As a popular girlhood educational ritual, sampler making declined by the mid-nineteenth century. The custom had spread over the expanding American nation, traveling westward with pioneer migrations, and though its heyday had passed, samplers continued to be made, though in decreasing numbers, to the end of the century. Several factors contributed to the decline of sampler making. In the 1840s indelible ink was introduced, providing a practical means of marking garments and linen. The sewing machine had begun to replace reliance on hand sewing. Most importantly, though, feminine education had evolved. The number of public schools, teaching boys and girls together, increased. In the 1820s the first free public high schools were opened for girls. Even in the eighteenth century, voices of reform had urged a rejection of "the graces" as a curriculum specially suited to girls (Swan 46). By the 1840s these voices were being heard. Plucked from their educational context, the late-century samplers became more ornamental than functional—a pastime rather than a lesson.

Yet the sampler ritual in early America gives witness to girlhood life in that era. "The twining texture of this thread," so a sampler verse declares, "may speak of me when I am dead." These threads do speak of happy hours spent together performing a valued task and of girlhood ideals: virtue, duty, obedience, faith, usefulness, truth, charity, humility, a sober sense of transience. For—in the words that complete this verse— "But grace, not art, survives the tomb / And gives the soul immortal bloom." The sampler ritual began linking from early childhood both practical skill and spiritual growth, implying that both were necessary for a girl to thrive. This careful task established a habit of diligent attention, satisfaction in accomplishment, and thoughtful reflection. Sampler verse themes reflect the social, religious, and pragmatic character of the era that this early form of values education prepared a girl to meet. As we picture the many young girls who worked at the window or by lamplight, friends at her elbow, this portrait is not without its charm, despite the confined sphere it suggests. Indeed, its grace—as well as its art—has survived the tomb. It testifies to the enduring spirit of the feminine world:

> Since beauties bloom to time must bow
> And age deform the fairest brow
> Let brighter charms be yours.
> The female mind embalmed in truth
> Shall bloom in everlasting youth
> While time itself endures.
> (Grafton Historical Society, Grafton, VT)

WORKS CITED

Alcott, Louisa May. *Little Women.* New York: Grosset and Dunlap, 1947.

Bolton, Ethel S., and Eva Johnston Coe. *American Samplers.* 1920. Reprint, New York: Weathervane, 1973.

Edmonds, Mary Jaene. *Samplers and Samplermakers: On American Schoolgirl Art, 1700–1850.* New York: Rizzoli, 1991.

Edwards, Joan. *Joan Edward's Small Books on the History of Embroidery: Sampler Making, 1540–1940.* Surrey, UK: Bayford Books, 1983.

Harbeson, Georgina Brown. *American Needlework.* New York: Bonanza Books, 1938. *Historical Statistics of the United States: Colonial Times to 1957.* Washington, DC: U.S. Bureau of the Census.

Hoffman, Ronald, and Peter J. Albert, eds. *Women in the Age of the American Revolution.* Charlottesville: University Press of Virginia, 1989.

Martineau, Harriet. *Society in America.* 1837. Reprint, ed. and abridged by Seymour Martin Lipset. Gloucester, MA: Peter Smith, 1962.

Ring, Betty. *Girlhood Embroidery, American Samplers and Pictorial Needlework, 1650–1850.* Vol. 1. New York: Knopf, 1993.

Swan, Susan Burrows. *Plain and Fancy: American Women and Their Needlework, 1700–1850.* New York: Holt, Rinehart and Winston, 1977.

Tocqueville, Alexis de. *Democracy in America,* ed. J. P. Mayer and Max Lerner. Trans. George Lawrence. New York: Harper and Row, 1966.

6

The Journey to School

Illustrations from Popular American Magazines, 1900–1962

BARBARA MARTINSON

A life is made of birth, birthdays, comings of age, marriages, more births, acceptings, passings on, and death. Institutional life requires entering, passing through, and learning; so we have initiation and welcomings, graduations and promotions, expulsions, resignations, firings, and retirements, dinners and parties and reunions . . . these are all rites, ceremonies, conventions, and celebrations; both the progress and the cycle of time are marked by them. These are all rituals and rituals are the key features of social life of every known society

Eric W. Rothenbuhler, *Ritual Communication*

Just as April showers bring forth the flowers of May, so do the falling autumn leaves bring forth fleets of school buses and flocks of children bearing lunch boxes. Children, teachers, and all of those involved in the educational process take part in the autumnal ritual called "Back to School." This annual migration has been documented on the covers of American popular magazines. Illustrations from 1900 to the 1950s tell the story of going to school. In these images we can get a glimpse of what going to school was like in the first half of the twentieth century.

Illustrations of schools, teaching, and learning occur frequently in popular literature. Illustrations were the visual mainstay of American magazines until the 1960s, when photography became dominant. These images were seen by millions of viewers, and as popular media, they are an indicator of shared beliefs and ideologies and are presumed to have considerable influence in shaping attitudes (Emmison and Smith 66). Erving Goffman describes cartoons and illustrations as "public pictures," and certainly these illustrations on the front of national magazines were very visible to a wide audience (Prosser 253). Theodor Adorno criticizes the "easy" style of popular culture that he says lulls the consumer into an unthinking, uncritical state (Walker and Chaplin 37). There is no question that these images are sweet, perhaps even trite, representations of everyday life, but their value lies in this very fact—that they represent an everyday reality for millions of people. Popular culture helps to explain the general status of human action in society. It is the everyday vernacular culture that comprises much of our lives (Browne).

Illustrated magazine covers were a form of public art. The rising middle class would purchase a magazine not only to read but also to look at and to value the pictures as reflections of daily life. Publishers knew that the commercial appeal of children would sell magazines. The content was accessible to the general public, and the genre scenes resembled those taking place in many a home and school. Magazines represented daily life and became "arbiters of convention" (Janello and Jones 166).

The illustrations in these magazines are lifelike, but unlike photographs, they were not images of real people. The representations provide a narrative look at an annual event, and each child is every child who goes back to school each fall. No picture is "pure image—'all are talking pictures'" (Warburton 253). Pictures articulate and contribute to social processes. Social processes determine these representations and are also influenced or altered by them (Walker and Chaplin 1). The images use key signifiers—visual devices that are central to reading the illustration's meaning. These signifiers frequently become stereotypes that synthesize and promote the cultural narrative. Public recognition of these stereotypes amplifies meaning and resonates within the cultural context. The combination of stereotypes and context becomes a system of signs, and the forms develop a social history.

Emmison asserts that most forms of visual data are based on stereotyped conventions—they should be thought of as something that offers us insight into the idealized character of relationships between groups and or institutions rather than an accurate source of information about behavior or lifestyle (63). He calls for a structural approach to analysis—we should focus not on content but on the messages to be gleaned from the interactions or relationships that they depict.

The images become archetypes for a shared experience in visual culture. Illustrators such as J. C. Leyendecker, Norman Rockwell, and George Hughes captured children in lifelike settings—searching for a lost shoe, bullying classmates on the school bus, and trying to impress friends with new accomplishments. Magazine covers preceded the TV screen in reflecting America back at itself as well as projecting what it wanted to be. In our reading of these illustrations we will look at specific images associated with the ritual of going to school. In this way, a ritual framework is developed that provides for an analysis of the media through identification of repetitive patterns that serve to define the world and "legitimize" the social order (Rothenbuhler 87). These actions become ritual in their depiction of ongoing activities. The ritual aspects of ordinary social activities are just as serious as big, special events. Rothenbuhler defines rituals as customary behavior—stereotyped and typical, repetitive in the sense that others have done it this way before. Rituals occur regularly, they are calendrical, and they are made up of repetitive actions. It is the voluntary performance of appropriately patterned behavior that allows one to symbolically participate "in the serious life" (Rothenbuhler 27). Magazine illustrations, like advertising of the early twentieth century, are a ritual display of approved social roles and relations. As communication vehicles they emphasize meaning and the sustenance of social roles over time. Through an analysis of the image we can see the archetypal act of going to school. Together images weave a narrative, as Barthes describes, that can tell the story of a common coming-of-age ritual.

Getting Ready for School—The Ritual Cleansing

The journey to school begins with preparation. In a 1932 *Saturday Evening Post* cover we see a matronly figure bathing a young boy (fig. 1). This could be the routine Saturday cleaning before the Sabbath, or perhaps the boy has been playing in the mud. Our clue to the occasion of this bath is the caption—"September Morn." What we have here is the removal of a summer's worth of grit and grime in preparation for school.

Figure 1. "Saturday Night Bath" by J. C. Leyendecker. © 1932 SEPS: Licensed by Curtis Publishing, Indianapolis, IN. All rights reserved. www.curtispublishing.com.

The words give us a context for the scene. Scrubbed clean, the lad will make his way to school.

Other typical September cover illustrations show familiar scenes of getting ready for school. A mother searches for a missing shoe—a frequently occurring scene in American homes. The boy is dressed in his new sweater and short pants. Book in hand and cap on head, he waits while mother searches; he is in no hurry to begin another school year (*Saturday Evening Post*, September 8, 1951). Another illustration presents two boys, in crisp new suits, who are on their way to school. They carry books and lunch boxes. But they have left behind a summer's worth of mess. Mother surveys the aftermath of her progeny's activities (*Saturday Evening Post*, October 22, 1955). Does this signify the leaving behind of chaos (ignorance) for the order and structure of educated life (knowledge)? Symbolic considerations aside, we know how this 1950s housewife will spend her day. Stereotypical gender representations of mothers as housewives and fathers as businessmen were dominant in the 1950s. Women stayed at home and served their families, while men ventured into the world to earn a living and support wives and children. Representations of girls often depict them learning or mimicking defined cultural roles—caring for dolls or playing house. Boys are more likely seen outdoors roughhousing or helping Dad in the garage.

Leaving Home

Cleaned and dressed, the students leave home and parents for school. A 1916 *Women's World* illustration presents an idyllic scene: four children walking hand-in-hand, make their way through the rural countryside on their way to school (fig. 2). Wearing hats or sunbonnets, they carry their books and are dressed in dresses (the typical schoolgirl plaid) and the traditional short pants. Black leggings are worn by all. They are about to cross a bridge. Is this crossing of the bridge a transport from ignorance to knowledge? Their procession from the frontal plane of the illustration to the depth contained in a circle seems symbolic of passing from one state of being to another. The exaggerated perspective represents the long road ahead in terms of both life and learning. The visual convention of the circular frame was a popular illustration technique for leading the viewer into the scene.

There are more than *Two Million subscribers to*

WOMAN'S WORLD

September 1916   *Five Cents*

CHICAGO

Figure 2. "Walking to School" by Marguerite Meacham. September 1916, *Woman's World*.

Figure 3. "Slow, School Ahead" by George Brehm. © 1925 SEPS: Licensed by Curtis Publishing, Indianapolis, IN. All rights reserved. www.curtispublishing.com.

A boy in a 1925 *Post* illustration is not so eager to get to school (fig. 3). He carries his books in a leather strap. His gray suit looks new and scratchy. A dapper red bow is at this neck. New socks and shoes adorn his feet—the freedom of summer and shoeless feet must be abandoned. His cap is pulled fiercely over his brow as he moves on at a snail's pace. Indeed, he reminds us of Shakespeare's "schoolboy with satchel creeping like snail unwillingly to school" (*As You Like It,* act 2, scene 7). He is only following orders, as the sign beside him says, "Slow, school ahead." An older student, he knows what lies ahead and moves on at a disgruntled pace.

In another household, swept up the flurry of last-minute preparations to catch the bus, a child has forgotten her lunch (*Saturday Evening Post,* March 5, 1955). Mom is chasing the bus down the street, arms outstretched. The scene is a quiet residential street (named Joy Street), replete with cozy homes and picket fences. The Hamilton school bus moves away from the stop as a toddler watches the mother try to catch the bus. This juxtaposition of the child leaving the mother's care with the smaller child still at home depicts the first leave-taking, that initial step out of the nest. The nourishment of home and mother are left behind. The child will have to think and fend for herself at school. The mother will have to learn to let go. This type of scene has become a stylistic convention used in representing the one who stays home and the one who ventures out to school or work. When Hillary Rodham Clinton left for her first day as a freshman senator, a video spoof showed President Clinton running after her limousine with a bag lunch.

Socialization on the Way to School

The journey to school provides an opportunity to develop friendships and learn social skills. Walking to school provides informal learning situations for children in life lessons. They compare their clothes and physical development to see how they are positioned within their peer group. Who has lost a tooth? Who has new shoes? Carrying a girl's books—a recent counterpart to ancient courting rites—is traditional on the way to school. A *Saturday Evening Post* cover from 1928 presents suitors meeting under the guise of study. The girl seems a bit doubtful, while the boy sings of his love, accompanying himself on a ukulele. Books are scattered on the ground, and a roguish William Shakespeare

keeps watch over the pair. Education not only gives one opportunities to mingle with opposite sex, but expanded knowledge also gives one music and poetry with which to woo.

"School Bus Stops Here" signs are gathering points for students waiting for the bus to take them to school. On a 1929 *Country Gentleman* cover (fig. 4), seven children are looking down the road in anxious anticipation of the bus. Their facial expressions exhibit their attitudes toward the new school year. The older boys' faces are disgruntled. The middle-grade children look eager to renew old acquaintances. The youngest children appear apprehensive. Their companion, the dog in the background, looks equally apprehensive of what lies ahead—long days without his playmates. Arms tightly clutch books and bags. Small hands grasp apples and flowers for the waiting teachers. The scene implies a small town with a white-steepled church in the background.

The level of everyday experience is where we find much of the social order of the world (Rothenbuhler xiiii). In this order are social stratification and class. Those in the controlling group are in a position to impose particular meanings on actions that the media create or to reinforce cultural categories resulting in a consensus of values, thus extending hegemony into the world of images. Artworks help us see the reality of the ideology of the world they describe. While ideology is the glue that binds different cultural components of society (education system, legal system, family, etc.) into an overall structure, images can help us see the inequalities in a social structure and work to change the system. Such images can contribute to a social argument (Walker and Chaplin 3).

Arriving at School

The journey complete, the student arrives at school. Here we see that two parents have dropped off their young son for his first day of school (fig. 5). The mother falls apart, right into the stoic father's arms. The woman is weak; the man a pillar of strength. Emotionality and rationality are dialectically opposed in the embracing pair. Meanwhile, Junior runs up the stairs of the massive building, grasping his lunchbox in one hand and his pink rabbit in another. We are seeing a transition in the boy's life—from preschooler to schoolboy. The wide, high steps literally raise the boy to new heights. Low windows on the building are covered with simple cutouts, probably indicating primary grade levels. Someone

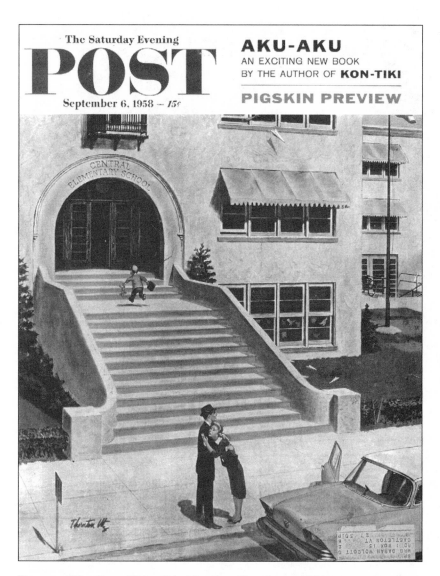

Figure 5. "First Day of School" by Thornton Utz. © 1929 SEPS: Licensed by Curtis Publishing, Indianapolis, IN. All rights reserved. www.curtispublishing.com.

Figure 6. "Late for School" by J. C. Leyendecker. *Saturday Evening Post*, September 19, 1914.

Figure 7. "Give Me Liberty" by J. C. Leyendecker. *Saturday Evening Post*, September 18, 1909.

is flinging paper airplanes from the third floor, most likely an older student trying his hand at paper engineering.

A 1914 *Saturday Evening Post* cover depicts a young man entering the schoolroom (fig.6). He is late for school. The clock indicates that it is 9:24, and the teacher beckons him forward with an intimidating finger. With his finger in his mouth, he hesitantly stands before the school marm, clutching his slate and his cap. His oversize shoes (he'll grow into them) anchor him to the floor. The teacher's bell sits on a table nearby. In the early part of the century, teachers were expected not to marry, and the stereotype of the spinster schoolmarm is common. This teacher is a visible example. The enormous silk ruffles encompass her bony physique. We can almost hear her nasal interrogation of the boy—"Why were you late?" This interaction becomes ritualistic. According to Rothenbuhler, "aggregates of performances constitute recognizable characters, aggregates of similar performances by different people constitute recognizable roles, aggregates of different roles constitute recognizable social organizations" (4).

Teacher and student are engaged in a ritual order of interaction that continues today in most schoolrooms.

Inside the Classroom

Part of the school day was spent in recitation, learning how to speak properly. Pronunciation and appropriate gestures were rhetorical necessities. A young boy is reciting "Give me liberty or give me death." The tiny orator is standing in a classic stance (fig. 7). He is dressed in a good school suit, red bow tie, and black leggings. The teacher, a kinder and gentler version of the schoolmarm, watches carefully over the edge of her book. An apple rests on the corner of her desk.

A sleeping student has caught the attention of his teacher in a 1918 illustration (fig. 8). This boy is dreaming of being at the war front. His dream self carries a small gun and the helmets of enemy soldiers. His toothless grin is a sign of victory. The teacher stands behind him, ruler in hand (in medieval times a body-striker was used). Had this been the stricter schoolmarm viewed earlier, we would have no doubt of the outcome. This teacher is less threatening and more contemplative. She is almost gentle in her observation of the boy.

Figure 8. "Daydream" by Robert Robinson. *Saturday Evening Post*, September 12, 1918.

Conclusion

By observing these images we catch a glimpse of how the ritual of going to school has been represented in popular U.S. magazines. The audience for these publications is obviously a white middle-class demographic group. They reflect a homogeneity that is certainly not representative of the entire population, but they do display events that surround one of our most common American experiences—going to school. One of the most treasured aspects of democracy is the opportunity to attend school and attain an education. The idealized nature of the illustrations portrays this value. This annual ritual of returning to school each fall is perhaps our most common heritage and experience.

WORKS CITED

Barthes, Roland. *Mythologies*. London: Jonathan Cape, 1972.

Browne, Ray B. *Digging into Popular Culture: Theories and Methodologies in Archeology, Anthropology, and Other Fields*. Bowling Green, OH: Bowling Green State University Popular Press, 1991.

Emmison, Michael, and Philip D. Smith. *Researching the Visual*. London: Sage, 2000.

Janello, Amy, and Brennon Jones. *The American Magazine*. New York: Harry M. Abrams, 1991.

Prosser, Jon, ed. *Image-Based Research*. London: Falmer Press, 1998.

Rothenbuhler, Eric W. *Ritual Communication*. Thousand Oaks, CA: Sage, 1998.

Walker, John A., and Sarah Chaplin. *Visual Culture: An Introduction*. Manchester, UK: Manchester University Press, 1997.

Warburton, Terry. "Cartoons and Teachers: Mediated Visual Images as Data." In *Image-Based Research*, ed. Jon Prosser, 252–262. London: Falmer Press, 1998.

PART 4

PLAY

Americans like to play; thus, games occupy integral positions in our culture. Sports, both amateur and professional, embody qualities of a quasi-religion, replete with chanting masses, godlike heroes, and ritualized behaviors. Children growing up in a sports-dominated society learn about winning and losing, skill and luck, and heroes and losers by watching and playing games.

Although organized sports are the most dominant manifestations of children's play patterns, they are not the only ones. All children's games, those played alone as well as in groups, contain ritualistic elements as they are reenacted generation after generation in varying ways. Games assert the mindset of a society—its values, rules, and taboos—and gaming practices help to maintain social boundaries. For example, a child playing a popular board game such as *Monopoly* learns about the joys of capitalism, the power differential between the "haves" and the "have-nots," the unacceptability of cheating, and the dynamics of careful decision making coupled with pure chance. How children play and the toys they use for play also speak to the role of the consumer in an industrialized nation. Children's leisure time increasingly is controlled by the manipulation of manufactured objects, such as video and computer games. In an age of product merchandising, the most popular child is often the one who has acquired the most, making him or her the envy of the neighborhood.

The two examinations of play practices that are recounted here demonstrate the lessons that play and games communicate to children. In "The Ritual of Doll Play: Implications of Children's Conceptualization of Race," Sabrina Thomas studies the history of doll play in America with an eye toward racial identity and the development of social roles. Sally Sugarman, in "Playing the Game: Rituals in Children's Games," considers a broad range of children's games, from traditional games to board games to playground games involving merchandised characters, exploring the axioms transmitted regarding power and gender.

The way children see themselves has a great deal to do with the way society views them and constructs their experiences. Although the games that children play may involve self-initiated rituals, more often than not they represent a perpetuation of the same value-laden activities practiced by generations before.

7

The Ritual of Doll Play

Implications of Understanding
Children's Conceptualization of Race

SABRINA THOMAS

Play is one of the most well known rituals of childhood. The image of play as an innocent context in which children manipulate toys—and of-tentimes each other—obscures children's play as an activity influenced by current social and political ideologies and, to some extent, discour-ages an examination of children's pretend world as a "society" in which conceptions of human relations are produced and reproduced. Race is one of the most salient social categories in which children's conceptual-ization of self and others unfolds. An examination of children's under-standing of race within the ritual of doll play, as opposed to play more generally, is appealing because it is within this context that the primary object of play functions as a racialized object of human representation.

G. Stanley Hall and A. Caswell Ellis's 1987 project titled *A Study of Dolls,* based in Worchester, Massachusetts, and the 1987 Margaret Woodbury Strong Museum's doll oral history project in Rochester, New York, documented what individuals thought about their dolls and how they played with them during the late nineteenth century and the early to mid twentieth century, respectively. Both the Strong Museum's doll oral history project and Hall and Ellis's *A Study of Dolls* provided serendipitous

insight into the ritual of doll play as a context in which children develop
and manifest an understanding of human relations based on race and
underscored the significance of dolls as messengers of race relations.[1]

A Brief Review of Dolls as Messengers of Race Relations

In 1939, the research of Mamie and Kenneth Clark served as a catalyst
for more than four decades of research investigating children's doll
choice behavior and its implications for their understanding of race relations. The different "skin" colors of the dolls, one black and one white,
represented individuals of different racial group memberships. Black
and white children's overwhelming preference for the white doll when
asked questions such as "Which doll is the pretty doll?" or "Which doll
would you rather play with?" was assumed to indicate children's perception of themselves in relation to others and their awareness of the racial hierarchy within the broader society that placed black people as inferior to white people. Black children's preference for the white doll was
interpreted as evidence of a low self-esteem and black inferiority complex. White children's preference for the white doll was interpreted as
evidence of a higher self-esteem, and the implications for a white superiority complex went unaddressed, according to Clark.

The history of dolls as racialized objects that produce and reproduce
society's dominant race ideology has been carefully examined. Myla
Perkins, a black doll historian, suggested that doll advertisements reflect
the social status and image of different races of people. Perkins identified the following nineteenth-century advertisements that illustrated
dolls as messengers of race relations in the broader society:

> Bisque dolls are most liked because they are less easily defaced than
> those of wax, and these are now shown of any complexion from the
> fairest blonde to the darkest brunette, and there are *also bisque negresses,*
> *with woolly hair, to be dressed as maids to fairer dolls.* (1885, *Harper's Bazaar,*
> qtd. in Perkins 4:20; emphasis in original)

A second advertisement read:

> Whole families of china dolls only two or three inches high to people
> doll houses are among the favorites of little girls; there are also boy dolls
> dressed as sailors or soldiers, and the *colored dolls are arrayed as cooks with*
> *gray turbans or in coachman's attire.* (1885, *Harper's Bazaar,* qtd. in Perkins 4:
> 20; emphasis added)

Finally, in a later issue:

> In the toy shops are seen 'all sorts of conditions' of dolls, from the gor-geously attired ladies in Directoire or Empire gowns down to the hum-ble mulatto nurse with her bisque *face most naturally colored, a gray bandana on her head, and in her arms her infant charge.* (1888, *Harper's Bazaar*, qtd. in Perkins 4:20; emphasis added)

Perkins argued that black dolls were not marketed as primary dolls in children's play. Instead they "were used as supplementary [servants] for the white dolls" (20). Nineteenth-century doll advertisements identified the acceptable positions of blacks in the broader society and, in turn, re-produced race and social class within the context of children's doll play. More specifically, Perkins argued that such advertisements encouraged children to assign black dolls "play" roles reflective of their placement and image in the broader society (20).

In *Skin Trade*, Ann DuCille supported Perkins's suggestion of dolls as messengers of race ideologies within the broader society. She argued that Mattel's manipulation of dyes and clothing to indicate racial and cultural diversity among its "Barbie" dolls merely underscored the cen-trality of whiteness in American society and concomitantly in children's doll play.[2] Darlene Powell-Hopson and Derek Hopson, in *Different and Wonderful: Raising Black Children in a Race-Conscious Society*, stated that toys "help children use and expand their imagination. Their attitude toward their toys, dolls especially, tell us much about how they see themselves and the world in general" (126). They suggested that doll playing was a significant context in which to combat the negative racialized imagery of black people.

Scholars who have addressed the influence of the social construction of race in children's play have not observed children's doll play behav-ior per se but have instead argued a more general premise of cognitive psychology, that negative imagery nurtures negative perceptions and treatment of the object or persons being represented. Thus, negative imagery of blacks in white children's—as in black children's—doll play encourages a negative race-based treatment of black dolls.[3]

Despite the spirit of intellectual debate that the past research has brought about dolls as objects of race representation and its implica-tions for children's psychological well-being, the significance of the rit-ual of children's doll play as a context in which to gain insight into chil-dren's understanding of race relations has been overlooked. The Strong Museum's doll oral history project and Hall and Ellis's *A Study of Dolls*

offered distinct contributions regarding the nature of race relations
between 1900 and 1940 and its implications for what doll players thought
about and how they played—if they played—with dolls that represented a racial group other than their own.[4]

The Margaret Woodbury Strong Museum's
Doll Oral History Project

The 1987 Margaret Woodbury Strong Museum's doll oral history project interviewed ninety-seven local women who were born between
1884 and 1928. The doll oral history project documented women's recollections of their childhood doll play during 1900–1940. Some doll
players who reported "no" to ever owning a black doll suggested that
the absence of a black doll in their play was related to the amount of exposure they had to black people in real life. Mary commented, "In the
town we lived in there weren't any black people. None. Ten thousand
population with no black people (Strong Museum, record 21:9). Jenell
echoed a similar memory: "There were never any black people around
us. We weren't exposed to black people at all in anyway[—] church,
school, or etcetera" (Strong Museum, record 32:20). Mae, another doll
player, suggested that she may have occasionally seen a black person,
but because the experience was so rare she was surprised when she saw
them symbolically represented through dolls. She stated that "There
weren't many black dolls sold in the stores. . . . I was so amazed to see a
black doll. We didn't have many black people around, you see, when I
was a little girl. You didn't see them, that was all" (record 23:7). Finally,
Joan simply responded, "No, oh no. And of course, that's sad but we
didn't see any black dolls or children" (record 39:24). The responses of
the doll players indicated that the existing laws of racial segregation nor-
malized the absence of their daily social interactions with blacks, which,
in turn, supported their understanding of the absence of black dolls in
their doll play.

Rushia, one of the doll players who reported "yes" to ever owning a
black doll, implied a hesitation to play with her black doll in public. She
reported that "[I] had the black china doll and the white china doll. . . .
You were disgraced if you carried a little black doll then (Strong Museum, record 14:5). The sentiments of Rushia were stated with greater
elaboration in an excerpt from the mother and daughter interview of
Ester and Shirley. Ester and Shirley reported that neither of them had

owned a black doll but that a relative purchased a black doll for the granddaughter as a birthday present. They both seemed perplexed by the relative's behavior:

ESTER: I can't imagine why they bought it?

SHIRLEY: One of the relative bought it.

ESTER: I can't imagine why did she select a black doll? . . . I was nervous because we had a black lady working for us. . . . Because we were so crazy about this lady that I think she felt flattered that we had a doll like that. . . . [People] were curious as to why she has a black doll.

SHIRLEY: Wherever she went she took that doll it was one of her favorites.

ESTER: Remember we used to go into restaurants?

SHIRLEY: Yes. She wasn't embarrassed with it. We were. (record 30:12–13)

Rushia, Ester, and Shirley suggested that a black doll within the context of a little white girl's doll play was socially inappropriate. The inappropriateness of the black doll, however, was not based on a lack of social interaction with black people, per se. (Ester acknowledged having a black woman working in her home). The inappropriateness of a black doll was more related to the affective attributions of black association—disgrace and embarrassment. Such attributions appeared to be domain specific. The presence of blackness in the servant capacity in the home did not evoke the same feeling of embarrassment as did the presence of blackness in the social capacity of her granddaughter's play.[5]

For other doll players, feelings of embarrassment and disgrace from being seen with a black doll were replaced by the advantage of social promotion among peers. When asked how she played with her black doll, Jeanne responded:

I played with the baby buggy, it [the black doll] went right along with all the other dolls and babied the same as all of the dolls. I think it was so special because *I was the only one in the neighborhood that had a black doll.* This was a special doll as far as I was concerned. . . . I think the black doll was so different from anything that anybody else had that there was a certain importance within the childish community, you know, so that you would remember this and be pleased that you had it. (Strong Museum, record 12:3–4, 8; emphasis added)

Susan, another doll player, shared the following comment about her black doll:

[S]he had a red and white polka dot skirt and a red top and a red bandana and wooly black mohair hair and gold earrings, not real gold but you know what I mean. . . . *I was the only one that had one.* She was in great demand because it was different and we had little tea parties and, you

know, and everyone had Effie as her guest because Effie was different
and Effie had gold earrings. (record 16:8; emphasis added)

The specialness that Jeanne and Susan attributed to their black dolls
was not based on any particular function of the dolls. The specialness of
the dolls was due to the rarity of black representation in their doll play.
They each were the only little girls that owned a black doll among their
respective friends.

Emily and Elizabeth could not remember playing much with their
black dolls but vividly recalled the physical characteristics of the dolls.
Emily recalled that "I had a pair of [black] porcelain dolls. Seated.
Pickaninnies eating watermelon" (Strong Museum, record 6:16).

Elizabeth remembered:

I did have a gollywog. . . . I think it was named from a book—and it was
a black person with very frizzy hair, like a big afro. And another doll I
had . . . that was shaped like an arrow like a spear, you see, at the top.
That, I think was made of green felt, might have been a premium from
the Spearmint gum for all I know. But I remember those two as offbeat
ones that I kinda liked because they were different.

When the interviewer asked Elizabeth how did she play with them.
Elizabeth responded, "I have no idea. I think we just propped them up
and looked at them" (record 65:15).

In a discussion of the racist imagery in children's play, Cross stated
that "Racist images of blacks persisted and found form in toys of all
kinds during the 1890s and 1900s. This was the height of Jim Crow leg-
islation. . . . These toys surely passed on racist stereotypes to children
through mockery and demeaning poses and situations. But they were
also emblems of the exotic and unknown" (98–99).

Elizabeth's conceptualization of blackness appeared to have been
framed within the exoticism mentioned by Cross. She and her playmate
viewed the black doll as something outside of the norm of doll play;
therefore they just "propped [it] up and looked at [it]." The children's
state of bewilderment or amazement was based on the exclusion of
blacks from their daily social interactions. Martha Mahoney argues that
white exclusivity promotes the perception of whiteness as the "dominant
norm" in society and the standard by which all other races are evaluated.
White exclusivity promotes the social construction of whiteness as the
norm of human representation and human social interaction. Children

whose racial schemata are formed on principles of white exclusivity are more likely to view black representation as exotic or "special" (Mahoney).

How the Strong Museum doll players actually played with their black dolls is speculative at best. The doll players' memories of their black dolls reflected more affective memories regarding the "blackness" of the doll as opposed to episodic memories of how they actually played with them. Or more specifically, the Strong Museum doll players' reported memories do not clearly indicate if the manner in which they played with black dolls was influenced by the race of the doll.

A possible explanation for the absence of doll players' memories of a race-based treatment of their black dolls is the simple fact that such treatment did not occur. The historic period of the doll players' childhood, however, makes this explanation improbable. The Strong Museum doll players were born between the years 1884 and 1928 and were bequeathed with the legacy of slavery and the Civil War and with an existing Jim Crow social structure. Their childhood unfolded within a society whose social infrastructure promoted the separation of races—save labor-related interactions—and whose constitutional interpretation upheld it.[6]

A Study of Dolls by G. Stanley Hall and A. Caswell Ellis

G. Stanley Hall and A. Caswell Ellis conducted a survey for *A Study of Dolls* during 1894–1896 in Worchester, Massachusetts. They surveyed women and children who played with dolls during a childhood period similar to that of the Strong Museum doll players. Hall and Ellis circulated a doll questionnaire among eight hundred teachers and parents in Worchester. The teachers were instructed to recall their own childhood memories with dolls as well as to distribute the questionnaire among their students. Their findings suggested that the Worcester doll players, as well as other children of historically comparable childhoods, engaged in race-based doll play.

After surveying the doll players' reports of playing "dress-up" and "washing" with their dolls, Hall and Ellis observed that the hygienic care of dolls had different implications for the treatment of black dolls than for white dolls. Some of the doll players believed that "Colored dolls sometimes need no clothing." One doll player expressed the view that black dolls did not need clothing "because they are so black nobody can see" (11). The darkness of the black doll suggested dirtiness to some children. A doll player reported, "I could not get my doll clean because he was so black" (33).

Social events such as family gatherings, weddings, the schoolhouse, visiting, minstrel shows, and deaths were regularly reported and described in the Hall and Ellis project. Children's reports of their dolls' deaths suggested that dolls often died once the children grew tired of them. One respondent, however, caused the death of her black doll because she feared it. She "burnt it in the fire, and for a long time could not look at the fireplace without fear its ghost would appear in the smoke" (30). Implying the importance of physical resemblance in establishing kinship, one of Hall and Ellis's respondents reported, "All my dolls were sisters except one I didn't like, which was a servant" (34). The social entertainment "value" of blackness was confirmed in one respondent's statement: "My darkey doll could dance a jig and sing Uncle Ned" (31). Hall and Ellis further reported that "Slave-selling" was a social play "described fully once and often hinted at more times" (34). In addition, black people were not the only racial group symbolically represented or victimized in the course of doll play. Hall and Ellis quoted one respondent's memory of being influenced by literature about "Indians." She stated, "After reading of Indians, my brother and I scalped my dolls head and it was beyond remedy" (27).

Hall and Ellis observed that not only dolls were a salient aspect of children's play. Other objects were used as substitutes for anthropomorphic dolls and referred to accordingly. The Hall and Ellis doll players reported that they treated objects such as flowers, clothespins, bottles filled with different colored water, pillows with a string tied around the middle, vegetables, or a chicken as dolls, or doll substitutes. One doll player described a somewhat elaborate play system for her flower dolls:

> I took pansies for dolls because of their human faces; the rose I revered too much to play with, it was like my best wax doll, dressed in her prettiest. . . . I loved these nature dolls far better than the prettiest store dolls and ascribed special psychic qualities to them. . . . The hepaticas seemed delicate children to be tenderly cared for, but which soon drooped and faded. . . . Violets were shy, good natured children, but their pansy cousins were often naughty and would not play. The hepaticas were invalids and cripples who watched their livelier brothers and sisters. . . . *The dahlias were colored servants and mammies;* yellow violets

mischievous fun-loving boys. . . . I often made little boats to give my flower dolls rides on the river. (cited in Hall and Ellis, 10; emphasis added)

The doll player personified her flowers based on ascribed personality traits. Her classification of the roses as the most elite and the dahlias as the *colored* servants and mammies clearly illustrated her awareness of both social class and race. In general, the "roles" that the Hall and Ellis doll players assigned their black dolls within the context of their doll play, as well as the actions they took upon their black dolls, reproduced social class and race hierarchies in the broader society.

Despite comparable childhood periods, the Hall and Ellis doll players were more open regarding descriptions of race-based doll play than the Strong Museum doll players. As mentioned earlier, it is possible that the Strong Museum doll players did not engage in race-based doll play. The historical address of their childhoods, however, suggests that the absence of race-based doll play memories relate more to the method of data collection and the time period in which the data was collected. The Strong Museum doll oral history project was conducted via face-to-face interviews as opposed to the survey approach of the Hall and Ellis project. The face-to-face interview at the Strong Museum offered less anonymity, which may have fostered less openness. Relatedly, the doll players were questioned during different historic periods. The Strong Museum doll players were senior citizens at the time of their interview and during a time period—the 1980s—when racial discourse and politics were less encouraging of blatant negative race-based comments or behavior. The Hall and Ellis doll players were questioned during their childhood and, more importantly, during the 1890s, when racial discourse and politics was more encouraging of negative race-based behavior and comments. In addition, the survey approach offered more anonymity and perhaps more honesty.

Conclusion

The exclusion of black dolls from the play of some of the Strong Museum's doll players did not fail to communicate perceptions of blackness or black people. Instead, it created the centrality of whiteness within the context of their doll play as the norm of human representation

and social interaction. Janet Helms, in her model of white racial identity
development, argues that in the absence of contact with black people,
the social construction of whiteness is most easily formed and never
addressed as a racial issue (54). Mahoney, in "Segregation, Whiteness,
and Transformation," suggests that the exclusion of black dolls in white
children's doll play is what allows whiteness to be constructed as both
exclusive and a dominate norm "that defines what attributes of race
should be counted, how to count them and who . . . gets to do the count-
ing" (65). Any characteristics that deviate from the dominant norm are
considered inferior or inappropriate. Thus, the social construction of
blackness is not mutually exclusive from the social construction of
whiteness (65).

An examination of children's understanding of race, or race relations, as manifested within the ritual of doll play is important not because of what it suggests about the Strong Museum or the Hall and Ellis
doll players but because of what it suggests about the ritual of doll play
as a context in which children develop and manifest an understanding
of themselves and others on the basis of racial group membership.
Children's development of racial schemata is informed by the symbolism and images of human relations as constructed in the broader society
as well as in the immediate home environment. Janet Helms argues, in
Black and White Racial Identity, that racial symbolisms in society nurture
children's "vicarious awareness" of others based on race.[7] Children's
racial schemata, regardless of the source of their information, govern
their willingness to interact and the manner in which they interpret
their experiences with individuals they perceive to be racially similar, or
different, from themselves. In "Socialization and Racism: The White
Experience," Dennis argues that pre-adult race socialization is transmitted in conscious and unconscious ways that are usually quite subtle.
He claims that adult racial intolerance, or acceptance, is oftentimes
in response to an idea of blacks that is transmitted through the ritual
of race socialization in childhood rather than the adult's independent
knowledge about the respective group. Doll play is a context in which
subtle messages of race and race relations in the broader society are ignored or only theoretically addressed.

Both doll manufacturers and scholars have recognized the ritual of
doll play as a context in which children develop conceptualizations of
race. Doll manufacturers routinely create multiracial representations
of their various doll lines with particular care given to ethnic clothing

and other accessories when appropriate. Scholars have argued that excluding black dolls from white or black children's doll play promotes whiteness as superior; the presence of only black dolls in white or black children's doll play, however, has not been argued to have the opposite effect—to promote black superiority. Thus, although the social construction of blackness and the social construction of whiteness are not mutually exclusive, nor are they symmetrical.

Of the many pathways of coming to understand race relations, children's doll play is one of the earliest and most salient. Naturalistic observation of children's doll play or examinations of children's memories of their doll play as a means for understanding their development of race consciousness has not been pursued energetically. An examination of the intersection of children's race, actual doll play, parental attitudes, and historical address would provide rich insight into children's conceptualizations of self and others on the basis of race, and it would underscore the complexity of children's development of race conceptualizations. Concomitantly, such an approach would contextualize children's doll play within a broader social order as opposed to a world of pretense and would provide insight into the processes by which children are socialized to understand race and race relations within the ritual of doll play.

NOTES

The research for this chapter was supported by a research grant from the American Association of University Women.

1. The discussion of the Strong Museum doll project is based on a direct examination of the 1987 interview transcripts in the museum's Doll Oral History Project. The original completed questionnaires of the Hall and Ellis study are not available; the discussion of the doll players is based on the reported findings of the published report, *A Study of Dolls*.

2. DuCille, *Skin Trade*, 8–59. DuCille argues that the consistency with which Mattel uses the white European phenotype for the facial features of their Barbie dolls implicitly undermines the importance of an accurate representation of members from diverse ethnic groups. Thus, the manipulation of "skin tones" and clothing offers superficial representation of nonwhite ethnic groups.

3. For a sampling of materials that address symbolism in children's play and its implication for children's conceptualizations of race, see Cross, *Kids Stuff*, 97–100; Balch Institute for Ethnic Studies, *Ethnic Images in Toys & Games;* Balch Institute for Ethnic Studies and Anti-Defamation League of B'nai B'rith, *Ethnic Images in Advertising.*

4. An examination of doll play among children of diverse ethnic backgrounds would contribute invaluable insight to our understanding of children's development of race relations. The Strong Museum doll oral history project and Hall and Ellis, *A Study of Dolls*, however, examine predominantly white subjects and mainly give reference to a "black" doll as the doll representing an ethnic group different from the doll players. Thus the present investigation is limited to white children's conceptualization of race within the black-white dichotomy.

5. Many researchers have examined the dual construction of blackness—black womanhood in particular—in white public and private space. The symbol of the black mammy throughout history has conveyed obedience and loyalty, and the presence of a mammy in the home was a visual index of white social class status. Beyond the parameters of domestic servant, blackness, in general, was defined as untrustworthy and inferior. Black women particularly were constructed as sexually promiscuous and lacking morality. Thus the comfort level of many white-black interactions was based on the context and implicit nature of the association or relationship. Mullings, *On Our Own Terms*, 109–130.

6. The 1896 case of *Plessy vs. Ferguson* legalized the existing practice of "separate and equal" governing use of public facilities or government-supported institutions and activities.

7. Helms, *Black and White Racial Identity*. Helms argues that children's vicarious awareness of blacks occurs with various forms of media or the opinions of significant others in the child's life as the primary source of that child's awareness of blacks (54).

WORKS CITED

Balch Institute for Ethnic Studies. *Ethnic Images in Toys & Games*. Ed. Pamela Nelson. Exhibit at the Balch Institute for Ethnic Studies, April 17–October 13, 1990. Philadelphia: Balch Institute for Ethnic Studies, 1990.

Balch Institute for Ethnic Studies and Anti-Defamation League of B'nai B'rith. *Ethnic Images in Advertising*. Exhibit at the Balch Institute for Ethnic Studies, 1984. Philadelphia: Balch Institute for Ethnic Studies and Anti-Defamation League of B'nai B'rith, 1984.

Clark, K., and M. Clark. "Development of Consciousness of Self and the Emergence of Racial Identification." *Journal of Social Psychology* 10 (1939): 591–599.

Cross, Gary. *Kids Stuff: Toys and the Changing World of American Childhood*. Cambridge, MA: Harvard University Press, 1997.

Dennis, R. "Socialization and Racism: The White Experience." In *Impacts of Racism on White Americans*, ed. Benjamin Bowser and Raymond Hunt. Beverly Hills, CA: Sage, 1981.

DuCille, Ann. *Skin Trade*. Cambridge, MA: Harvard University Press, 1996.

Hall, Stanley G., and A. Caswell Ellis. *A Study of Dolls.* New York: E. L. Kellogg, 1897.

Helms, Janet. *Black and White Racial Identity: Theory, Research, and Practice.* Westport, CT: Greenwood Press, 1990.

Mahoney, Martha. "Segregation, Whiteness, and Transformation." In *Critical White Studies: Looking behind the Mirror,* ed. Richard Delgado and Jean Stefancic. Philadelphia: Temple University Press, 1997.

Mullings, Lieth. *On Our Own Terms: Race, Class, and Gender in the Lives of African American Women.* New York: Routledge, 1997.

Perkins, Myla. *Black Dolls: An Identification and Value Guide, 1820–1991.* Paducah, KY: Collector Books, 1995.

Powell-Hopson, Darlene, and Derek Hopson. *Different and Wonderful: Raising Black Children in a Race-Conscious Society.* New York: Simon and Schuster, 1992.

Strong Museum, Margaret Woodbury. Doll Oral History Project. Margaret Woodbury Strong Museum, Rochester, New York, 1987.

8

Playing the Game

Rituals in Children's Games

SALLY SUGARMAN

Games are more than child's play. As metaphors, games permeate and reflect the cultures in which they are played. Contests of the schoolyard are transferred to arenas where professionals play childhood games for profit, rather than fun. Team players are valued on the football field, in business boardrooms, and in the corridors of political power. Learning the rules of the game matters. Play is one of the ways in which children learn, but it is also more than a way to absorb society's manners and morals. In play the individual reshapes the world. Play, through its symbolic nature, conceals as well as reveals the child's struggle for mastery.

Although play persists into adult life in the form of jokes, sports, fiction, festivals, and other entertainments, the play of children has been seen to have particular significance for the developing individual. Play, in this view, supports growth. However, it may do so more by its subversive and ritualistic nature than by serving as a preparation for life through adult-approved activities and role models. According to Brian Sutton-Smith and John Roberts, "in games, children learn all those necessary arts of treachery, deception, harassment, divination and foul play that their teachers won't teach them, but that are most important in successful human interrelationships in marriage, business and war" (100).

Studying games provides a window into childhood and into many children's lives. Although sometimes used interchangeably, *childhood* and *children* refer to different entities. Childhood is a construct by which adults organize their knowledge and attitudes about children. We know this construct changes over time. We have had the sinful child, the pure child, the child as redeemer, the child as bad seed, and as historical circumstances change, we will have different visions of childhood.

Children, however, do not exist in some abstract universe, but in special social circumstances and historical realities. They change over the course of time from infants to toddlers to school-age children to adolescents. They play their games in different places and with different objects. The city child and the suburban child have different landscapes in which to play. Even limiting an examination of children's play to the United States presents a complex mosaic of activities and experiences.

Children's play is like a kaleidoscope, revealing different patterns as one shifts the lens. For Piaget, the genetic epistemologist, play and games mark shifts in cognitive development. For Freud, Erikson, and other psychoanalysts, play and games are screens to enable children to master internal and universal conflicts. The historian Huizinga saw play as the source of the sacred in human life. Anthropologists such as Malinowski have seen play's function as enculturation and socialization. What is play to a child?

This question is more complex than it appears since both the play and the player vary according to age and activity. Corinne Hutt makes the distinction between the child's exploration and play. In exploration children find out what an object can do, but in play children find out what they can do with the object (231–251). Play is also described as being intrinsically motivated, self-directed, and without consequence. Roger Caillois organized play into four categories: agon, alea, mimicry, and ilinx. *Agon* is competition or contest, the source of sport. *Alea* is chance, operating in the counting-out games in childhood and in gambling in adult life. *Mimicry* can be observed in children's dramatic play and in theater, films, and television. *Ilinx* or vertigo is demonstrated by children spinning themselves or on roller coaster rides or in skiing (17–20).

Play may also be the reconciliation of opposites. As a player, I am a child and a mother simultaneously. I am a Power Ranger and a four-year-old. I learn society's songs, but I change the words.

Mine eyes have seen the glory of the burning of the school
We have tortured every teacher and we've broken every rule
His truth is marching on.

(Bronner 97)

This is the paradox that Gregory Bateson saw in play (261–266). While play helps children learn about themselves, about others, and about the world, it also provides opportunities to comment on the world, to control it, to mock it, to change it. Play is simultaneously socialization and subversion. Play is not so much a rehearsal for the child's future as an adult as it is a comment on the child's present condition. Play displaces control from the adult to the child. The powerless become, momentarily, for the length of the game, the powerful.

By definition, games are activities with rules. The source of these rules may vary, but the game depends upon people agreeing to, if not playing by, the rules. Rituals, however, have a deeper significance than rules. In rituals we see the spiritual significance of play that Huizinga posits in his historical and philosophical study of play. Rules may require consent, but rituals compel. Whether it is a chant for choosing players for different sides or the space in which the play occurs, the power of rituals is their persistence over time. The nonhierarchical circle games of toddlers are rooted in the sacred circles of tribal societies.

Rules may come from reason; rituals arise from needs. Patterns promise security and control. Rituals are repeated behaviors or interactions that have symbolic value beyond the experiences themselves. In an unpredictable world, early humans found ways to order their lives through repeated symbolic acts that they felt would protect or assist them. The vulnerability of childhood echoes that early condition, but not in simple recapitulation as suggested by G. Stanley Hall. Rather, children experience the psychological realities of physical and economic dependence. As relatively defenseless explorers in a new world, children may need the magic of ritual to safeguard them on their journeys. Although the geography of the terrains may change, children on these life journeys are still wary of stepping on a crack that will break a back.

Rituals persist into adult life. Ceremonies may change in some details, but the need for them does not. Marriages and funerals continue customs whose origins may be forgotten or add newly devised rituals. How are these manifestations different from the rituals in children's games? Unlike the rituals of childhood, these ceremonies have consequences that last beyond themselves. Playing house, children can be caring and loving as well as leave a doll or teddy bear outside in the rain or thrown downstairs. Adults might find themselves charged with abuse and neglect for similar behavior.

What are the unique features of children's game rituals? Children's games are serious to the players although they may not be to the observer. There is a continuum from the child to the adult that we can see as we look at children's games. Both the Little Leaguer and the World Series player are engaged in contests of skill that momentarily take them out of their ordinary experiences. The child, however, may operate with less awareness than the adult. The perspective that comes from experience is lacking. The rituals are less likely to be questioned and more likely to be seen as immutable.

As a part of children's play, games take many forms. They may be played out of doors, with a board indoors, as part of a team, with one other person or alone, as in computer games or solitaire. They may reflect the society in which children live; jump-rope rhymes incorporate the names of current celebrities. They may echo past societies; London Bridge falls down generation after generation. Traditional games, board games, and sociodramatic play are the focus of this examination.

Our knowledge of children's games is limited by the venues in which we see children and by the dismissal of games as trivial by many adults. Yet as the period of childhood expands along with the growing commercial toy and game market, greater attention is paid to this aspect of children's lives. With more children in group-based programs at earlier ages, there are more opportunities to observe play as well as to initiate traditional singing and rhyming games in early childhood education programs. Even children in the middle years of childhood spend more time in supervised settings than children have in the past. In after-school programs children's organized games are more accessible to adults' observations and influence. Iona and Peter Opie maintain that we see more violent games in the schoolyard than in neighborhoods because children are confined there, like animals in captivity (13).

When people talk of childhood, a common response is to yearn for bygone days when children had time to dream and to play with neighborhood friends. Adults perpetually seem to believe that childhood today is not what it was in their day. Television programs are not as good; toys are more easily broken; and no one plays the old games anymore. The Opies note this phenomenon in their book on children's games. Ask fourteen-year-olds about children's games, and they will say that nobody plays the old games now that they played a year or two ago (6).

This view of childhood is a distinctly modern one. Childhood was not always such a desired state. Hard work on farms and later in factories blurred the boundaries between adult and childhood. Games were shared between adults and children, as the Breugel painting *Children's Games* shows. Barbara Tuchman in her analysis of the fourteenth century noted that most of the adults at that time acted like children because they were, in fact, children. With an average life expectancy of thirty-six years and a high infant mortality rate, there was not much time to achieve wisdom and maturity (49–69). Some of the games Breugel painted are still played, but now primarily by children.

Folklorists have recorded street games, jump-rope rhymes, singing games, and team games. The school rather than the neighborhood may be the place now where chants and rituals are taught and performed, but children continue to hide and seek and run and tag each other. Each season brings its outdoor games, and despite the lure of the television set and the computer, children swarm onto the streets and fields and back alleys to play.

Barrie Thorne notes that ritual is an important part of children's play in school. As she observed boys and girls in the schoolyard, she saw the stylized nature of their play. Chasing games with their ritualistic challenges masked the sexuality behind the screeching playfulness. Assigning "cooties" to marginal children echoed pollution rites in which menstruating women were seen as contaminating the tribe. The game of tag is also a contamination game as players flee from the touch of the mysterious and all-powerful "it." In these "Central Leader" games, as Brian Sutton-Smith and John M. Roberts call them in *Cross Cultural and Psychological Study of Games*, the group dares the leader to catch them, as generations of children have done. Even the names of these games have a romantic and ancient air: Mother, May I? Red Rover, Red Rover; Jack, May I Cross Your Golden River? As children taunt the central figure, who some see representing God or the devil, "the players control the fear, the fear does not control the players" (501).

Rifka Eifermann contends that the rituals of these games are parallel to fairy tales and myths in the way they embody unconscious community fantasies (127–144). Internal conflicts are masked by the structure of the games. Because of the rules of the games, children can be freed from the responsibility of their aggressive actions. Eifermann also likens individual play within the structure of the games to that of the performer of musical compositions who can be creative within the limits of a form. Children may vary their individual performance of the game, just as musicians provide unique individual interpretations of a score. Since children have usually taught games to other children, Eifermann believes games might be considered a "pure form" of children's culture (129).

This tradition of child transmission of games may be modified in a society when one of the functions of game collections is to enable adults to teach games to children. Many college students recall learning traditional games in school or in camps. However, the illicit children's play Nancy R. King describes suggests that children at times find adult tutelage and control oppressive. King shows that the giggling, note passing, and play fighting in classrooms are games devised by children to challenge teachers' authority (149–151).

Among the types of verbal games children learn without adult instruction are riddles, jokes, song parodies, and insults. Snaps or Dozens is a ritual insulting game that African American children, mostly boys, play. The version played by white children is called Cutting or Ranking. The idea of these games is for the players to top each other in negative comments, most often about the other person's mother.

> Your mother's an autoworker.
> *Your mother's a baby elephant.*
> Your mother plays for the Jets.
> *Your mother plays for the Dallas cowboys.*
> Your mother plays ping pong with King Kong.
> *Your mother goes begging for surplus food.*
> Your mother wears sneakers to work.
> *Your mother has a waffle face.*
>
> (Hall and Adelman 5–6)

This game diffuses anger and binds the group together in a contest of skill and camaraderie much like the ritual insults exchanged among friendly adults. Whether one is an imitation or an outgrowth of the other, the purpose seems to be the same, and the model seems close to Bateson's idea of play actions having simultaneously different meanings. This is an insult and not an insult.

Within the United States most traditional games seem to be British in origin. However, other cultural groups have made their contribution to the repertoire of singing games and ritual plays. The African American tradition has notably enriched the playing lives of children. In recording games and songs from the African American heritage, Bessie Jones and Bess Lomax Hawes note how differently European Americans and African Americans approached these ritual games. When teaching games from the black tradition to white teenagers and adults, the black teacher's emphasis was on cooperation, whereas for the white students it was on competition. The culture from which these African American games emerged stressed mutual support and general participation. For European Americans, a game without winners or losers hardly seemed to be a game (xiv).

If outdoor games, singing, and circle games have connections to the deeper workings of the human psyche and to the developmental tasks of childhood, are board games, manufactured by adults, more culturally specific and less meaningful to the child? Probably not. Just as the Opies report the singing and outdoor games adapted to the latest fads, so are board games structurally the same whatever their contemporary themes.

Huizinga talks about the sacred space set aside for play. Although it may be difficult to think of a Monopoly board as sacred, its space is as rigidly defined and controlling as any ball field or ceremonial stage. The layout of the board is integral to the action of the game. The players' moves are determined as much by the configuration board as by the rules.

Most modern board games are cast in traditional forms that determine the players' actions. Playing spaces are square, rectangular, or circular. Within those spaces, play follows either a column or row, a cross within a circle, or a spiral pattern. Examples of the column/row model are *Cows and Leopards, Fox and Geese, Checkers*, and *Stratego. Parcheesi, Ludo, Nyout*, and *Trivial Pursuit* are variations on the circle/cross form. *The Game of the Goose, Around the World with Nelly Bly, Candy Land*, and *The Game of Life* are spiral games. Some games like *Monopoly* are played on the borders of the board, but they are variations of a race game where the goal is to be the first to win.

Board games do not have the fluidity of street games in terms of entrances and exits. Once started, a player cannot leave without ending the game for everyone. In board games the throw of the die to see who goes first is an important ritual, as is the subsequent order of the play. There is order and predictability in these routines, which are similar in all board games. In the use of the die, we see an example of Caillois's alea; chance takes precedence over skill. For players of mixed ages, this is advantageous for the younger players.

Rituals are inherent not only in particular games such as *Parcheesi* but in the process of gaming itself. Opening the board box, any board box, initiates the child into a wonderful world of possibilities. The world may be one of fantasy, such as *By Jove*, or one that bears a resemblance to the adult world, as does *The AAA Safe Driver Game*, or one like *Careers* that ridicules the adult world. The appeal of Chris Van Allsburg's children's book *Jumanji* may be that it shows the wildest animals of children's imaginations tamed by closing the box, thereby returning control to the children.

The theme of the journey appears frequently as a motif of board games, as it does in fairy tales, even if it is only in the journey around the board. Just as hopscotch, an ancient Roman game adopted by Christians, is based on a journey to heaven, so *Chutes and Ladders* is a journey to perfectibility with the original snakes of the Indian game representing vices and the ladders representing virtues. During the nineteenth century, journey games provided the opportunity to teach children geography. In games such as *Monopoly* and *The Game of Life*, the journey leads to the acquisition of worldly goods. The player with the most money wins. In newer games like *Billionaire* and *Trump*, the amounts of money are greater than the Depression-inspired *Monopoly* provided its players. Concern for the lessons being learned in these games led to the creation of games like *Anti-Monopoly* and new cooperative games such as *Community*, in which "we try to develop a happy, complete village.... If we succeed in building a community, we all 'win' together," according to the description of the game. The focus, however, is not shifted away from winning, but from the individual winner to the group.

Besides these overt messages about the world, games teach children to lose. *Monopoly* does not teach children how to become ruthless tycoons, but how to accept fate by losing or winning everything with a hotel on Broadway. Reversals are characteristic of board games, enabling losers to become unexpected winners. These reversals are based on chance. Chance softens the blows of losing and tempers the joys of winning. Since luck can change, the games are worth playing and replaying. This may be why games of chance are more commonly played among groups with little sense of power or control, such as children and the poor.

Cheating must take place within the rules of the game and is usually permitted only by the youngest player. Such allowances usually consist of permitting a player to throw again if the dice land off the board or not keeping close count of the number of spaces the player moves. Players may agree to change the rules, but the frame of the game must be maintained. Leaving the game before the agreed-upon conclusion is worse than cheating. Board games exist not only in a specific ritualized space but also within a ritualized time frame. They are designed with different levels of complexity to maintain time frames appropriate to the ages of the children. *Candy Land* is a simple race game that does not involve decision making, unlike *The Game of Life*, which is a more sophisticated version of a race game. *Clue for Little Detectives, Clue Jr.,* and *Clue* are other examples of how games are modified to fit different ages. *Clue for Little Detectives* is a race game like *Candy Land. Clue Jr.* is much closer to the adult *Clue*, requiring decision making and inferences about the clues, but on a smaller scale.

Games come into and go out of fashion. Bernard Mergen notes changes in the games children play in a study of play preferences (272–283). Since his sample size of fifty-two teenagers was small, the strength of Mergen's study is its relationship to other studies of trends in play. In a study of play preferences, Mergen compared his study to studies done in 1896, 1898, 1921, and 1959. Although board and video games were high on the list of activities done for fun by Mergen's respondents, they reported that their favorite games five years earlier included traditional games such as jump rope, tag, hopscotch, clapping games, and hide and seek. Television was important for the children in both their teenage years and five years earlier. Yet, as Mergen points out, television is often more of a social than a solitary activity.

Probably most important was his finding that there currently was a greater similarity between the games played by boys and girls than there was in the past. Changes in girls' behaviors drove this convergence. More games were available to girls as they crossed previous gender boundaries. Cards, swimming, basketball, and computer games displaced jump rope, hopscotch, and singing games. Girls now also play soccer and Little League baseball. Boys, however, find it more difficult to cross the line between boys' and girls' games. Boys' play has become more circumscribed. They avoid games boys played in earlier periods, such as dolls, hopscotch, jacks, house, school, and singing games.

Games are often contrasted with sociodramatic play as constraining children more than their imaginations do. On closer examination, however, it appears that even in contemporary sociodramatic play, a need for order persists. Often what appears as free-form spontaneous dramatic play, unhindered by rules, is the replaying of scenarios as tightly structured as any formal game. B. B. Haslett notes that in playing McDonald's, if children do not pretend to pay before they eat their pretend McDonald's food, the play will be restarted by the children so that the play sequence correctly mimics the actual experience (1–19). While early childhood educators become disturbed by the repetitive nature of superhero play, they often overlook the stylized actions within traditional house play. Activities named by the children, as in "Let's play McDonald's," and repeated in a particular form over time, gain the features of games in that spontaneity is replaced by a formal structure that children need to learn.

William Cosaro describes the access rituals that preschool children employ to join play. In his extensive observations of children's play, he sees nonverbal entry where children put themselves into the physical area of the play as the most frequently used technique. If there is no response to their presence, children produce behavior similar to the behavior of those children they wish to join. If children are making sand cakes, the entering child also makes sand cakes. Entering ongoing play requires children to use appropriate access rituals similar to the adult's verbal strategies (315–336).

Brian Sutton-Smith says in *The Ambiguity of Play* that in adults, play and ritual are separated, whereas in children they are entwined. He describes Meckely's study in which she explored the construction of play by a group of preschool children (169). These children developed shared play worlds with recurring details and plots. Games such as prisons, floods, houses, and dressing up were played repeatedly in the same way at the same time each day. Playing bombs and playing dolls were highly consistent in their content and structure from day to day, whereas water play and sand play were of very low consistency. This sociodramatic play assumed the quality of a formalized game; the play was conservative rather than innovative. Children needed to learn the structure of the play in order to participate. Even self-directed play by children has within it the reassuring repetition characteristic of thematic board or traditional games. Children, so often seen as carefree and spontaneous in their play, are less so. Whether in fantasy or imitative sociodramatic play, children engage in patterned behaviors with symbolic meanings.

In a study done in 1989 in Bennington, Vermont, 157 informants were interviewed about their favorite or most frequently played games in the categories of outdoor play, board games, sociodramatic play, and solitary play. This study revealed more sociodramatic play than was evident in Mergen's study. This may have resulted from the use of interviews rather than questionnaires. The informants ranged in age from 10 to 68, with 100 of them between 10 and 22. Since most of the games were described as having been played by youths between the ages of 7 and 14, the heavy emphasis on sociodramatic games indicates that symbolic play may continue for a longer period of time than a theorist like Piaget suggests. These games were rule governed and were repeated in detail and form over time. They were characterized by ritual, not by spontaneity.

Differences between males and females were evident in games like Cowboys and Indians. Over and over, when females reported playing this game, they had assumed the Indian role. Indeed, sometimes the game was called Indians, and cowboys were non-existent or imaginary. As one girl said, "No one was killed so no one would be left out." With females, Indian games focussed more on survival, costumes, and domestic life. In one female-reported game that included cowboys, the most the Indians did was sneak up on the cowboys and surprise them.

Boys' games of Cowboys and Indians, Cops and Robbers, and Army had their rules, often derived from the group's agreement. A ten-year-old reported, "You couldn't always say my guy's everything-proof." That would have been unfair and would have slowed the action. The action was chasing and shooting at enemies, real or imagined, with real or pretend guns. As boys got older, some of these games were combined with bike riding or other outdoor activities.

A game popular with both boys and girls, usually called Boat, was played in the living room or bedroom. Children piled on a piece of furniture that they had to imaginatively maneuver through a shark-infested sea. Stuffed animals were often thrown overboard to be devoured. Sometimes the game required the players to risk moving to another piece of furniture. Repeatedly, subjects noted that the fun of this game was that it was scary. This format was also used in a game called Rocket in which interplanetary dangers threatened.

Barbie was important in the play of preadolescent girls. The scenarios described by many of the girls emphasized issues of sexuality. One college student commented, "Sometimes we would have murders and scandals. Sometimes we would just get them married." One girl with many Barbies and only one Ken explained that some of the Barbies had to be lesbians. Another girl revealed that Barbie was date-raped by

Ken. Rape was a recurrent theme for these prepubescent girls. Pregnancy, incest, and abuse represent the darker side of Barbie that these girls enacted. In *Barbie Culture*, Mary F. Rogers reports similar accounts of violence on Barbie dolls by both boys and girls. Barbie's status as a symbol of femininity, Rogers suggests, may be the reason for working through conflicts around sexuality (29–34).

Boys also reported ripping apart their toy soldiers. In their sociodramatic games, they tended to play games like Snow Man Murder or Terrorism. Although the girls' focus on sexuality and boys' on violence in their games showed gender differences, there was some indication that, as in other areas of play, girls were including boys' themes in their play as well. Since college students interviewed these children and adolescents, the informants may have felt more comfortable dwelling on the more sensational aspects of their play.

Although originated by the children, these games had strict rules. The play had to proceed according to the scripts that had evolved. These games have much in common with the Dead Baby and the Name-the-Deformed Jokes that Simon J. Bronner has collected. The grossness of sick jokes appeals to children in the same way as do other challenges to adult value systems. Children are often commenting on the hypocrisy of adults. Gary Fine addresses this dark side of play in discussing dirty play, a subject about which little is written. By dirty play, Fine means aggressive pranks, such as throwing eggs at passing cars, vandalism, and sexual and racist invective. These are ritual acts of passage into manhood performed by boys who will become upstanding, law-abiding citizens. These acts are not impelled by the rage that will lead other children to prison, but by a playing at bad behavior (43–56).

The elements that Fine sees as driving dirty play are similar to the mechanisms that appear to be operating in the sociodramatic games described by children and young adults in the Bennington study. Fine observed five Little League teams over three years. The boys were white and middle-class and exhibited these dirty play behaviors in the company of peers.

These activities are a way of asserting control over situations, as well as achieving status and solidarity within a group. Playing Ding-Dong Ditch, which involves ringing a doorbell and running away, is a demonstration of a willingness to take risks. Sexuality in our society is problematic for males as well as females. Controlling and being controlled by taunts of being gay is another aspect of the male adolescent conflict over sexuality. Flaunting adult values and learning the rules by breaking them are stages in the growth of children.

As the values of society are mocked in rhymes and games, children assert themselves through these group rituals. Although children's culture cannot exist separate from adult culture, it can be a distorting mirror. Perhaps adults' claim that no one plays the old games anymore is because it is too disturbing to think that the anarchy of childhood continues.

Some games may not change because some of the conditions of childhood do not change. Children still depend upon adults for physical and psychological survival. Children in the United States have little power outside of their families. As universal as some aspects of childhood may be, other experiences are historically unique. Children at the beginning of the twenty-first century in the United States are required to attend school later into adolescence than any children previously. Laws target them as a special group with limited civil rights. Conversely, children in the United States probably have more access to consumer goods and leisure time than any other generation of children has had or than children in other countries presently have.

In her essay "Continuities and Discontinuities in Cultural Conditioning," Ruth Benedict contrasts the child and the adult in American society on three dimensions: responsible/nonresponsible, dominance/submission, and the contrasted sex role (302–312). In our society children are not given responsibilities, are expected to be submissive, and are generally considered asexual. Benedict compares this to other societies that prepare children for the transition into the adult role more gradually than we do. Since Benedict wrote this essay in 1938, cultural critics such as Joshua Meyrowitz and Neil Postman claim that the line between the adult and the child in our society has become less rigid, with the adult becoming more childlike, rather than the reverse. There are differences, however, between today and the fourteenth century. An extended life span, children's isolation from direct experience with a variety of adults and their work, changing family structures, and technological transformations in communication and transportation are elements that provide a unique challenge to the maturing child. Television and movies tantalize children and adolescents with fantasy images of power and sexuality.

The greater the gap between the child and the adult in opportunities and responsibilities, the longer children need to play their games. The rituals of adolescent fantasy games like *Dungeons and Dragons* indicate how play builds community among its players. Play makes the conflicts within a complex society easier to confront. Not only are the consequences delayed, but delay is made more bearable.

In games, risk and safety are balanced. The circle and the square provide clear paths. The rules equalize the players. The leadership role of "it" is fluid, and chance may transform losers into winners. Time and space are set aside for the game's reality to supercede the reality of daily life. All the games children play—outdoor, traditional, board, and pretend—are connected through these ceremonies of childhood, rituals that evolve and merge into the rituals of adult life.

WORKS CITED

Bateson, Gregory. "This Is Play." In *Child's Play*, ed. R. E. Herron and Brian Sutton-Smith, 261–266. London: John Wiley and Sons, 1971.

Benedict, Ruth. "Continuities and Discontinuities in Cultural Conditioning." In *The World of the Child*, ed. Toby Talbot, 302–312. Garden City, NY: Doubleday, 1968.

Bronner, Simon J. *American Children's Folklore*. Little Rock, AK: August House, 1988.

Caillois, Roger. *Man, Play and Games*. New York: Free Press, 1961.

Cosaro, William. "We're Friends, Right: Children's Use of Access Rituals in Nursery School." *Language in Society* 8 (3 Dec. 1979): 315–336.

Eifermann, Rifka. "Children's Games, Observed and Experienced." In *The Psychoanalytical Study of the Child*, ed. Albert J. Solnit and Peter B. Neubauer, vol. 42, 127–144. New Haven, CT: Yale University Press, 1987.

Fine, Gary. "Good Children and Dirty Play." *Play and Culture* 1, no. 1 (1988): 43–56.

Hall, Susan, and Bob Adelman. *Street Smart*. New York: McGraw-Hill, 1972.

Haslett, B. B. "Basic Concepts: Communication, Cognition and Language." In *Children Communicating: The First Five Years* by Beth Bonniwell Haslett and Wendy Samter, 1–19. Mahwah, NJ: Lawrence Earlbaum Associates, 1997.

Hutt, Corrine. "Exploration and Play in Children." In *Child's Play*, ed. R. E. Herron and Brian Sutton-Smith, 231–251. New York: John Wiley and Sons, 1971.

Jones, Bessie, and Bess Lomax Hawes. *Step It Down: Games, Plays, Songs and Stories from the Afro-American Heritage*. Athens: University of Georgia Press, 1987.

King, Nancy R. "Elementary School Play: Theory and Research." In *School Play*, ed. James H. Block and Nancy R. King, 149–151. New York: Teachers College Press, 1987.

Mergen, Bernard. "Ninety-Five Years of Historical Change in the Game *Preferences* of American Children." *Play and Culture* 4, no. 3 (1991): 272–283.

Meyrowitz, Joshua. *No Sense of Place.* New York: Oxford University Press, 1985.

Opie, Iona, and Peter Opie. *Children's Games in Street and Playground.* Oxford: Oxford University Press, 1984.

Rogers, Mary F. *Barbie Culture.* London: Sage, 1999.

Sutton-Smith, Brian. *The Ambiguity of Play.* Cambridge, MA: Harvard University Press, 1997.

———. *The Folkgames of Children.* Austin: University of Texas Press, 1972.

Sutton-Smith, Brian, and John M. Roberts. "The Cross Cultural and Psychological Study of Games." In *Cross-Cultural Analysis of Games,* ed. Gunter Luschen. Champaign, IL: Stripes, 1970.

Thorne, Barrie. *Gender Play: Girls and Boys in School.* New Brunswick, NJ: Rutgers University Press, 1993.

Tuchman, Barbara. *A Distant Mirror.* New York: Knopf, 1978.

PART 5

MARRIAGE AND MOURNING

Birth, marriage, and death comprise the traditional rites of passage. Children's connection to the first of these is obvious, but what of the others? Cultures differ in their approaches to including children in marriage and death rituals. Some regard children as full-fledged members of a community who act as participants in adult-centered rituals. Others attempt to shield the young from events that they may not fully appreciate or understand, or consider children too poorly behaved and disruptive to be a part of solemn ceremonies. One thing is certain, though, children who are involved in marriage and death rituals in ways that are age-appropriate may be better able to understand the meaning of these rituals when they become adults. They also may benefit from the therapeutic value of rituals, enabling them to connect to a group, confront powerful emotions, and cope with changes in the family structure and interpersonal relationships.

The essays that follow speak to children's involvement in marriage and death rituals. Kathy Merlock Jackson confronts gender issues regarding what is considered to be one of the most joyous of rituals in "Petals and Patriarchy: The Flower Girl in American Weddings." On a more somber note, Vincent DiGiralomo takes a historical approach in "Newsboy Funerals: Sorrow and Solidarity in Urban America," examining a little-known ritual that exemplifies the ways in which lower-class youth mourned the death of one of their own. Both of these essays consider children as both participants in and observers of ritualized behavior and the ramifications of these experiences.

9

Petals and Patriarchy

The Flower Girl in American Weddings

KATHY MERLOCK JACKSON

> She strews petals of flowers in front of the bride, symbolizing fertility.
> Linda Otto Lipsett, *To Love and to Cherish*

Consider this traditional scenario:

A little girl, no more than five years of age, learns at a family celebration that her aunt is engaged to be married; she shares in her family's joy at the news. Shortly thereafter, her aunt asks her to be a flower girl in the wedding, and in the months that follow, the little girl becomes central to the wedding planning. As the youngest female member of the wedding party, she goes along with her aunt, the bride; her mother, the matron of honor; and her grandmother, the mother of the bride to choose her wedding finery. Finally, the women find the perfect flower-girl dress for the occasion. Like the bride, the flower girl is dressed in white, and her gown, in its fabric and design, is a miniature version of the bride's. On the day of the wedding, the flower girl leads the female procession down the aisle to meet the men at the altar. All eyes are upon this tiny child, perfectly coifed and attired, as she drops rose petals, matching

the pastel shade of the bridesmaids' gowns, from a small ribboned basket. Accolades of "cute" and "precious" fill the room.

Being a flower girl is for many little girls in America a memorable event
of childhood. As these girls prepare for and participate in the female-
centered wedding ritual, they are reenacting a practice that dates to
medieval times. They are also learning the definitions and values their
culture associates with weddings, as well as women's roles in them. In a
sense, acting the part of a flower girl brings the youngest female member of the family or community into the fold, making her a participant
in the wedding ceremony and introducing her to her society's patri-
archal views of gender and marriage. For this reason, the flower-girl experience can have an early effect on a young girl, imparting to her important cultural messages. In order to study the phenomenon of flower
girls, it is useful to consider the following contexts: the historical and
symbolic meaning of the flower girl, in conjunction with weddings and
with the lore of flowers; the perpetuation of the flower-girl tradition, as
reflected in the popular imagination and in bridal magazines; and the
ramifications of the flower-girl experience in American girlhood.

The Flower Girl as Symbol

> Four phases of the life cycle are represented in the wedding ritual
> through the association of these artifacts with the ritual participants.
> These ritual roles are recognized as cyclical although represented in
> the ritual as a linear development of women: the flower girl, the Bride's
> maids, the Bride, and the mother of the Bride.
>
> Pamela Frese, "Holy Matrimony"

The flower girl in weddings of today functions as a symbol in a traditional rite of passage and, as such, is charged with meaning. As Pamela
Frese points out, "As a rite of passage, a ritual provides the powerful
motive force to move individuals from one state of being to another, to
a new status in society, and to a different stage in the person's life"
(Frese, "Union" 97). In the wedding ritual, the bride is the focus, for it is
she who undergoes the greatest change in status and identity (Seligson
28), and the flower girl is included to represent the bride at the first stage
in her life: as an innocent child. In traditional weddings, this link is

clearly established: the wedding procession begins with the flower girl and ends with the bride, and only they may wear white, the color that symbolizes innocence and purity (Frese, "Holy Matrimony" 42). It is interesting to note that the wedding ceremony itself serves as a transitional state of liminality for the bride and therefore is characterized by a certain timelessness. At this moment of the bridal procession, seemingly frozen in time, one is reminded of the progression of stages in a woman's life.

The flower girl, although not a part of the first marriage rituals, was eventually added as a fertility symbol. According to Diane Ackerman in *A Natural History of Love*, marriages in Anglo-Saxon times were by capture, and the groom solicited a group of friends, known as "bridesmen" or "bride-knights," to assist him in snaring his bride. By the same token, the bride selected her own "bridesmaids" or a married "bride woman" to help her. It is also believed that in primitive marriages the bride and groom, so as not to be easily identified by evil spirits, surrounded themselves with "bridesmen" and bridesmaids" dressed similarly, a practice that led to the modern custom of matching costumes for bridal attendants. The flower girl did not appear in wedding ceremonies until medieval times; originally, she carried wheat, her function being to symbolize fertility. Later, she adopted flowers, which, in addition to representing fertility, emitted a fragrance that would mask any musty or unpleasant odors at the wedding site. The ring bearer, usually a page, was also added in the Middle Ages, possibly as a partner for the flower girl (Ackerman 271).

The tradition of the flower girl, heavily imbued with fertility symbolism, is also reflective of early pagan rituals that frequently contained symbols of males and females and the sexual union. The flower-girl custom is most reminiscent of the pagan May Day celebration in which the may pole and its surrounding ribbons and flowers symbolize the male and female anatomies respectively, and the dance around the pole represents sexual intercourse (Wright 2).

The Symbolic Meaning of Flowers

The flower girl represents the promise of fertility and through her association with the falling petals of the rose, represents a stage in the natural cycle of life. The Bride's maids and the Bride have already passed

through this stage as has the Bride's mother. This cycle is started by the
Bride's mother, who actually preceeds [sic] the flower girl down the
aisle.

Pamela Frese, "Holy Matrimony"

Weddings abound with symbols of fertility, such as the wedding cake
originally made of barley or wheat, the semen-like drop pearls decorat-
ing the bridal gown, and the rice showered upon the bride and groom as
they leave the reception. Of all, however, flowers are the most recognizable symbols of fertility, often arranged into a nosegay, which the bride
holds directly in front of her, level with her uterus, or an arm bouquet,
which she carries to one side, as if cradling a baby. The flower girl's association with flowers is obvious: not only does the flower girl scatter the
petals, but she herself, the product of a sexual union, embodies the
promise of children for the bride and groom.

By the nineteenth century in England, children, regarded by some
as magical charms ensuring fertility (Kirschenbaum and Rockwell 93),
were integral components in weddings, as were flowers. Linda Otto
Lipsett describes popular bridal flowers of the time and their meanings:

Orange blossoms
   Symbol of fertility, the orange tree being one of the most
   fruitful; if artificial they should be removed before the end
   of the first month of marriage

Roses
   Flowers of Venus, white roses represented virginity; red roses
   meant love, joy, and beauty

Myrtle
   Symbol of constancy in duty and affection; in Wales it was
   planted on both sides of the front door to bring harmony to
   the household

Rosemary
   Symbol of remembrance

Baby's breath
   Symbol of fertility (57)

On February 10, 1840, a royal wedding occurred in England that
secured the popularity of flowers and children in the marriage ritual.
Twenty-year-old Queen Victoria married Prince Albert in what

became, according to Lipsett, "the wedding of the century, the storybook wedding to change all weddings and to set the fashion for all brides of the future" (57). Queen Victoria, in her statement to the archbishop of Canterbury, indicated that "it was her wish to be married in all respects like any other woman" (quoted in Rusk 138). At her wedding, she adorned her hair with a wreath of orange blossoms and included a child in her processional. According to Reverend John Rusk's 1901 account of *The Beautiful Life and Illustrious Reign of Queen Victoria*, the third of the princess attendants to precede the queen down the aisle was "the Duchess of Cambridge, in white velvet, leading by the hand the lovely little Princess Mary, who was dressed in white satin and swansdown, the mother all animation and smiles at the applause which greeted her child" (Rusk 143).

Queen Victoria's royal wedding solidified the inclusion of flowers and children in the marriage ceremony, and the tradition has endured, affecting the style and tone of weddings. Even today American weddings retain elements from this earlier era. As Virginia bridal consultant Susan Hirsh observes, "Our brides are choosing the Victorian look, which is close-knit flowers in a hand-tied bouquet. . . . They are using white roses a lot" (quoted in Shepard X18). In modern times, roses have become the most popular of wedding flowers and are the type generally associated with flower girls. According to Pamela Frese, "Real or silk rose petals are thrown down in front of the flower girl, or she may simply carry a basket of flowers" ("Holy Matrimony" 42), the latter becoming more popular as church officials frown on loose petals on the carpet or flooring (Shepard, "Floral Bouquets," X18). Oftentimes flower girls, representative of the "bud" rather than the "full bloom," carry small sweetheart roses. Stirling Macoboy's *The Ultimate Rose Book* lists 1,500 varieties of roses — some in delicate shades of pink or creamy white with names such as Bridal Pink, Bridal White, Bridesmaid, First Love, and, not surprisingly, Flower Girl — enough to satisfy a wide diversity of bridal tastes and preferences. Also importantly, the rose, once used for garlands to decorate the statues of Cupid, Venus, Flora, and Hymen, maintains its traditional distinction as an emblem of love and life (Phillips and Foy 68).

The Perpetuation of the Flower-Girl Tradition

Whether there's just one or a gaggle, flower girls tend to steal the show.
"Budding Beauties," *Town and Country*

The flower girl has remained a recognizable participant in the wedding drama, although her popularity, reflective of cultural trends and personal tastes, has fluctuated. In the 1980s, for example, the flower-girl tradition appeared to be on the wane in America while, at the same time, the demand for wedding flowers for stepparents increased. This, according to Pam Frese, "indicates the rising number of divorces in American culture and the general tendency for newlywed couples to put off having children immediately so there is no reason to represent them in the ceremony" ("Holy Matrimony" 45). *Bride's* magazine, an important barometer of cultural attitudes regarding weddings, indicates other reasons for excluding flower girls from weddings. According to one bride-to-be, "When my best friend walked down the aisle last year, none of the guests paid as much attention to her as they did to the flower girls. . . . I decided then and there that the same thing wouldn't happen to me" (Osen 188). These words, reflective of the stereotype of female competitiveness and of a self-absorption that characterized the 1980s "me generation," also underscore the fact that not everyone finds children and their antics enchanting. Given this, *Bride's* offers another, even more pervasive, reason for keeping youngsters away from weddings: their unpredictable behavior. As one observer remarked, "My brother and sister-in-law still talk about the time their . . . kids practically ruined a wedding—and that was more than 10 years ago" (Osen 188).

By the 1990s, however, the flower girl, and her counterpart, the ring bearer, had once again become prevalent and have remained so in the new millennium. Chris Ames, manager of Ames Tuxedos in Hampton, Virginia, voices a national trend: "We were ready to get rid of our ring bearer tuxedo line a few years ago because so few weddings were using flower girls and ring bearers, but now they're back and selling well" (Ames, personal interview). At the same time, bridal magazines showed a proliferation of flower-girl dresses, indicating their appropriateness in various wedding settings. Finally, *Town and Country* magazine, a bellwether of style if ever there was one, published its splashy "First Special Weddings Issue" in February 1997, featuring ten photographs with flower girls, several of them the largest and most eye-catching photographs in the issue. The flower-girl photographs and the text accompanying them suggest that no wedding is complete without a little girl, dressed in frothy white, attending the bride. In one of several full-page color photographs capturing the intimacy between a flower girl and bride, a flower girl sits on the grass gazing at the long white train of the bride's wedding dress as the bride, stepping away, looks over her shoulder and laughs affectionately at the "bride in training" (98). In another photograph, a smiling flower girl is captured in close-up with the descriptor, "Simply adorable, Erin Friedberg embraces her Philip Baloun–arranged bouquet" (102). Erin's sister, also a flower girl, shares her sister's glee at being chosen for the role. According to the text, "When asked to participate, eight-year old Megan Friedberg said rapturously, 'I've been waiting for this moment my entire life'" (103). *Town and Country*'s 2001 issue on "Truly Perfect Weddings" reinforces the child attendant trend with a dozen images of flower girls, including six full-page photos, one on the magazine's cover.

This inclusion of and appreciation for child attendants may be tied to another trend: a return to traditional, classic weddings (Shepard, "Bridal Fashion" X2; Bezner 30). Of the approximately 2.5 million couples who marry in America each year, 84 percent opt for a more traditional, formal wedding (Bezner 19). In general, the larger and more formal the wedding, the more likely it is to include a flower girl. Although a flower girl may occasionally divert attention from the bride (perhaps to a shy bride's relief), the opposite is more likely to be true. Regarded as the ultimate wedding accessory, flower girls add to the anticipation of an elaborate processional, allowing the bride to make an even more grand entrance. They also amuse onlookers, providing a sense of whimsy to the solemn events of the marriage ritual. As the tony *Town and Country* reported, "Even if she throws her entire basket of rose petals before she toddles halfway down the aisle or sneaks a fingerful of frosting from the cake when she thinks no one is looking, a flower girl adds charm to any wedding" ("Budding Beauties"). This, according to children's dress designer Joan Calabrese, has sparked an American phenomenon: "More and more brides around the country are doing what's been done in Europe for years—including many little attendants in their weddings and not so many big ones" ("Budding Beauties").

Another reason for the inclusion of flower girls in modern weddings relates to changing demographics. In 1960, when Dwight Eisenhower was president, the median age for newlyweds was 20 for women and 23 for men. However, in the past decade, due to an uncertain economy and more women wanting to further their education and careers, the median age for marriage, according to census figures, has reached its highest level ever: 25 for brides and almost 27 for grooms (Davis A7). Jennifer Weiner reports that University of Pennsylvania demographer

Sam Preston found that among college-educated women, the figure was even higher, with a majority postponing marriage until their mid to late 20s. Pattie Winkler, a bridal buyer at the upscale Suky Rosan bridal shop in Philadelphia, estimates the average age of brides in her shop at 28 to 32 and notes, "We never see a 21-year old bride anymore . . . We send 'em home!" (Weiner D8).

An older marriage age creates an environment supportive of flower girls. Women mindful of the biological clock who marry later and want to have children will plan them sooner; thus, they may not be bothered by the symbolism of children in the wedding ritual. As one *Bride's* magazine respondent noted of children, "they're beautiful reminders of what marriage is about" (Osen 188). Also, older couples who have worked for a time prior to marriage often have more money to spend on their weddings and are intent on "having it all"—including a full entourage. Bridal magazines and their advertisers, intent on targeting this audience, enthusiastically promote this idea.

Finally, in an era where single parenthood, divorce, and remarriage are common, children are often included as attendants in their parents' weddings as a way of acknowledging and making children feel part of a blended family. While choosing a flower girl and ring bearer to be in a wedding has always been a way of honoring special children in one's life, this gesture takes on greater importance when they are one's own children. Thus, a traditional practice has been adapted to meet new societal needs.

The Influence of the Flower-Girl Custom in the Lives of Young Girls

> As a flower girl, . . . I enjoyed the attention I received and felt pretty. A flower girl, just as any young girl who attends a wedding, will probably think marriage and having a family is a fairy tale come true.
> Single, white female, age eighteen, who has been a flower girl once, Virginia Beach, VA

> Being a flower girl taught me about being a woman, to look forward to being married and how to function during the change of a girl to womanhood.
> African American female who has been a flower girl four times and who, at age nineteen, is engaged to be married, Chesapeake, VA

> It made me feel important, self-confident and beautiful. It is important in the life of a young girl. It gives young girls the idea that a wedding is the biggest event in a girl's life. It's also a time for families to come together.
>
> Single, white female, age eighteen, who had been a flower girl once, Virginia Beach, VA

The flower-girl ritual in American culture has a long history and symbolic meaning, as well as clear reasons for its perpetuation. What is most important, however, is the influence that such an experience has in the life of a young girl. In particular, what does it teach her about women's roles in weddings, the family, and the community? As Lili Corbus Bezner points out in her analysis of wedding photography, women in America traditionally have been socialized and primed for participation in the marriage rite, which "historically changes a woman's status more than a man's and makes graphically real that profound change in status" (Bezner 27). As a flower girl, a child undergoes her own rite of passage, embarking on the first of her designated wedding roles, later — if she so chooses — to be followed by junior bridesmaid, bridesmaid, maid of honor, bride, matron of honor, mother of the bride or bridegroom, and, finally, grandmother of the bride or bridegroom with appropriate seating and corsage.

In order to study the meaning of the flower-girl experience in the life of a young girl, fieldwork was conducted in Tidewater, Virginia, where twenty females with experience with the flower-girl tradition, as either a participant or a close observer, were asked to share their thoughts. Tidewater, although not representative of the nation as a whole, is a diverse, transient area, in part due to its high military population. Thus, people there tend to have lived in other places and have knowledge of other traditions. Although the respondents represent a variety of socioeconomic groups and ethnic, racial, and religious backgrounds, they cannot be considered a cross-section of American females; thus, the results are not fully representative or generalizable. Nevertheless, clear patterns emerge from the data, which, when combined with current literature on weddings, provide useful information on the role of the flower-girl experience in a child's life.

As can be expected, when asking those versed in the flower-girl ritual to comment on it, one is tapping an audience of many who, by their very involvement, have favorable attitudes. While horror stories abound regarding flower girls who were terrorized by the experience, no respondents had any to report, although they did relate minor mishaps. One flower girl was so excited that she ran down the aisle singing while another walked alongside the bride, holding her hand. Another "forgot to sprinkle her rose petals on the way down the aisle, but sprinkled some during the ceremony itself, to the amusement of onlookers." A respondent who had been a flower girl at a wedding in Norfolk when she was three had nothing to say about the ceremony but noted, "Two years after the wedding, the couple divorced. I felt like a bad luck charm for a while."

The flower-girl experience undoubtedly teaches young girls about weddings. Given this, it is useful to consider the types of weddings most likely to include flower girls. Some respondents stated that every wedding they had ever been to included flower girls. In the words of one African American from Chesapeake, Virginia, "It is as big a tradition to have a flower girl as it is to have a bride." The majority, however, provided responses that coincide with national data: the bigger the wedding, the greater likelihood of one or more flower girls. When asked what sort of weddings were most apt to have flower girls, respondents provided similar answers: "large weddings with many attendants," "fancy, expensive, traditional church weddings," "larger weddings, more elaborate weddings," "family-oriented weddings, or those who want to have a huge wedding and have as many people as possible be a part of it," and "big, formal . . . traditional, weddings." Words such as "large," "formal," "traditional," and "church" were common, perhaps because, as one woman noted, "After all, there has to be an aisle to toss petals in." Respondents overwhelmingly dismissed the flower-girl tradition as being associated with any particular geographic area or racial, ethnic, or religious group (although they appear to be absent in Jewish weddings); instead, they tied it to big weddings, which are, of course, expensive and reflective of the value the couple's family and community place on the event. The message the young child gets is twofold: first, weddings are important because they are elaborate, and second, because they are elaborate, weddings must be important. The flower girl also functions as an object of conspicuous consumption as the bride and groom and their families use the wedding as a means of displaying wealth and status.

The flower girl's role in the expensive wedding venture is telling. Dress designer Joan Calabrese urges a bride to pay as much attention to the flower girl's dress as her own, advising her to choose a flower-girl dress in "the same color and in keeping with the style of the bride's gown" ("Budding Beauties"). These dresses, often adorned with lace and organza, range from $100 to $200 (Shepard, "Bridal Fashion" X16), and, according to respondents, are for many girls the most memorable part of being a flower girl. In the words of one Norfolk woman who had been her sister's flower girl, "I was only three years old so I don't remember much about it except that I loved my dress. I remember thinking it was beautiful." Another girl was "nervous but loved her dress." One former flower girl, who referred to her attire as her "princess dress," wore it in two weddings and many times after to play dress up, pretending she was the bride. Her response echoes the sentiment of another woman whose dress made her feel "girly and beautiful."

Flowers add another $20 to the cost of outfitting the flower girl (Shepard, "Floral Bouquets" X20), and although they are not as memorable as the dress, they are indispensable to the role. Respondents, echoing national trends, cited roses as the wedding flower of choice, mindful of their association with love and romance. One former flower girl who had worn a flower head wreath planned to carry on the family tradition: "My flower girl is going to have a wreath of pink and white tea roses in her hair. Her bouquet will also be pink and white. I chose tea roses because they symbolize young love, and pink and white because they are innocent colors. Red would be too harsh on a little girl." Other respondents named daisies, lilies, and baby's breath, which they also associated with innocence, as flowers they had worn or carried. As a young participant in a wedding, then, the flower girl gains a solid lesson in buying the right products to create the perfect image.

She also learns about women's traditional roles, and this begins from the moment she is asked to be flower girl. One woman who chose her niece to be her flower girl remarked, "I wanted family to be part of my day." While most flower girls are selected because of their close relationship to the bride or groom—generally sister, niece, cousin, godchild, neighbor, or friend of the family—this is not the only criterion. Respondents were quick to note other flower-girl requirements. She should be "young and beautiful," "innocent," "cute," "*very* well behaved and patient," "reasonably poised," and have "an angel-like look to her face." In the words of one recent bride, "I picked my flower girl, Laura, because she is adorable, very well behaved, and a family friend. She is a pro, as she has been in many weddings. She was perfect flower girl material."

And what do these criteria suggest to girls? In the words of one young woman of English, Irish, and Scottish descent, "I learned the importance of looking 'just-so.' Being quiet during the ceremony and not being rowdy at the reception were very important to the bride." Thus, flower girls learn at a very early age the importance of looking pretty and being passive; they are socialized to be demure objects of beauty, much akin to the traditional role of the bride as she appears in formal bridal portraits gazing at herself in front of a mirror or looking sedately at her flowers with her head bowed and eyes lowered (Bezner 22, 28). As one woman remarked, the flower girl's function is to "[wish] the bride and groom luck in having beautiful children just like her."

The flower-girl experience also triggers many young girls' first awareness of weddings and marriage. Reflecting on this, one former flower girl noted, "It is important in the life of a girl. It gives young girls the idea that a wedding is the biggest event in a girl's life." Another said, "It can teach children what marriage is all about, its importance." Transformed into miniature versions of the bride, flower girls observe the wedding ritual from an unusual vantage point. In the words of one respondent, "[being a flower girl] just makes them think that one day they will be the bride." Another claimed that they observe "the importance of the bride during this ceremony, that all the time and attention are given to the bride." This glorification of the bride can be compelling to the youngest wedding participants, creating for them an ideal image to be emulated. Girls watching the wedding, one woman remarked, "will probably think marriage and having a family is a fairy tale come true." Knowledge of gender roles is established early in life, and a child's observation of the wedding, and especially the bride's role in it, may function as a catalyst for stereotyped views.

There is no question that the flower-girl experience is saturated with sexist overtones. Nevertheless, it can contribute positively to a girl's self-esteem and sense of belonging. Respondents recalling their flower-girl roles most frequently mentioned "feeling special." One mother captured the essence of her four-year-old's recent stint as a flower girl saying,

> For my daughter it was mainly an opportunity to be someone "special" for a few moments during the ceremony, and to be complimented by grownups for the rest of the evening. I think that for her, being asked to be a flower girl was a sign that she was considered a very good friend by the bride, part of the bride's inner circle. She was awed by the bride's

dress, but could also identify with her and with the bridesmaids, especially when dressing with the bridesmaids before the ceremony.

Other respondents echoed similar sentiments. One said, "I felt very special and needed as a part of the festivities." Another asserted that being asked to be a flower girl "means that you are special to the one that chose you." Still others characterized the flower-girl role as fostering self-confidence and making girls "feel special and important. It can be a big event for them. It can give them a feeling of responsibility." For a tiny, preschool child, the duty of having to lead the processional can be daunting; nevertheless, having done it, she feels a sense of pride and accomplishment.

Not to be underestimated, too, is the sense of "connectedness" that flower girls feel to another woman. As one woman noted succinctly, "Somehow they bond to the bride." Another offered this recollection:

> In my case, when I was a flower girl, I remember the whole experience made me feel closer to my uncle's new bride. I always felt that she liked me so much that she picked me to be the flower girl! I wasn't scared and I didn't feel as though the attention was placed on me. Basically, I felt honored that my new aunt picked me and my sister.

One recent bride referred to her flower girl as "[her] pal all day long," while another said, "She thought she and I were princesses." Finally, in the case of a second marriage, a woman observed of her niece, "She did a wonderful job [as flower girl] and was happy to be a part of her mother's wedding." One function of weddings is to bring together members of a family and community for the purpose of celebration. As a participant in the wedding ritual, the flower girl is taken into the fold, where she bonds with the bride and other female players; this experience can contribute to a child's feelings of importance and belonging.

Conclusion

It is a cultural reality that many females gain attention and acceptance by acting out traditional, stereotyped roles. This begins early in life, and the flower girl is a prime example. Like many wedding elements, the flower girl was first incorporated into weddings as a kind of bridal

surrogate, to symbolize fertility, since the bride's role was to take leave
of her family, join her husband's family, and procreate. Although the
original meaning of this practice is largely forgotten, the practice itself
still prevails. Today flower girls, often chosen for their cuteness and
good behavior, serve as accessories in elaborate weddings, where they
also symbolize the youth and innocence that the bride is about to sur-
render. As active participants in the wedding, flower girls are afforded
attention, responsibility, and an opportunity to bond with other women,
all of which can enhance their self-esteem. At the same time, however,
they are primed to regard marriage and the bridal image as ideals. It is
interesting to note that many respondents who had been flower girls
were married or engaged by their early twenties, several years younger
than the current median age for marriage, perhaps because they were
socialized at an early age to accept this model.

Socialization is, of course, the key, and parents—especially
mothers—interpret and shape experiences for their daughters. If a child
is to be a flower girl, it is crucial to emphasize not one's expensive dress
and perfect appearance, or the fairy-tale quality of marriage, but rather
the honor, responsibility, and sense of community inherent in the role.
As one woman observed of flower girls, their charge is to "honor [the
bride] as she has honored them by choosing them."

Reflective of new ideas and circumstances, the flower-girl tradition
in America may slowly be changing. Respondents noted variations in
the modern wedding, such as children of both genders leading the processional by ringing bells or blowing bubbles to celebrate the joy of the
occasion. Also, as the demographics of America continue to shift, so do
its rituals. In the words of one respondent,

> As more people embark on second marriages and work to blend their
> families, I expect we'll be seeing more flower girls and junior brides-
> maids in the future, along with more ring bearers and junior ushers. . . .
> I think there will need to be more roles for school-age children in wed-
> dings of their parents as people have more and more blended families.

Thus, the flower girl represents an old tradition being transformed to
fit the new; she becomes a ritualistic component in the re-creation of
family.

Whether leading the processional in her aunt's large, traditional
church wedding or standing alongside as her mother takes a new husband in a brief civil ceremony, the flower girl gets her first lesson in

weddings and marriage. As one respondent noted, "She presents a 'happy' beginning." One hopes that the ending will turn out as well.

WORKS CITED

Ackerman, Diane. *A Natural History of Love*. New York: Vintage Books, 1995.

Ames, Chris. Manager, Ames Tuxedos, Hampton, VA. Personal interview. Norfolk, VA, 14 Dec. 1996.

Bezner, Lili Corbus. "'Divine Detritus:' An Analysis of American Wedding Photography." *Studies in Popular Culture* 18.2 (April 1996): 19–33.

"Budding Beauties." *Town and Country*. http://tncweddings.com/flowergirl .html. Feb. 1997 (accessed Nov. 1, 1996).

Davis, Marc. "Americans Waiting Longer to Marry." *Virginian-Pilot* (Hampton Roads, VA), 29 June 2001, A7.

Frese, Pamela R. "Holy Matrimony: A Symbolic Analysis." Ph.D. diss., University of Virginia, Department of Anthropology, Aug. 1982.

———. "The Union of Nature and Culture: Gender Symbolism in the American Wedding Ritual." In *Transcending Boundaries: Multi-Disciplinary Approaches to the Study of Gender*, ed. Pamela R. Frese and John M. Coggeshall, 97–112. New York: Bergin and Garvey, 1991.

Kirschenbaum, Howard, and Stensrud Rockwell. *The Wedding Book: Alternative Ways to Celebrate Marriage*. New York: Seabury Press, 1974.

Lipsett, Linda Otto. *To Love and to Cherish*. San Francisco: Quilt Digest, 1989.

Macoboy, Stirling. *The Ultimate Rose Book*. New York: Harry Abrams, 1993.

Osen, Diane. "Bride's Basics: Should You Invite Children to Your Wedding?" *Bride's*, April/May 1996, 188.

Phillips, Roger, and Nicky Foy. *The Random House Book of Herbs*. New York: Random House, 1990.

Rusk, Reverend John. *The Beautiful Life and Illustrious Reign of Queen Victoria*. [Chicago]: K. T. Boland, 1901.

Seligson, Marcia. *The Eternal Bliss Machine: America's Way of Wedding*. New York: William Morrow, 1973.

Shepard, Charlotte. "Bridal Fashion Harkens Back to the '60s." *1996 Nuptials, Published by the Virginian-Pilot*, X2, 16.

———. "Floral Bouquets Have Traditional Tones." *1996 Nuptials, Published by the Virginian-Pilot*, X18, 20.

Town and Country. "First Special Weddings Issue." February 1997.

———. "Truly Perfect Weddings Issue." February 2001.

Weiner, Jennifer. "Bridal Couples Come Older and They Hope Wiser" Knight-Ridder News Service, *Albany Times Union*, May 1996, D8.

Wright, Betsy Mathews. "Paganism: An Ancient Religion Lives On." *Virginian-Pilot*, 12 Oct. 1996, E2.

10

Newsboy Funerals

Tales of Sorrow and Solidarity in Urban America

VINCENT DIGIROLAMO

In a small write-up about the death of a newsboy, the *Boston Globe* observed in 1890 that there was "nothing more pathetic in all the 'short and simple annals of the poor' than some of the scenes connected with the burial of one of their number." The reporter noted that "the surviving members of the fraternity gladly forego their meals for an entire day, if necessary, for the sake of bringing flowers to lay upon the cheap coffin." The writer then described the exchange between a "deputation" of newsboys and a prominent florist over the order of a ten-dollar wreath:

> "And, Mister, we want his name fixed in it somehow," said the spokesman.
> "Certainly," said the obliging clerk, "what is his name?"
> "We allus called him 'Skinney,' cos he was a lean little rat."
> The clerk demurred against embalming in flowers this somewhat striking cognomen, on the ground that the feelings of the family might be hurt.
> "He ain't got no family," stoutly maintained his comrades. "He b'longs to us fellers as much 's anybody, and we won't have nothin' but

Skinney—that or nothin'. We pays for it, and we've got a right to boss it. Who'd know who 't was by any other name?"

The article ended with a direct appeal to *Globe* readers: "Do something besides drop a sympathizing tear. The tear is all right if it materializes into dollars and cents." Signed, "THE NEWSBOYS' FRIEND."[1]

While many Bostonians no doubt skimmed over this little item unmoved by its blatant sentimentalism, such a callous response can only blind modern readers to its deeper meanings. The story's value no longer rests in its capacity to elicit tears or tips, but to reveal the historical significance of one of the more obscure rituals of childhood—newsboy funerals.

Newsboy funerals were pitifully elaborate rituals of pomp and poverty. Most children of the poor were buried as members of a family, church, or ethnic group, not a trade. But between the 1850s and the 1910s dozens of orphaned or homeless newsboys in Boston, New York, Brooklyn, Philadelphia, Louisville, St. Louis, Chicago, and other cities were publicly laid to rest by their peers and the institutions that ministered to them. In addition to flowers, newsboys took up collections for coffins, plots, and gravestones. They hired hearses, undertakers, and ministers. They drafted letters of sympathy, passed resolutions of condolence, and marched in funeral trains through the same streets in which they sold their papers.

If we take the view that newsboy funerals were stories that young people told about themselves, then what exactly were they saying, to whom were they speaking, and for what purpose? One way to answer these questions is via an ethnographic reading of several such funerals. Most historical studies of child mortality and mourning practices have focused on the home, but newsboy funerals compel us to expand our understanding of children and death beyond the domestic and into the public sphere.[2] Indeed, they enable us to see children's grief not simply as products of familial loss, religious faith, or even journalistic convention, but as expressions of class feeling.

Take the story about Skinney. While the haggling between the florist and the newsboys reads more like fiction than reportage, it demonstrates that the boys regarded themselves—and were regarded by others—as a "fraternity," as members of an organized body that had a right to mourn a fellow trader. When the florist objected to their request because it might offend the feelings of relatives, the boys asserted the primacy of their own feelings, the value of their own relationship with the deceased, and the power of their own money to "boss" the job. Their streety dialect served to contrast the lowness of their station with the nobility of their gesture. The fact that Skinney's friends knew him by a nickname speaks not to the superficiality of their association, but to its totality. "Who'd know who 't was by any other name?" they asked. Who indeed? To this day we know the boy only by his nickname and through the tribute of his friends, among whom the journalist counted himself. The writer's closing appeal for charity further shows how a newsboy's death occasioned concern not just for the deceased, but for all members of the trade.

Given their association with the press, it is not surprising that stories of newsboys' short lives, tragic deaths, and humbly ostentatious funerals occasionally found their way into the papers. Yet they were also the subject of tracts, sermons, poems, memoirs, illustrations, and not a few Tin Pan Alley tearjerkers. These sources are all part of the vast consolation literature that nourished what Karen Halttunen refers to as "the sentimental cult of mourning."[3] So lachrymose are works of this genre that Ann Douglas has called them "exercises in necrophilia."[4] Such phrases unfortunately imply that middle-class Americans were deluded, if not perverted, in their most cherished beliefs. Sentimentalism, argues Douglas, was the way the bourgeoisie, particularly women and ministers, feigned concern yet evaded responsibility for the evils of a capitalist industrial order they were helping to usher in. It was an unconscious strategy, says Halttunen, for middle-class Americans to distinguish themselves as a class while still denying the class structure of their society. Working folks who adopted these forms and rituals, she says, were simply trying to establish a public claim to bourgeois gentility. Newsboys were both exemplars and casualties of capitalism and thus could hardly avoid being sentimentalized in song and story. Yet even these sources suggest a more complex pattern of cultural influence. Moreover, if we read between the lines of these tracts and songs and human-interest stories, we can glimpse the social and emotional lives of working-class kids.

Historians have only recently begun to write an emotional history of the United States, to trace how people's feelings of love, anger, jealousy, and grief are not so much natural, immutable impulses as reflections of changing social structures and movements, passing fads and fancies, new ideas and technologies.[5] Capturing such reflections is difficult, especially when dealing with poor youths who did not often commit their feelings to paper. Newsboys usually were literate; some did write letters and even memoirs. But most expressed their sorrow ritualistically, and so it is to these rituals we must look if we wish to discover who they were and how they really felt about matters of life and death.

Newsboys were legion in nineteenth-century America, and they came from the lowest ranks of society. They were the sons—and occasionally the daughters—of day laborers, piece workers, and petty traders. Many were immigrants or the children of immigrants. In the 1850s and 1860s New York and Philadelphia claimed between five hundred and six hundred newsboys, most of whom came from poor Irish or German families. This juvenile labor force swelled in the 1880s and 1890s as the number of daily and Sunday newspapers quadrupled, circulations doubled, and eleven million new immigrants (mainly Jews and Italians) poured into the country.[6] By the beginning of the twentieth century there were more than five thousand newsboys in big cities like New York, Boston, and Chicago, and two thousand in smaller cities like Detroit, St. Louis, and Cincinnati.[7] Most newsboys were between six and fifteen years old, the age when working-class children typically entered the adult labor force. But adults also sold papers if they had lucrative routes or corners or if they needed to get through hard times.

Unlike Skinney, relatively few newsboys were orphans. Most lived in cramped apartments with one or both parents, but any number of events—the arrival of a new baby, the loss of a job, money disputes, and domestic violence—could send parents and children reeling in opposite directions. Thousands of children wound up living or working on the streets of New York in the 1850s. They were feared and reviled as street rats and guttersnipes, vagrants and beggars. Yet they were also admired and ministered to. In 1854, the Reverend Charles Loring Brace opened the first Newsboys' Lodging House, a kind of cheap hotel for working boys, and dozens of similar institutions sprang up across the country.

Whether they lived with or apart from their families, young people of all classes were familiar with death. In the 1870s nine out of ten Americans over fifteen had lost a parent or a sibling.[8] Child mortality rates were high, though declining, throughout the second half of the century. In Massachusetts, for example, infants died at a rate of 205 per thousand in 1865 and 190 per thousand in 1900. The odds of survival improved as one got older, but the average life expectancy in the United

States then stood at 47 years. Death rates were higher for the working class than for the general population due to their more dangerous jobs and less adequate medical care, sanitation, and diet.[9] Skinney, if his name is any indication, may well have died from the effects of malnutrition. Nationwide, the biggest killers of children were infectious diseases such as diphtheria, tuberculosis, pneumonia, typhoid, and measles. Accidents accounted for about 10 percent of deaths of children. Statistically, children of working, renting, unemployed, illiterate, foreign-born, African American, or city-dwelling parents died at a much higher rate than did other children. In short, poverty killed, and urban poverty killed the most.[10]

Some commentators thought such familiarity with death inured poor children to the ravages of grief. This was the message of a sketch in *Frank Leslie's Illustrated Newspaper* that depicted a tenement funeral in New York's notorious Five Points slum district in 1865 (fig. 1). Neighbors watch impassively from stoops, sidewalks, and upper-story windows as four men load a small wooden coffin into a horse-drawn hearse. Oblivious to the solemnity of the moment, three boys drag a dog through the mud by its hind leg.[11] A generation later the crusading police reporter Jacob Riis took perverse consolation in the heartlessness of the slum child. "If the delights of life are few, its sorrows do not sit heavily upon him either," he wrote. "He is in too close and constant touch with misery, with death itself, to mind it much. To find a family of children living, sleeping, and eating in the room where father or mother lies dead, without seeming to be in any special distress about it, is no unusual experience."[12]

Riis mistook distress shown for distress felt. He also failed to recognize that sitting with the dead at home was part of Irish, Jewish, and other ethnic mourning customs.[13] Yet he accurately observed that these customs differed according to the age of the deceased and the resources of the survivors. Infants were often buried in anonymous paupers' graves or, in cases of extreme poverty, were abandoned. "Seventy-two dead babies were picked up in the streets last year," wrote Riis of New York in 1890. "Some of them were doubtless put out by very poor parents to save funeral expenses."[14] Older children, whose individuality was more manifest, usually merited a humble service and their own grave. Working men received the biggest funerals, for they died at a more rapid clip than women and school-age children, and the economic repercussions of their death were more devastating to their families.[15]

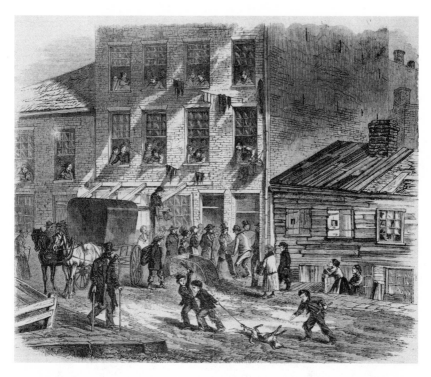

Figure 1. "End of the Poor—funeral from a tenement house in Baxter Street, Five Points, New York," *Frank Leslie's Illustrated Newspaper,* July 1, 1865. Peter J. Eckel Collection, Department of Rare Books and Special Collections, Princeton University Library.

Children also encountered the mysteries of death outside the family. They listened to fire-and-brimstone sermons in church and read stories about fallen heroes in school. Some boys and girls incorporated these teachings into their play, reciting morbid nursery rhymes and staging funerals for their pets or dolls.[16] Newsboys supplemented these lessons with those learned on the job and in the cheap theaters they patronized almost religiously. Newsboys virtually trafficked in death, shouting headlines of "'orrible murders," "bloody battles," and "tragic accidents." On slow news days children such as Henry Dockter in New York would invent shocking or humorous cries to attract customers: "Extra! Extra! Big shipwreck in the subway! Two dead men found alive!" Death to them was a commodity, a source of profit. Yet the reported death of a beloved president or a famous general could also be a deeply felt vicarious experience similar to that engendered by a novels or a play."[17]

Figure 2. Sol Eytinge, "The Streets of New York—A Tragic Story," *Harper's Weekly*, Oct. 11, 1879, 801.

Newsboys loved the theater and therein formed their most basic ideas about death, damnation, and resurrection. Those who frequented the gallery of the Bowery Theatre were called "aficionados of death" because they so enjoyed a bloody finale.[18] They would recite the last words of the expiring hero or villain right along with the actors, never failing to point out a missed line. The boys were generous with their applause, yet they would hiss and boo if a character expired too quickly or without sufficient agony or pathos. The most talented boys would later reenact their favorite death scenes on the street or in declamation contests at the Newsboys' Lodging House (fig. 2).[19]

The play that made the biggest impact on the spiritual thinking of newsboys in the antebellum era was *Uncle Tom's Cabin*. The New York stage adaptation of Harriet Beecher Stowe's sensational 1852 novel led to the formation of the "O-de-Ram Society," a club open to all newsboys who vowed to be good enough to become angels in heaven like Little Eva. It took its name from the boys' mispronunciation of the hymn Uncle Tom sang to Eva on her deathbed, "O, de Lamb, de bressed Lamb." According to one journalist:

> The tender-hearted little fellows used to cry, as all the rest of us did, over Eva's dying advice and farewell to Uncle Tom; and they also resolved, with Uncle Tom, to meet the dear child in Heaven. That vision of innocence and beauty was the absolute incarnation of angelhood; and the scene amid which she nightly took her mimic departure for the Land of the Blessed was to them an actual foretaste of eternal life.[20]

Not only did *Uncle Tom's Cabin* stir the moral imagination of newsboys, but it also taught them to grieve together in public, which they did whenever one of their own died.

Some accounts of newsboy funerals come to us via evangelical reformers such as Brace. The deaths and burials they recorded in most detail were usually of children who died as a result of their years on the street or from some selfless act. For example, "Mickety," the first boy to sign the ledger of the Newsboys' Lodging House and the first to expire there, died of consumption, "perhaps brought on by exposure in early days," said Brace, "when he slept in boxes or on the damp ground." In one of his many short sermons to newsboys Brace told how Mickety grew so weak one afternoon that he had to lie down on the counter of a newspaper shop. His friends wanted to call a carriage, but he would not let them, "feeling too modest to ride in a carriage in the day." According to Brace, "The boys clubbed together and bought a handsome mahogany coffin, and buried him in Greenwood, paying the whole expenses themselves."[21]

Greenwood was one of the lush new suburban cemeteries or "memorial gardens" that had begun to replace overcrowded churchyards. Fancy hardwood caskets were another new phenomenon in the 1850s. Protestants in the antebellum era regarded ostentatious funerals as vain and sinful. Rich and poor alike buried their dead in simple fashion, with friends and neighbors—usually the womenfolk—taking responsibility for laying out the body and arranging the service. The Civil War, which claimed nearly 620,000 men and left tens of thousands of widows and orphans, profoundly changed Americans' attitudes toward death and mourning. Death declined as a theme in popular literature and, when taken up, was treated much more euphemistically. Funerals became more elaborate, especially in cities. Families started hiring undertakers to prepare the deceased for burial. A "decent" funeral came to include a lacquered hearse, ornate casket, floral wreaths, and rented banners, crape, gloves, and sashes.[22] It was this commercialized funeral that the newsboys—symbols of commerce themselves—saw as the ideal.

Another newsboy who realized this emerging ideal was John Ellard in Philadelphia (see fig. 3). Nicknamed Didley Dumps, Ellard was a small hump-backed boy who slept in newspaper bags in printing offices before churchmen founded a Newsboys' Home in 1858. Ellard lived at the home for a year and a half; he attended Wednesday classes and Sunday services, saved and loaned money to his colleagues, and eventually became proprietor of a little newsstand next to the county building. Never of strong constitution, Ellard had to be carried back and forth to work on the shoulders of the other boys. In November 1859 he caught a severe cold from which he never recovered. A biography written by a director of the home, F. Ratchford Starr, and published by the American Sunday School Union describes his last days in great detail. Starr refused to withhold the doctor's grim prognosis from Ellard:

> I felt it my duty to acquaint him with it at once. The poor lad revolted at the thought of death, and irritably denounced the physician and declared he would go out the next day. But this was not to be. The hand that now held him was the relentless hand of the angel of death. I felt most sensibly that much was to be done for his soul, and that there was but a brief and uncertain period in which to do it.[23]

Figure 3. Frontispiece. F. Ratchford Starr, *Didley Dumps, or John Ellard the Newsboy* (Philadelphia: American Sunday School Union, 1884).

Ellard died a "happy death" in the manner of Little Eva. During his last days he prayed with his friends and guardians, forgave two outstanding loans, and made up with a boy with whom he had quarreled. Three newsboys were praying at his bedside when he died on December 15, 1859, at the age of sixteen. He was given a "grand" funeral that included a cortege of fifty-six newsboys, six of whom carried his body from the home on Pear Street to St. Joseph's Church. At Sixth and Chestnut they passed Dumps's newsstand, which had been draped in black crape and tied with white ribbon, "indicating that the adornment was for one of tender years."[24]

Processions, according to the *Atlantic Monthly*, were "a source of great gratification to the street boy," and funeral parades were no exception.[25] Most memorable were the corteges of prominent soldiers or statesmen. Newsboy funerals were self-conscious imitations of these lugubrious ceremonies. In 1861, Brace explicitly compared newsboy Johnny Morrow's funeral procession with that of Colonel Elmer Ellsworth, the twenty-four-year-old commander of New York's Eleventh Regiment and the first Union combat fatality of the Civil War. While Ellsworth's "grand funeral procession, with slow and mournful step, and wailing music was following down Broadway," said Brace, "another coffin was being followed, with many tears, by little children and poor boys, in the city of Brooklyn" (fig. 4).[26]

Morrow was seventeen when he died. His family had emigrated from England when he was about ten. They were poor; his father was a hard-drinking, frequently out-of-work carpenter. Morrow, who limped due to a childhood accident, helped support the family by peddling newspapers and matches, scavenging for coal and wood, and selling little stools that his father made. Nevertheless, his father beat him regularly for his low earnings and growing appetite. Morrow and his brother eventually ran away from home. They ended up at the Newsboys' Lodging House, where Morrow befriended theological students, attended classes, and dreamed of becoming a clergyman himself. At age sixteen he published his life story, *A Voice from the Newsboys*, to earn money for college. Unfortunately, he died the next year after undergoing surgery on his bad leg. He bled to death when he tried to change the dressing himself rather than trouble the doctor to do it.

Morrow's funeral procession started from the State Street Congregational Church, which had been filled to capacity with students from three Sabbath schools and the Newsboy's School in New York. After

Figure 4. Frontispiece. Johnny Morrow, *A Voice from the Newsboys* (New York: A. S. Barnes & Burr, 1860).

Figure 5. Peter J. Eckel, Johnny Morrow's gravestone, Evergreen Cemetery, Brooklyn, New York, 1977.

eulogies by Brace, two ministers, and Morrow's attending physician, the mourners marched to Evergreen Cemetery. His gravestone identified him by occupation: "Johnny Morrow, the Newsboy, died May 23, 1861, aged 17" (fig. 5).[27]

Newsboys had two things in common with the more celebrated recipients of public funerals. One was their sex: the funeral cortege appears to have been an exclusively male privilege. The other was their hero status. During the postwar years New Yorkers of every age and rank witnessed impressive memorial parades for President Lincoln (1865), Admiral Farragut (1870), Horace Greeley (1872), and Ulysses S. Grant (1885).[28] Their effect on children's inchoate notions of mortality and propriety cannot be overestimated. Although news selling was an unreliable form of subsistence labor, it had been idealized in art and literature since the 1840s as a patriotic, character-building occupation in the tradition of Benjamin Franklin. As the market for children's literature burgeoned in the 1860s and 1870s, stories featuring newsboy heroes proliferated in books and magazines.[29] Real boys like Mickety, Ellard, and Morrow were easily cast as heroic figures. In eulogizing Morrow, the Reverend W. A. Bartlett of the New York Theological Seminary unabashedly asserted that he "was no less a hero than any who ever fell on the field of battle." Morrow himself evoked a military allusion in his autobiography when he wrote, "the newsboy's cause is a warfare on the battle-field of life, where he who fights the *hardest* comes off triumphant from strife."[30]

Another advocate of newsboys was Colonel Alexander Hogeland, a military man himself. Hogeland was one of the many emulators of Brace's pragmatic form of child saving. He founded the Newsboys' and Bootblacks' Association and Night Schools in Louisville, Kentucky, and like Brace, he was a well-traveled lecturer and author. He, too, published an account of his years among the newsboys and compiled a book of inspirational readings for young people. His most dismal duty was burying indigent members of the association. He said he was often the only adult present besides the undertaker or a widowed parent. Among those he buried in 1881 were Fred Fisher, who had asked that his life savings of thirty-three dollars be spent on his funeral; Jimmy Hart, who died after his foot was crushed in an accident; and twelve year-old Robert Maxie, who for some reason was buried outside the fence of the local Cave Hill cemetery. Hogeland tried to persuade the newsboys that it didn't matter how or where they were buried:

> No, boys, our heavenly Father cares as much for the soul of little Robert as for the richest in the land, and will cause the moon and stars to shine there as brightly as if it rested under a monument of marble on the Cave Hill side of the fence.[31]

It is doubtful that many of the boys were convinced. Ellard, Morrow, and Fisher all revealed their fear of being buried in a potter's field. Such fears were widely shared by working-class youth, as is evident in this little street rhyme from Milwaukee in the 1880s: "Rattle his bones over the stones. He's only a pauper nobody owns."[32] It was all too common, Riis observed, for "the "little army of waifs" to be reunited "in the

Figure 6. Jacob Riis, The Potters Field, Harts Island, Bronx, ca. 1890, lantern slide, Museum of the City of New York. Jacob A. Riis Collection. 92. 13. 2. 45.

trench in the Potter's Field where, if no medical student is in need of a subject, they are laid in squads of a dozen" (fig. 6).[33]

In contrast to these stark burials was the princely funeral of fifteen-year-old Sammy Stout in Louisville in 1883. Hogeland described it as "one of unusual solemnity."[34] The service was held at the association's headquarters on West Jefferson Street. "Sympathizing friends sent quite

Figure 7. C. F. Reilly, "Burial of a Newsboy," in Alexander Hogeland, *Boys and Girls of 100 Cities* (Louisville, KY, 1886), 60.

a supply of blooming flowers," said Hogeland, "while eight of the newsboys' late companions acted as pall-bearers." An illustration of the burial shows the eight boys carrying Stout's flower-laden ebony casket from a horse-drawn hearse toward an open grave (fig. 7).[35] Each boy is wearing a dark suit and clutching a cap in his free hand as he trudges over the snowy ground. Above them looms the association banner, properly draped in mourning, followed by the boy's aunt, also heavily veiled, and still more boys. Their lame dog Jack watches the procession while the grave digger, shovel in hand, stares into the glass walls of the hearse. Hogeland and the officiating minister stand over the grave ready to lead the final prayers. There is no telling if the picture captures the ceremony with any degree of accuracy. What it does depict is a vision of the ideal funeral. Hogeland's express purpose in dwelling on these matters was to encourage righteous behavior by helping youths to appreciate "the uncertainty and shortness of life."[36]

Songs about dying newsboys conveyed a similar message to a different audience. They typically sought to instill a sense of noblesse oblige among the middle class—those who could afford pianos and parlors. One of these songs, "Found Dead in the Street," written in 1882 by the music instructor of the Louisville House of Refuge, was dedicated to Hogeland. Its climactic verse goes:

> Once more hear him cry, "My papers, who'll buy?
> Oh! Is there not some one that cares though I die?"
> A shivering chill, and then all is still,
> While softly the snow-flakes come down from the sky.[37]

Other songs were tributes to real boys. The 1893 song "The Little Newsboy's Death," for example, documented in verse the *esprit de corps* of those who worked with newsboy Johnny Vantanno (fig. 8). According to the song's dedication, shortly after Vantanno was struck down by a street car his friends "took his bundle of evening papers and sold them, turning the money over to his mother, one of the boys remarking, 'She needs de stuff, see?'"[38]

Pathetic deaths and pitiful rhymes also characterized much of the poetry written about newsboys during this period. Poems such as Miss H. R. Hudson's "The Newsboy's Debt" (1873), Mrs. Emily Thornton's "The Dying Newsboy" (1886), Madeline S. Bridges's "The Newsboy" (1900), and Irene Abbott's "Only a Little Newsboy" (1903) appeared in *Harper's*, *Leslie's*, and other popular magazines.[39] Written primarily by women, these works sought not to expose and ameliorate deadly social conditions but to remind readers of their sacred duty to aid the least of God's children. Thus these poets and songwriters shared much in common with evangelical philanthropists like Brace, Starr, and Hogeland: they all saw newsboys' deaths as opportunities for moral instruction.

Figure 8. Benjamin C. and Gus B. Brignam, "Little Newsboy's Death" (Chicago: National Music Company, 1893). Eckel Collection.

The 1880s and 1890s witnessed dramatic changes in philanthropy, trade unionism, and the funeral industry, all of which affected newsboys' mourning rituals. A new generation of professional charity workers appeared; many of them were college-trained women who practiced "scientific philanthropy" in settlement houses, orphan asylums, juvenile courts, and reformatories. They saw street trading by children as part of the problem, not the solution, to urban poverty, delinquency, and homelessness. They accused newsboy homes and associations of perpetuating that which should be abolished.[40] Meanwhile, the labor movement, hobbled during the depression of the 1870s, bounced back. The Knights of Labor increased its membership sevenfold among skilled and unskilled workers in the mid-1880s. It led colorful marches for the eighthour day, advocated producer cooperatives, and ran candidates for political office. Newsboys also formed unions and mounted strikes during this period. Their unions were usually short-lived and their strikes unsuccessful, but their identification with organized labor was strong.[41]

Undertakers also professionalized at this time. They formed the National Funeral Directors' Association in 1882 and promoted embalming and other changes in funeral services. Most morticians were small businessmen who earned $4,000 to $5,000 a year, but some had grown into large companies. One establishment in New York occupied an entire building on Eighth Avenue. It had salesrooms on the ground floor, vaults in the basement, and an auditorium, "larger than a village church," on the second floor. Fitted with pews and an organ, it was the site of four to five services a day, some of which were officiated by the president of the company, an ordained minister. The upper stories housed a floral shop and a casket factory. The firm had only one hearse, but it was considered "the most remarkable one outside of India." Long as the longest electric streetcar, it carried mourners on the inside, bore the casket atop the roof, and required a team of eight horses to pull it.[42] At the other end of the spectrum were "circular" hearses, smaller, lightly built vehicles named for their rounded corners and elliptical windows. Those painted white were used exclusively for the funerals of children.[43]

The floral arts also evolved and sometimes featured innovative occupational designs. In 1886, William Henry Ortel, better known in St. Louis as "Dutch Hiney, King of the Newsboys," received an arrangement that included copies of the *Post-Dispatch*, *Globe-Democrat*, *Republican*, and other local papers, all bordered by half-opened buds of white roses. Placed diagonally across the arrangement were the words "Latest

Edition" in purple immortelles, surrounded by white carnations. Created by Tony Faust, the city's leading florist, it measured sixteen by fourteen inches and rested on a small stand. It is not clear who paid for the offering, but it may well have come from Ortel's fellow workers. According to the *Post-Dispatch,* "A large number of newsboys of all age and descriptions attended the funeral service and followed the body to its last resting place."[44]

There were six thousand funerals a day in the United States at the turn of the twentieth century, and they cost Americans a hundred million dollars a year.[45] In 1897, the *New York World* estimated that one poor family on the Lower East Side spent over $140 on a funeral, which included $60 for the casket, $30 for five coaches, and $10.50 for the hearse.[46] Middle-class reformers decried the fact that poor families paid between $75 and $300 for a "proper burial." Many of these critics advocated cremation as a cheaper alternative. But cremation was never popular with the working class. Many regarded it as a repulsive form of scientific management, the aim of which, according to one Pittsburgh labor paper, was to reduce "the body to a shovelfull of ashes" and thereby bury people in smaller packages.[47]

To meet the rising cost of burying their dead, many working-class families took out burial insurance or joined burial clubs, which, for a few cents a week, offered similar protection. Between 1882 and 1902 more than three million children were insured for burial, earning insurance companies a hundred million dollars a year in premiums.[48] Jacob Riis and Benjamin Waugh, president of the English Society for the Prevention of Cruelty to Children, were two of the many reformers who wanted to ban children's insurance on the grounds that it gave parents incentive to let their children die, or, in Waugh's words, to finance the "little funeral" and the "big drink."[49] Child insurance plans continued nonetheless. In 1892, a group of prominent citizens established the News Boys Association of Detroit to promote the boys' "moral, social, personal and intellectual and religious welfare" and to provide for the "relief of the sick" and "the burial of the dead."[50] Participating newsboys paid weekly dues, and thus became accustomed to saving for their death and that of their comrades.

The custom of buying family plots was also popular at this time. When Chicago newsboy Ole Jacobson, better known as Young Waffles, died of exposure on a government pier in 1894 at the age of twenty-five, he was found with only one possession: a water-soaked deed to a grave in a family plot in Graceland Cemetery. Except for his spot, it was fully occupied by his parents and four siblings. As historian John Gillis has noted, such plots made modern cemeteries into domestic spaces devoted to the symbolic reconstruction of the family. This shift matched middle-class perceptions of heaven itself as a domesticated haven.[51]

Nevertheless, it was Waffles's comrades, not his family, who laid him to rest. A "soliciting committee" of three boys secured the coffin at cost and raised money for other expenses. The *Chicago Tribune* reported that fewer than half the city's usual number of newsboys were on the streets the day of his funeral. Waffles had been a fixture downtown for fifteen years, and one hundred of the older news vendors gathered at the morgue for a final look. Also in attendance were several ex-newsboys who had become regular employees of the newspaper. "They were the forerunners of the entire craft," reported the *Tribune*, "and for two hours a steady steam of individuals from the old man who sells papers at the entrance to the La Salle Street tunnel to the four-year-old beginner, filed by the coffin, and many a one came out with two white streaks down an otherwise dirty face."

Viewings were rarely held at city morgues, but apparently an exception was made in this case. Waffles's funeral is also noteworthy in that his fellow newsboys did not deem it necessary to invite a minister to conduct the service. Despite the massive turnout, and a funeral that included a hearse, casket, and all the trimmings, no clergyman was in attendance. The boys said they were afraid to ask a minister for fear of being refused. They conducted the ceremony themselves; as the casket was lowered into the grave, one of the pallbearers picked up a handful of earth, threw it on the coffin, and said, "Dust to dust." The others followed his example, said the *Tribune*, "and the obsequies of 'Waffles' were over."[52]

Although working-class and middle-class males generally regarded excessive grieving as effeminate, there is little to suggest that newsboys held back tears or felt embarrassed at expressing their sorrow. According to Brace, sobbing and singing went hand in hand at Johnny Morrow's funeral: "sobs sounded in the stillness as the news boys, with voices hoarse with feeling, sang—"There's a rest for the weary—A rest for thee."[53] On learning of Ellard's death, a former colleague wrote from Memphis, Tennessee, to say that "it made the tears come out, and I could not stop for half an hour."[54] Likewise, a letter from the mother of New York newsboy Willie Crawford acknowledging the receipt of his life savings of

$40.50 had a similar effect when read aloud at the lodging house. "Many of them were moved to tears, for they all had a rough affection for Willie," said one news account. Another reported that the boys "sobbed and cried as if they had lost their only friend on earth, and in their simple, rude way expressed their regret for their lost companion."[55]

If newsboys ignored masculine prescriptions against mourning too hard, they generally conformed to those against mourning too long. On the walk home from Morrow's funeral, for example, rival gangs from Brooklyn and New York clashed in a rock-throwing "war" that left one boy with a bloody head and sent another to jail for twenty days.[56] Such were the limits of their unifying inconsolability.

Like members of any respectable labor fraternity, newsboys sometimes passed resolutions of sympathy when a prominent person or one of their own passed away. They sent them to newspapers for publication and saw that they were forwarded to relatives of the deceased. When Ulysses Grant died, for example, Chicago newsboys expressed their sorrow both publicly and collectively. On July 30, 1885, several hundred of them marched to city hall seeking an audience with the mayor. Since he was out of town they met with the chief of police. The boys presented him with a unanimous resolution stating, in part, "whereas, we, the newsboys of Chicago, though comprising the most humble of the callings, trades, or professions, feel that it is our privilege to give expressions of regret and sympathy so universal." They ordered a copy to be sent to Grant's family, bowed their heads for a final prayer, and left. Their action was taken seriously. Within weeks Grant's son, Colonel Fred Grant, acknowledged receipt of the resolution and thanked the newsboys on behalf of his mother and family.[57]

New York newsboys passed a similar resolution after the death of fifteen year-old Willie Crawford in 1898. They wrote:

Whereas, Willie Crawford was a good fellow, and
Whereas, He was always square and honest, and
Whereas, He should have lived longer, we, his partners and friends when he was alive,
hereby
Resolve, That it is no more than right to let his mother know what a good fellow he was when he was with us, and
Resolve, That we feel just as bad about his going so far away as we can, and
Resolve, That we sympathize with his mother.[58]

Conversely, some resolutions reveal newsboys' shame over the failure of fellowship. Such was the case with Little Joe Every, who was routinely robbed of his papers and otherwise "misused" by the bigger boys. The night he died in 1895, one hundred boys met in front of city hall and passed a resolution declaring that "Everybody is sorry he has died." Afterward, the boys took up a collection and chose four delegates to accompany Joe's small, plain coffin as it was transported in a donated hearse from the county hospital to Holy Cross Cemetery at Flatbush. There was no funeral service, but each delegate placed a flower on the coffin, which bore a metal plate purchased by the boys. It read, "Little Joe, Aged 14. The Best Newsboy in New York. We All Liked Him."[59]

Cleveland, Ohio, newsboy Alfred Williams also received a plaque from his comrades after he killed himself. The eleven-year-old drank poison and died on October 11, 1900. His friends buried him nine days later in Erie Cemetery under a memorial that sought to put his last act in perspective. It reads, "This boy committed suicide because of the hardships of life."[60]

One death and burial that demonstrated interracial working-class solidarity was that of nineteen-year-old Aaron "the slave" Charity, a black newsboy from Wilmington, South Carolina (fig. 9). Charity lived in the Newsboys' Lodging House and worked on the New York side of the Brooklyn Bridge. He was engaged to be married to "a pretty mulatto girl" when he took sick in the winter of 1899. As he lay on his deathbed Charity expressed his fear of the potter's field. The *New York World* and Steve Brodie, a famous ex-newsboy, spared him that fate by treating him to a "first class funeral." Charity's body was laid in state at the lodging house, where scores of his former colleagues filed past to pay their last respects. A minister gave a funeral oration on "The Value of Manliness," and a chorus of newsboys sang "Nearer My God to Thee." Two hired carriages carried a delegation of newsies to Mount Olivet Cemetery on Long Island, where Charity's body was interred in a private plot.[61]

Newspapers were frequently called upon to help bury newsboys. In 1880 George W. Peck, publisher of the *Milwaukee Sun*, furnished an omnibus so newsboys could accompany the remains of their friend, "little" Dan Palmer, to the grave. This philanthropic act was reported not by the *Sun* but by its competitor, the *Sentinel*. Similarly, in 1893 Lucius Nieman of the *Journal* granted the request of a delegation of newsboys who showed up in his office, "hands washed and hair combed,"

Figure 9. Hooper, "Aaron, The Slave," *New York Evening Journal*, Feb. 6, 1899. Heig Scrapbook, Eckel Collection.

to borrow money to save fourteen year-old Freddy Munk, one of twenty-five *Journal* newsboys, from burial in a potter's field. "And if I lend you the money, how will you pay it back?" Nieman reportedly asked. "We're willing to donate our pay for the next two months, sir," one of them said. "That ought to be enough to do it." Nieman feigned that it was a sound business proposition and agreed to go along with it if he could make a small donation. His contribution paid for the entire funeral.[62]

Running obituaries was another way newspapers paid tribute to newsboys. Most big city dailies published death notices only for its more prominent citizens, but newsboys were the exception. Ellard's demise was reported by two newspapers in Philadelphia and one in Baltimore; Morrow's exit was written up by the *New York World, Sun,* and *Tribune,* as well as the *Brooklyn Daily Eagle.* And Crawford's losing battle with consumption was the subject of no fewer than four articles in New York City papers. They told of his origins in Goldsboro, North Carolina, and the fact that he was a champion speller at the Newsboys' Lodging House.[63]

Some newsboys took the initiative of writing the obituaries themselves and submitting them to the periodicals they sold. In July of 1900 the editors of *Success* magazine ran one such notice saying, "This morning, one of our faithful newsboys handed us the following, which we publish in all its originality:

> Joseph Rathburn, beter known as "Whistlin' Jo," dide last nite, he was a delicate litle feller and was sick only a week. Us fellers wanted him to go to the hospital or hav a doctor, but he dident bleve in them he said. His folks was dead but he was workin hard to get a educaitn and be a big musician like he said his father was, but he couldent make it go, an' we are all aful sory he dide cause we had great hopes for him.[64]

Crawford the spelling champ could surely have helped polish up this draft, but what's noticeably absent from this obituary besides proper spelling and grammar is the religious rhetoric of their middle-class protectors. In the resolutions, too, the boys' language is secular not sacred. There is no mention of the deceased going to their heavenly reward, enjoying eternal rest, meeting their Maker, joining the angels, or even reuniting with relatives. The boys simply praise their companions' qualities and unsentimentally lament their death, which in their cosmology was mainly just a big gyp. "He should have lived longer," declared Crawford's friends.

In whatever literary form they have survived, such utterances ought to be taken seriously as vernacular expressions of genuine sentiment. The same principle applies to newsboy funerals, for even sentimental accounts of them can provide a way into the heads and hearts of working-class youth. Their words and rituals are just the surface ripples of a vast inner ocean of emotion that historians have long found inaccessible. To be sure, many newsboy funerals reflect the influence of the middle-class adults who helped the boys bury each other, but newsboys did not simply ape bourgeois standards of propriety and spirituality. Rather, they drew on a host of cultural influences, both bourgeois and plebeian, to develop their own codes of affection and rituals of mourning. Just as in their strikes and boycotts, newsboys demonstrated a kind of craft and class consciousness when they laid a fellow hawker to rest. This is most apparent if we define class consciousness broadly, along with Raymond Williams, as "a structure of feeling."[65] Newsboy funerals clearly show how poor children *felt* in class ways.

These rituals also compel us to reconsider just how injurious or ennobling life was on the streets. Most Americans have learned to distrust Horatio Alger's formulaic novels in which plucky street boys pull themselves up by their bootstraps, progressing from rags to respectability in each and every volume. The death and burial of real newsboys described by writers, reformers, and the children themselves remind us that a certain "downward mobility," measurable in six-foot increments, was the fate of more than a few of them. Moreover, their funerals force us to redefine respectability not as some vague middle-class virtue but in concrete working-class terms as the boys defined it themselves. Respectability, to them, was taking care of their own, which somehow became more important in death than in life.

This caring is best symbolized by their efforts to save each other from the potter's field. Johnny Morrow was most articulate about what such an ignominious ending represented. In comparing his parents' graves, he wrote:

> I thought of my own precious mother, whose remains had slumbered
> for years in a quiet and beautiful spot, marked with a clean and tasteful

slab of marble; and then of my dear father, who was buried in a very
different way almost uncared for, in the Potter's Field. Some very sad
thoughts came up in my mind.[66]

Morrow was an atypical newsboy for having attended seminary and
written a book, but he was able to half-express what many of them may
have felt—that there was a correlation between the quality of one's
grave and the condition of one's soul. They felt that to be buried in a
potter's field was to be denied eternal rest. A pauper's funeral was not
just the last indignity; it was an everlasting one. Newsboys wanted better
for their families and for each other, and expressed such feelings in their
words and actions.

A hero's funeral, however humble, allowed newsboys to assert their
collective and individual identities. It was their way of saying that they
were not just street rats and guttersnipes, but human beings; not just vagrants and beggars, but members of a trade; and not just anonymous
hawkers, but individuals who had names. That's why Skinney's friends
were so intent on honoring him by the name they knew him by, even if
inscribed in such an ephemeral form as flowers. The fact that we can
still remember obscure boys like Skinney, Mickety, John Ellard, Johnny
Morrow, Fred Fisher, Jimmy Hart, Robert Maxie, Johnny Vantanno,
Dutch Hiney, Young Waffles, Willie Crawford, Little Joe Every, Alfred
Williams, Aaron "the slave" Charity, Dan Palmer, Freddy Munk, and
Whistlin' Jo Rathburn suggests that the efforts of those who buried
them were not in vain. Only through ritual could the death of one enhance the status of all.

This essay is dedicated to the memory of Peter J. Eckel. I would like to
thank April Masten for her extraordinary help in writing it, and Margaret
Darby, Jennifer Delton, Bert Hansen, Eric Love, Bruce Pegg, Peter Stearns,
Dror Wahrman, and participants of the New England Seminar in American
History at the American Antiquarian Society in Worcester, Massachusetts, for
their valuable comments.

NOTES

1. *Newsboys' Reading Rooms of Boston* (Boston, 1890), 5.
2. See Richard A. Kalish, "The Effects of Death upon the Family," in

L. Pearson, ed., *Death and Dying* (Cleveland, 1969), 79–107; David E. Stannard, "Death and the Puritan Child," *American Quarterly* 26, no. 5 (1974): 456–476; Peter G. Slater, "'From Cradle to the Coffin': Parental Bereavement and the Shadow of Infant Damnation in Puritan Society," in N. Ray Hiner and Joseph M. Hawes, eds., *Growing Up in America: Children in Historical Perspective* (Urbana, IL, 1985), 27–43; and Peter Uhlenberg, "Death and the Family," in Hiner and Hawes, *Growing Up in America*, 243–252. On the significance of public mourning rites among the poor in England during the early industrial age see Thomas Laqueur, "Bodies, Death and Pauper Funerals," *Representations* 1, no. 1 (Feb. 1983), 109–131. See also the essays in Gillian Avery and Kimberley Reynolds, eds., *Representations of Childhood Death* (New York, 2000).

3. Karen Halttunen, *Confidence Men and Painted Women: A Study of Middle-Class Culture in America, 1830–1870* (New Haven, CT, 1982), 130, 195.

4. Ann Douglas, *The Feminization of American Culture* (New York, 1977), 200, 12. See also Douglas's "Heaven Our Home: Consolation Literature in the Northern United States, 1830–1850," in David E. Stannard, ed., *Death in America* (Philadelphia, 1975), 49–68.

5. See Peter N. Stearns and Jan Lewis, eds., *An Emotional History of the United States* (New York, 1998).

6. The number of U.S. dailies rose from 574 in 1870 to a high of 2,600 in 1909; two-newspaper towns became four-newspaper towns, and their average circulation more than doubled from 4,532 to 9,312. Six cities set the pace; New York, Chicago, Philadelphia, Cleveland, Boston, and San Francisco boasted 277 daily and Sunday newspapers in 1909 with a combined circulation of over 16 million. See Alfred McClung Lee, *The Daily Newspaper in America: The Evolution of a Social Instrument* (New York, 1937), 65, 718–719, 728, 732. For immigration figures see Alan M. Kraut, *The Huddled Masses: The Immigrant in American Society, 1880–1921* (Arlington Heights, IL, 1982).

7. "The News-Boys," *Child's Paper* 3, no. 10 (Oct. 1854): 37; Ninth U.S. Census (1870), table 65, Occupations, 604–615; John F. Fitzgerald, "Street Life in Boston in the '70s," *Hustler*, 1 (March 1911): 3. See also David Nasaw, *Children of the City: At Work and at Play* (New York, 1985), and Vincent DiGirolamo, "Crying the News: Children, Street Work, and the American Press, 1830s–1920s," unpublished Ph.D. diss., Princeton University, 1997, 3–4, 305–306.

8. Daniel E. Sutherland, *The Expansion of Everyday Life, 1860–1876* (New York, 1989), 127.

9. *Historical Statistics of the United States, Colonial Times to 1970*, pt. 1, series B, 193–200, 201–213, 63.

10. Samuel H. Preston and Michael R. Haines, *Fatal Years: Child Mortality in Late-Nineteenth-Century America* (Princeton, NJ, 1991), xviii–xix, 4–5, 86, 99, 117, 119, 125–126.

11. "End of the Poor," *Frank Leslie's Illustrated Newspaper* (July 1, 1865), Peter J. Eckel Collection, Department of Rare Books and Special Collections, Princeton University Library.

12. Jacob Riis, *The Children of the Poor* (1892), reprinted in Francesca Cordasco, ed., *Jacob Riis Revisited: Poverty and the Slum in Another Era* (Garden City, NY, 1968), 163–164.

13. See Richard E. Meyer, ed., *Ethnicity and the American Cemetery* (Bowling Green, OH, 1993); Richard A. Kalish, *Death and Ethnicity: A Psychocultural Study* (Los Angeles, 1976); and two interesting case studies, Joan Moore, "The Death Culture of Mexico and Mexican Americans," in Kalish, *Death and Dying: Views from Many Cultures* (Farmingdale, NY, 1980), 72–91, and Maurice Jackson, "The Black Experience with Death: A Brief Analysis through Black Writing," in Kalish, 92–98.

14. Jacob Riis, *How the Other Half Lives: Studies among the Tenements of New York* (New York, 1989; orig. pub. 1890), 142. On this phenomenon in an earlier period, see Paul A. Gilje, "Infant Abandonment in Early Nineteenth-Century New York: Three Cases," in Hiner and Hawes, *Growing Up in America*, 109–117.

15. In Pittsburgh between 1870 and 1900, for example, male workers between 15 and 24 died at a rate of 12 per thousand, or about twice the rate of females in the same age group. Nearly a third died as a result of industrial accidents. The mortality rate of younger boys, between 5 and 14 years old, was 8 per thousand. See S. J. Kleinberg, "Death and the Working Class," *Journal of Popular Culture* 11, no. 1 (Summer 1977): 194/56–196/58.

16. New York newsboy Johnny Morrow recalled that when his cat died back in his native England, "I made a little grave for it, and put a tombstone at its head with this inscription, which I had persuaded some one to write upon it:—'Here lies poor puss, who died in the year A.D. 1847; may she rest in peace!'" Johnny Morrow, *A Voice from the Newsboys* (New York, 1860), 21. On doll funerals see Miriam Formanek Brunell, *Made to Play House: Dolls and the Commercialization of American Girlhood, 1830–1930* (Baltimore, 1998), 20–23.

17. Gail Goodman, interview with Henry Docktor, 1989, in author's possession. On death as news, see Robert V. Wells, *Facing the "King of Terrors": Death and Society in an American Community, 1750–1990* (New York, 2000), 245–253.

18. Madeline Leslie, *Never Give Up; or, The News-boys* (1863; reprint, Chicago, 1881), 46. Cornelius Mathews also observed that newsboys had a "profound passion for the Theatre" and would carve their names into the benches of the Chatham or the Bowery, securing a right to the spot no less sacred than that guaranteed by the pew rents at Grace Cathedral or St. Patrick's. Newsboys preferred dramas with "thunder and lightening long-swords, casques, and black-whiskered villains," he said, and were devoted to actors who demonstrated a "convulsive, awful manner of yielding up the ghost on the stage." See Mathews, *A Pen-and-Ink Panorama of New-York City* (New York, 1853), 187–188.

19. Sol Eytinge, "The Streets of New York—A Tragic Story," *Harper's Weekly*, Oct. 11, 1879, 801.

20. Oliver Dyer, "The New York Sun; Its Rise, Progress, Character, and Condition," *American Agriculturalist*, Dec. 1869, 463–467, Eckel Collection.

21. Charles Loring Brace, *Short Sermons to Newsboys* (New York, 1866), 234–236.

22. On the evolution of the funeral and the diminution of the religious aura surrounding death, see James J. Farrell, *Inventing the American Way of Death, 1830–1920* (Philadelphia, 1980); Charles O. Jackson, "American Attitudes to Death," *Journal of American Studies* 11 (Dec. 1977): 297–312; Lewis O. Saum, "Death in the Popular Mind of Pre–Civil War America," in Charles O. Jackson, ed., *Passing: The Vision of Death in America* (Westport, CT, 1977), 65–90; Lewis O. Saum, *The Popular Mood of America, 1860–1890* (Lincoln, NE, 1990), 104–133; and Maris A. Vinovskis, "Death," in Mary Kupiec Cayton, Elliott J. Gorn, and Peter W. Williams, eds., *Encyclopedia of American Social History*, vol. 3 (New York, 1993), 2063–2070.

23. F. Ratchford Starr, *Didley Dumps, or John Ellard the Newsboy* (Philadelphia, 1884), 148.

24. Starr, 160.

25. Charles Dawson Shanly, "The Small Arabs of New York," *Atlantic Monthly* 23, no. 137 (March 1869): 281.

26. Charles Loring Brace, "Reminiscences" and "The Little Newsboy's Funeral," *N.Y. Evangelist & S.S. Times* (June 1861), in Morrow, *A Voice from the Newsboys*, 137–139. Both articles appear in later editions of Morrow's memoir that still bear the 1860 publication date. For other versions see "A Newsboy's Funeral," *New York Independent*, June 6, 1861; *Ninth Annual Report of the Children's Aid Society*, Feb. 1862, 34–37; and *Short Sermons to Newsboys* (New York, 1866), 238–244.

27. Brace, "The Little Newsboy's Funeral," 140. Peter J. Eckel located and photographed Morrow's grave in 1977.

28. Brooks McNamara, *Day of Jubilee: The Great Age of Public Celebrations in New York, 1788–1909* (New Brunswick, NJ, 1997), 110–117, 130–136. On the gender politics of public ceremonies see Mary P. Ryan, *Women in Public: Between Banners and Ballots, 1825–1880* (Baltimore, 1990).

29. See, for example, Horatio Alger, *Rough and Ready; or, Life among the New York Newsboys* (Boston, 1869); James Otis, *Left Behind; or, Ten Days a Newsboy* (New York, 1884); and Oliver Optic [William Taylor Adams], *Watch and Wait; or, The Young Fugitives* (Boston, 1866). Among the leading juvenile publications that featured newsboy stories were *Harper's Young People*, *St. Nicholas for Young Folks*, and *Oliver Optic's Magazine*. Cheap serials such as Ornum's & Co.'s Fifteen Cent Romances, Beadle's Half Dime Library, and Fame and Fortune Weekly also made newsboy protagonists a stock in trade.

30. Morrow, *A Voice from the Newsboys,* 144, 128. One casualty of this battle-field was newsboy Giuseppe Margalto, who died Feb. 14, 1891 when a fire broke out while he was sleeping in the ventilation chute of a New York post office. Jacob Riis poignantly recalled this was the same night that General William Tecumseh Sherman died. Riis, *The Children of the Poor,* in *Jacob Riis Revisited,* 29.

31. Alexander Hogeland, *Boys and Girls of 100 Cities* (Louisville, KY, 1886), 117–118.

32. Cited by David Overstreet in "Children of Poverty: The County Paupers' Cemetery and Milwaukee Children," a panel at the Children in Urban America Conference, Marquette University, Milwaukee, May 6, 2000.

33. Riis, *How the Other Half Lives,* 142. New York had several potter's fields until 1869, when the city acquired Hart Island, a forty-five-acre site in the Long Island Sound. About a million indigents have been interred there in graves numbered but otherwise unmarked. See Edward F. Bergman, "Potter's Field," in Kenneth T. Jackson, ed., *The Encyclopedia of New York City* (New Haven, CT, 1998), 931.

34. Hogeland, *Boys and Girls of 100 Cities,* 60, and Alexander Hogeland, *Ten Years among the Newsboys* (Louisville, KY, 1884), 31–32.

35. C. F. Reilly, "Burial of a Newsboy," in Hogeland, *Boys and Girls of 100 Cities,* 60.

36. Hogeland, *Ten Years among the Newsboys,* 118.

37. Thomas P. Westendorf, "Found Dead in the Street" (Nashville, TN: H.A. French, 1882), Eckel Collection; Hogeland, *Boys and Girls of 100 Cities,* 39–40.

38. Benjamin C. and Gus B. Brignam, "Little Newsboy's Death" (Chicago: National Music Company, 1893), Eckel Collection.

39. Miss H. R. Hudson, "The Newsboy's Debt," *Harper's New Monthly Magazine* 46, no. 276 (May 1873): 876–877. Thanks to Christine Stansell; Mrs. Emily Thornton, "The Dying Newsboy," Eckel Collection; Madeline S. Bridges's "The Newsboy," *Leslie's Popular Monthly,* reprinted in *The Book and News-Dealer* 11, no. 136 (Dec. 1900): 31; and Irene Abbott, "Only a Little Newsboy," *The Ministry of Love* (Topeka, KS, 1903), 103–104.

40. See Walter Trattner, *From Poor Law to Welfare State: A History of Social Welfare in America,* 5th ed. (New York, 1994), esp. chs. 5 and 6; and Trattner, *Crusade for the Children: A History of the National Child Labor Committee and Child Labor Reform in America* (Chicago, 1970).

41. DiGirolamo, "Crying the News," 393.

42. Gilson Willets, *Workers of the Nation,* vol. 2 (New York: Collier, 1903), 1043. See also Robert Wesley Habenstein, *The History of American Funeral Directing* (Milwaukee, 1955), and Robert Wesley Habenstein and William M. Lamers, "The Pattern of Late Nineteenth Century Funerals," in Jackson, *Passing,* 91–102.

43. One such vehicle may be found at the Farmers' Museum in Coopers-town, New York.

44. "'Dutch Hiney's' Funeral," *St. Louis Post-Dispatch,* May 3, 1886, 7. Thanks to Bert Hansen.

45. Willets, *Workers of the Nation,* vol. 2, 1043.

46. *New York Evening World,* May 6, 1897, cited in Irving Howe, *World of Our Fathers: The Journey of the East European Jews to America and the Life They Found and Made* (New York, 1976), 221.

47. Kleinberg, "Death and the Working Class," 203/65; Rev. Quincy L. Dowd, "Burial Costs among the Poor," *Proceedings of the National Conference of Charities and Corrections,* June 12–19, 1912, 121. I am also indebted to Eric Love's unpublished paper, "Fire or the Worm: Cremation and Burial in Fin de Siecle America," presented at the Princeton University Graduate History Conference, Oct. 7, 1995.

48. Viviana A. Zelizer, *Pricing the Priceless Child: The Changing Social Value of Children* (New York, 1985), 116.

49. Benjamin Waugh, "Child Life Insurance," *Contemporary Review* 58 (July 1890): 41. Cited in Zelizer, *Pricing the Priceless Child,* 124.

50. Articles of Association of the News Boys Association of Detroit, Feb. 20, 1892.

51. John R. Gillis, *A World of Their Own Making: Myth, Ritual, and the Quest for Family Values* (New York, 1996), 203; Douglas, *Feminization of American Culture,* 220–222.

52. "'Waffles Is Buried,'" *Chicago Tribune,* May 26, 1894, reprinted in *Newsboy* (HAS) 24, nos. 9 and 10 (March–April 1986), 3. The soliciting committee included Robert McMara, William Swaufield, and Severs Johnson, who, along with Bennie Ross, George Campbell, and Epper Kenna, served as pall bearers.

53. *New York Independent,* June 6, 1861.

54. Starr, *Didley Dumps,* 163–164.

55. "Newsboys Wept for Lost Chum," *New York Journal,* Feb. 7, 1898, Heig Scrapbook, Eckel Collection.

56. "War among the News Boys," *Brooklyn Daily Eagle,* May 27, 1861.

57. *Chicago Evening News,* July 31, 1885, in Hogeland, *Boys and Girls of 100 Cities,* 17, 19.

58. "Newsboys Regret Willie," *New York Times,* Feb. 8, 1898, Heig Scrapbook, Eckel Collection.

59. Carter J. Beard, "The Newsboys of New York: A Study from Life," *Demorest's Family Magazine* 31 (May 1895): 381–382, Eckel Collection.

60. Unidentified clipping. Eckel Collection.

61. "Brodie Will Bury Aaron 'The Slave,'" *New York Evening Journal,* Feb. 6, 1899; "Evening World Buries a Boy," *New York Evening World,* Feb. 8, 1899, Heig Scrapbook, Eckel Collection. (The *World* identified the deceased as Aaron Clarity.)

62. *Milwaukee Sentinel,* Jan. 28, 1880, 4; Robert W. Wells, *The Milwaukee Journal: An Informal Chronicle of its First 100 Years, 1882–1982* (Milwaukee, 1981), 43–44.

63. Undated clipping Heig Scrapbook, Eckel Collection. See also "Pluck Boy's Brief Career," *New York Times,* Feb. 7, 1895, 5.

64. Rosebud Folsom, "Whistlin' Joe, 'the Best Feller 'T Ever Live," *Success,* Jan. 1900, 15. Eckel Collection.

65. See Raymond Williams, *The Long Revolution* (London, 1960), and *Marxism and Literature* (Oxford, 1977), 128–135.

66. Morrow, *Voice from the Newsboys,* 109.

PART 6

LITERATURE

Literature teaches children about life. Whether realistic or fantastic, children's stories contain blueprints for how to make sense of the world and cope with life's day-to-day perils. Rituals can offer therapeutic advantages, and because of this many authors knowingly or unknowingly include them in their works for and about children. Truman Capote recalls his own childhood in "A Christmas Memory," as he tells how his and his elderly cousin's holiday practice of making fruitcakes taught him more than culinary skills. In *Wait till Next Year: A Memoir*, Doris Kearns Goodwin shows how her nightly pattern of tracking the progress of the Brooklyn Dodgers formed an integral part of her childhood, enabling her to develop a deep bond with her father, master a body of information, and come to terms with changes in her own life. Harry Potter's magical world, as popularized in America by the books of British writer J. K. Rowling, contains many examples of ritualized behavior that captivate young readers.

Perhaps no author better understood the function of physical and verbal rituals for children than Mark Twain. In the first essay that follows, "*The Adventures of Tom Sawyer* and *The Great Brain*: Liminality, Ritual, and Race in the Construction of the 'Real American Boy,'" Leona W. Fisher demonstrates the influence of Twain's classic on a later boys' story, John D. Fitzgerald's *The Great Brain*, focusing on the childhood ritualistic behavior, especially involving games and language, that characterizes both books. In the next essay, "The Many Faces of Childhood: Costume as Ritualized Behavior," Jamie McMinn and H. Alan Pickrell address the rituals inherent in "dressing up," including the role of disguise in the theories of Oscar Brockett, Claude Lévi-Strauss, Sigmund Freud, and Carl Jung. Knowledge of these theories better enables us to understand the dynamics of Halloween, masquerades, and popular plot devices in children's series books. Just as patterns of behavior characterize children's lives, so too do they find their way into juvenile books, both literary classics and popular pastime reading.

The Adventures of Tom Sawyer and The Great Brain

Liminality, Ritual, and Race in the Construction of the "Real American Boy"

LEONA W. FISHER

The Two Texts: Liminality, Ritual, and Race

John D. Fitzgerald's 1967 book *The Great Brain* foregrounds its debts to Mark Twain's classic *The Adventures of Tom Sawyer*, written almost exactly one hundred years before. Fitzgerald pays obvious tribute to his illustrious forerunner in the genre of the "boys' book" and the construction of what Leslie Fiedler was to call the "Good Bad Boy" in American fiction (259–290), in multiple ways.[1] His protagonist, though not his central "consciousness," is also named Tom, although he is more often called simply "the Great Brain" (in implicit tribute to both "heroes") by his Sid-like narrator brother, J. D. Both books are set in the romantic, small-town American West, although in his late-nineteenth-century setting, Fitzgerald has appropriately moved westward from Missouri to Utah. Both central characters are smarter, intellectually and practically, than their peers and the adults in their lives; both are consummate "con artists" who oppose themselves to the naïveté and, sometimes, injustice that surrounds them; both suffer appropriate pangs of "conscience" when they have gone too far, and seem to know when to bend the rules and rituals in complex moral situations.

Structurally the books present themselves as picaresque adventure stories that require episodic challenges, a gang, a leader of that gang, and opposition to adult institutional authority (school, church, family). These rituals of rebellion and cleverness on the part of the central Toms involve such repeated motifs as adult stupidity; children plotting and eavesdropping; and boys learning to fight, excluding girls from all meaningful activity, exploring caves, playing games, testing superstitions, and being introduced to death. Both texts succeed in conflating the innocence of childhood, a temporal phenomenon, with nostalgia for the fading frontier, a spatial construct: that is, they construct boyhood as quintessentially "American"—and American energy as residually boyish.[2]

But there, as we will see, the similarities end. Whereas Tom Sawyer somewhat unconsciously appropriates the ritual wisdom of the slaves' oral culture as well as the lore he has learned in key books of Western civilization, Tom Fitzgerald self-consciously exploits oral lore as well as conventional adult rhetoric for his own selfish ends. Thus, while the second novel seems to be a modern rewriting of the classic text, it actually explodes both ritual and traditional American values in ways that betray Twain's risky experiment. *Tom Sawyer,* for all the antics of its iconic protagonist, remains a communal experience, while *The Great Brain* privileges and celebrates a divisive form of American individualism.

Victor Turner's by now famous distinction between "liminal" (characteristic of oral and pre-literate cultures) and "liminoid" (characteristic of post-industrial and literate societies) rituals offers a useful way to understand the differences: *Tom Sawyer*'s rituals are liminal whereas *The Great Brain*'s, emptied of their content and symbolism, barely qualify as liminoid—that is, as rituals at all. The former provides an opportunity for marginal people, in this case children, to attach themselves to other liminal people and together to produce a temporary critique of the normative. For Turner, the liminal ritual (from *limen,* meaning "threshold" in Latin [Turner 24]), produces *communitas* through the experience of shared "marginal" activity. Such activity soon becomes a *memory* that in turn strives to replicate itself within the stable social structure. Liminal rituals occupy the middle of three stages in adolescent rites of passage, according to Turner (following Arnold Van Gennep's structure as formulated in *Rites de Passage,* 1908): *separation, transition,* and *incorporation* (Turner 24).[3] As marginal experiences, liminal rituals produce

> an alternative and more "liberated" way of being socially human, a way both of being detached from social structure—and hence potentially of periodically *evaluating* its performance—and also of a "distanced" or "marginal" person's being more attached to *other* disengaged persons—and hence, sometimes of evaluating a social structure's historical performance in common with them. Here we may have a loving union of the structurally damned pronouncing judgment on normative structure and providing alternative models of structure. (Turner 51)

In this process of bonding as outsiders, there is a predictable "lack of stress on individuality" (Turner 43); further, tribal liminality relies on "topsy-turveydom, parody, abrogation of the normative system, exaggeration of rule into caricature or satirizing of rule" (43), but never produces "more than a subversive flicker. It [the liminal ritual] is put into the service of normativeness almost as soon as it appears" (44–45).

Thus, both the liberation and the subversion are temporary, although they may have permanent effects on the social structure, as Twain, of course, hoped his satire would have. In other words, the ritual never entirely abjures social normativity, even though the participants collectively call into question its customs and forms; the goal of such activity is always re-incorporation. The slippage from "primitives" to children is easy enough to apply to the case of Tom Sawyer and his gang, whose challenge to adult bourgeois values both succeeds brilliantly and signals its temporariness: boys will be boys, but they will grow out of it.

Seen as liminal activity undertaken with the understanding that its dangers or subversions are only temporary, play-as-ritual can help us to understand the tension in Twain between rebellion and conformity, unconscious necessity and conscious creativity. As play theorist Steven J. Fox has suggested, "Play, as a ritual form, is the process through which participants assume 'the role of the other" (Fox 54), thus linking it to directly to Twain's themes. Other scholars have determined that "play" among children, as relatively unconscious, would qualify instead as (ritual) "work" in Turner's sense of the nonvolitional and would therefore fall outside their purview (Csikszentmihalyi 21).[4] But, for my purposes, the two different forms of play help to inform our comparison: if the liminal is unconscious and obligatory (hence more like "work" than "play"), the liminoid *is* volitional, a matter of selected ritual activity (Turner 32–33). As we examine the two texts, therefore, it should become clear that if *Tom Sawyer* is primarily liminal in its play activities, *The Great Brain* utilizes "play" in precisely the willed and willful ways that would define it as consciously chosen, individualistic, and liminoid—thereby emptying it of some of its capacity to interrogate social normativity in a communal way.[5]

Another important element in the rituals of these books is the legacy of the verbal "trickster" passed down to Fitzgerald through Twain. The construction of the American boy hero depends not on freewheeling adventure but on elaborate verbal schemes and the continual manipulation of linguistic formulas. Even more significantly, this prowess with language is inextricably intertwined with racial and ethnic traditions and considerations—in the case of Twain, with slaves and "injuns"; and of Fitzgerald, with Jews, Greeks, Mormons, Catholics, and Indians, a melting pot of American ethnicity at the turn of the century. Both books construct the "real American boy" as defined both in opposition to these "others" and, paradoxically, in dependency on them.[6]

Citing Turner, Jeanne Rosier Smith notes that tricksters themselves are "'liminal phenomena . . . betwixt and between'" normative origins and social changes (7). She also incorporates William Lenz's discussion of the "nineteenth-century confidence man" in Twain and others as "'a distinctly American version' of the trickster" who disappears because "the closing of the frontier constrains his speculative schemes" (8–9). According to Smith, tricksters in the Anglo-Saxon tradition run to the individualistic, while writers of color have preserved the "strong communal values" of the nonwestern trickster figure (9).

Twain's child con-man, Tom Sawyer, would seem both to validate this distinction and to explode it: what does one do with a white American con-boy who operates liminally in *communitas* with other marginal persons—and where did he come from? Drawing as he does for his rituals and tricks on *both* the Anglo-Saxon tradition of children's games *and* the African American superstitions and lore that sustain so many of his schemes, Tom serves as an imaginative alternative to both white culture and adult bourgeois responsibility. Like Turner's liminal subversives within tribal cultures, Tom Sawyer occupies a creative, unique, temporary space/time between childhood and adulthood, community and individuality, fantasy and realism, opposition and assimilation, blackness and whiteness.[7] As children, as outsiders (if only temporarily), and as creatures co-identified with slaves as "Noble Savages," Tom and his gang can be seen to act as "surrogates" for those marginal others.[8] Despite its superficial imitation of Twain, *The Great Brain* fails to achieve Twain's complexity in its own representation of "surrogation."

The Adventures of Tom Sawyer: The Ur-Text of American Boyhood

When Twain's Tom taunts her with "'You'll tell,'" the new love-of-his-life Becky Thatcher replies with an apparently ritual oath: "'No I won't—deed and deed and double deed I won't'" (ch. 6, 55). In the dropping of the "in-" from "indeed," the jingle inadvertently but symbolically represents one of *Tom Sawyer*'s central ideological confusions. In the shift from the abstract "indeed" (i.e., certainly, of course, emphatically) to the concrete signifier of action—the "deed"—Becky articulates what the book enacts in its entirety; the movement from the importance of the *word* to the apparent (but, as we will see, illusory) significance of the *deed*. It is the same shift—from the intellectual origins of this country to the activist spirit of western expansion—that could be said to be taking place in American frontier life in the nineteenth century.

As a girl, of course, Becky does not genuinely represent either a relationship to the wilderness or any life of (even temporary) significant action.[9] But ironically, neither does Tom Sawyer represent the active adventurer who escapes bourgeois domesticity and "civilization" through deeds of daring and lawlessness—though he engages with temporary enthusiasm in the roles of prankster, military officer, Robin Hood, pirate, wilderness adventurer, even intermittent hero. And, perhaps most importantly, he flirts temporarily with the person and status of the ultimate romantic "outcast," Huck Finn. Many have pointed out that Tom is "romantic, imaginative, and well read," the literate and literary Don Quixote to Huck's Sancho Panza (for example, Gerber in Twain 270). What appears to be a "boys' book" of active adventure, it would seem, is only a "mock adventure" (Green 133), filled with verbal byplay and childish lore, the linguistic and cultural rituals of competitive "call and response" rather than the manly "American" ideals of rough-and-ready confrontation, male bonding, and symbolic rapes of the virgin landscape.[10]

I am arguing a related but rather different point: that the intrinsically and structurally *linguistic* and *ritualistic* basis for Tom's and the others' adventures, as well as their liminal status as children identified with other outsiders, ensures the "mock" nature of their escapades—although that is a misleading word, suggesting falsity and even mockery. In other words, the mimicry of these rituals constitutes a kind of "performance" or parody on Tom's part that is both a tribute to the culture and a criticism of it; in Turner's terms, Tom's largely unconscious embodiment of ritual serves to critique normativity even as he expects to re-enter the social order someday as an adult.

Furthermore, if this text can be seen as foundational and mythic, then its influence must be regarded as fundamentally multicultural in its incorporation of racial and ethnic elements, no less than verbal and intellectual. For Twain, the construction of American identity is not monolithic—racially, geographically, or temporally. Far from the simple "boys' book" of its reputation, then, Twain's text becomes a paradoxical guidebook to a problematic and contradictory American past and future: where space (the retreating American frontier) must be read as time (encroaching mortality)[11]; where boys stand for the "unmarked case" of innocent childhood *and* enduring maleness[12]; and where "injuns" and slaves simultaneously function as "others" who remind the white residents and readers of their power and help provide the book's defining verbal texture and cultural vitality. With male childhood as his liminal topic, Twain can represent both escape and return, transgression and capitulation, abolitionist sentiments and embedded racism, with impunity.[13]

In a reversal of Becky's unconsciously ironic oath, then, Twain can represent each of these themes by means of its apparent opposite: action can be represented "'by the book'" (ch. 8, 67), as Tom tells the boys whom he leads at playing Robin Hood; deep moral and supernatural fears can submit to the arbitrary and inherited traditions of superstitious incantations and jingles; and, perhaps most importantly, egalitarian "Americanness" can be yoked to that horrific countertradition of colonialism (the Native American rout) and slavery. As Twain states in the preface, "The odd superstitions touched upon were prevalent among *children and slaves* in the West at the period of this story" (emphasis added). In this straightforward and apparently unironic statement, Twain both provides us with a means of deconstructing the opposition between these two populations (hence between whites and blacks) and signals his own simultaneous attraction to and separation from both groups. Although neither population of "outsiders" will come in for the venomous and hilarious criticism that he levels at the white adults "showing off" for dignitaries or being duped by Tom, Twain's narrator does gently mock both children's self-delusions and slaves' tendency to "lie" and to reduce complex experience to repetitive *mantras* for survival.[14]

Where, then, do children's (and African Americans') "lore and language" (to use Iona and Peter Opie's phrase, the title of their book) figure in the structure of this complex and contradictory chain of meanings? Whether playing Robin Hood according to the rules, curing warts, exacting revenge, conning his fellows, effecting a "swap," swearing to keep a secret, tracking a buried treasure, or planning for a collective life of crime, Tom Sawyer reveals himself to be a ritualistic and precise wordsmith. He knows (or pretends to know) all the rules and undertakes to instruct the others, usually Huck, about the proper procedures. For example, after introducing the word *orgies*, Tom answers Huck's question, "'What's orgies?'" with the assertion, "'*I* dono. But robbers always have orgies, and of course we've got to have them, too'" (ch. 33, 247). If he is not citing "the book" as his authority, then he simply conflates "'the general thing'" (ch. 33, 258) with his own opinion or manipulative preference: "'But Huck, we can't let you into the gang if you ain't respectable, you know'" (ch. 33, 258). In matters of dress, behavior, demeanor, even linquistic appropriateness, Tom Sawyer consistently plays Miss Manners to his less articulate crew—or the writer reshaping "reality" to suit his own cultural construction and cautious rebellion.

Even in the opening chapter of the novel (after brief bouts of stealing sugar and practicing a "valued novelty in whistling, which he had just acquired from a negro"), Tom's preference for words is immediately revealed, as he welcomes the well-dressed "new boy" to town with a ritual exchange of verbal taunts and formulaic challenges, what Iona and Peter Opie call "Having the Last Word" (65).[15] Twain's hero is certainly no inarticulate Billy Budd who needs to lash out in a primitive gesture of frustrated violence or feels the mute powerlessness of childhood. Indeed, the actual fight (described merely as "rolling and tumbling") takes precisely "the space of a minute" while the exchange that precedes the physical contact occupies several pages. With Tom clearly dominating, the two boys proceed in ritualistic fashion: from the challenge ("'I can lick you!'") to the introduction ("'What's your name?'") through the ritual boasts and, ultimately, the drawn line in the dust and the "'dare'" (ch. 1, 6–8). The new boy presumably emerges from this exchange and pummeling with a clear and systematic idea of his adversary and the general attitude of the town toward dandies like himself. Tom's power is established.

Without examining the passages that refer to Tom's romance with Becky or the Robin Hood games, it is clear to an adult reader, if not to a child, that the diction and fictional stance of the courtly lover, pining from afar, and the hero of medieval romance, champion of the poor,

dominate these intertextual discourses. But the rituals of boyhood in the
novel are dominated increasingly by the supernatural and superstitious
lore associated with African Americans, the only population besides
criminals and Indians who presumably occupy a lower status than the
children. From the beginning of America's "peculiar institution," slaves
were conveniently regarded and represented as a species of "child," so it
is not surprising that the racially enlightened Twain would yoke the two
as romantic liminal subversives. That such appropriation of a subaltern
population can easily slip back into racism has, of course, been attested
to by generations of Twain readers who have also objected to the realism in his use of the "n" word.[16]

Yet slaves also figure as recurring authorities on life's mysteries. A
"Negro," therefore, has taught Tom a new technique for whistling (ch.
1, 5).[17] Chains of valuable information involve the "word" of slaves:
Huck reports to Tom on the properties of "spunk-water" for curing
warts, for instance: "'Why he [Bob Tanner] told Jeff Thatcher, and
Jeff told Johnny Baker, and Johnny told Jim Hollis, and Jim told Ben
Rogers, and Ben told a nigger, and the nigger told me. There, now!'"
And Tom responds, singling out the slave: "'Well, what of it? They'll all
lie. Leastways all but the nigger. I don't know *him*. But I never see a nigger that *wouldn't* lie'" (ch. 6, 49).[18]

Similarly, blacks are authorities on all kinds of superstitious "signs":
"'That's what the niggers say, and they know all about these kind of
things, Huck'" (ch.10, 83). Implicitly, then, the sources for all knowledge
of witches and devils and supernatural phenomena are indeed the slaves
whom the boys both identify with and differentiate themselves from—
with some ambiguity as to their own status as "surrogates."

Huck Finn, a more permanent kind of outsider who helps mark the
spatial and temporal limits of Tom's own benign rebellion, appropriately articulated the author's double view toward blacks. Huck here is
speaking of Ben Rogers's allowing him to sleep in his family's barn:

> He lets me, and so does his pap's nigger man, Uncle Jake. I tote water
> for Uncle Jake whenever he wants me to, and any time I ask him he
> gives me a little something to eat if he can spare it. That's a mighty
> good nigger, Tom. He likes me, becuz I don't ever act as if I was above
> him. Sometimes I've set right down and eat *with* him. But you needn't
> tell that. A body's got to do things when he's awful hungry he wouldn't
> want to do as a steady thing. (ch. 28, 200–201)[19]

By refusing (through ignorance and naïveté) to comprehend its linguistic and ideological rules, Huck—the permanently liminal figure—condemns the normative society on Twain's behalf.

The most light-hearted examples of Twain's implicit tribute to African Americans predictably come in the boys' discussions of "correct" behavior in situations of relative powerlessness: whether over warts, marbles that insist on staying lost, ghosts, or treasures that resist discovery. Both dead cats and stump-water (not to mention beans) are debated by Tom and Huck as cures for warts, with meticulously described details and incantations included: "'Down bean; off, wart; come no more to bother me!'" and "'Devil follow corpse, cat follow devil, warts follow cat, *I*'m done with ye!' That'll fetch *any* wart" (ch. 6, 50). Later Tom feels so frustrated at the failure of his marble incantation that his "whole structure of faith was shaken to its foundations." Turning to a new remedy, he enjoins a small black bug to confirm his guess that "some witch had interfered and broken the charm," "'Doodle-bug, doodle-bug, tell me what I want to know!'" (ch. 8, 65–66), and concludes when the bug appears that "'it *was* a witch that done it'" and "He well know the futility of trying to contend against witches, so he gave up discouraged" (ch. 8, 66).[20] The narrator's reality checks and irony let us know, here and elsewhere, that Tom is inconsistent in his belief structure, that he both manipulates reality to suit his superstitious worldview and adapts his perspective to practicalities. In terms of play theory and ritual studies, Tom is using his imagination and memory to stretch the rules and exert power over his and Huck's fate.

But Twain also delights in the recounting—and succeeds in representing—the hopefulness that Tom's remedies signify: Twain, like Tom, plays with the possibility that the ritual might have some potency. The culminating vindication of Tom's optimism about portents *and* rules is, of course, his and Huck's actual discovery of the buried treasure. After laboriously instructing Huck and reassuring himself about the rituals involved in the burial and retrieval of buried treasure (e.g., to Huck's question, "'Do they always bury it as deep as this?'" Tom backpedals rapidly: "'Sometimes—not always. Not generally. I reckon we haven't got the right place'" [ch. 25, 180]), Tom builds up his excuses for moving their search to the haunted house: "'They most always put in a dead man when they bury a treasure under a tree, to look out for it. . . . S'pose this one here was to stick his skull out and say something! . . . Huck, I don't feel comfortable a bit" (ch. 25, 181). Huck doesn't like haunted houses, but Tom wins him over by pointing out that "'ghosts travel around only at night—they won't hender us from digging there in the daytime'" (ch. 25, 192).

In their different understandings of competing superstitions, Tom is bound to win because of his logical powers, even though Huck also reveals common sense and the occasional brilliance of an idiot savant; besides, they share a deep knowledge of the shared rituals. Nowhere is their relative supernatural competency demonstrated more graphically than in their swearing of an "oath in blood" not to tell about Injun Joe's framing of Muff Potter. As the Opies point out, important promises are frequently accompanied by such phrases as "Cross my heart and hope to die / Drop down dead if I tell a lie" (145), but in this case the situation indeed could result in the deaths of one or both eavesdroppers.[21] This time it is Huck who senses the urgency and rejects Tom's bland suggestion that they "'just hold hands and swear'" not to tell. Instead, he reveals his rather more "savage" origins and deeper sense of cosmic, not to mention social, evil: "'O, no, that wouldn't do for this. . . . there orter be writing 'bout a big thing like this. And blood'" (ch. 10, 79). Persuaded instantly, Tom composes the following (although using red chalk rather than blood, demonstrating his sense of the performative nature of the undertaking): "'Huck Fin and Tom Sawyer swears they will keep mum about this and they wish they may Drop down dead in their tracks if they ever tell and Rot'" (ch. 10, 80). Later they "'swear again'" because "'It's more surer'" (ch. 23, 167), but this is right before Tom breaks the oath unilaterally and goes to the authorities with the truth. Twain deals with this betrayal in only half-ironic tones, empathizing with Huck's righteous sense of disorder even as he affirms that Tom has plainly done the right thing in saving Muff Potter's life: "Since Tom's harassed conscience had managed to drive him to the lawyer's house by night and wring a dread tale from lips that had been sealed with the dismalest and more formidable of oaths, Huck's confidence in the human race was well nigh obliterated" (ch. 24, 173).

The arrogant mistake Tom makes, in both moral and ritual terms, is not to share the decision with his partner—but the reader already understands Huck's intransigence on the subject, even though he himself can break large societal rules when he is desperate, as when he eats with Uncle Jake.[22] Again, Tom is heralded as a "hero" because he knows when and how to remain silent or to speak, how to invoke the ritual

"rules," and when to break them in the interests of either expediency—
or a higher principle.

All the repetitive verbal rituals in *Tom Sawyer,* except perhaps the
overtly literary ones, portray the liminal power of childhood as inti-
mately connected to the rituals and life struggles of the outsider classes—
those who depend on their superstitions and formulaic procedures to
survive. In relation to children, this invocation of the wisdom of the dis-
possessed can be both comic and deadly serious—suggesting a double
audience for the book. Children, after all, will grow up to become practical, skeptical, white, male, law-abiding citizens and readers, Twain
implies. Thus Huck, though white, represents the permanent "outlaw"
who believes in the literal reality of the oath, while Tom, as the temporary "American boy" outsider, recognizes intuitively its fictitious and
ritual qualities. In contrast to Tom's safety from outsiderhood (and re-
incorporation into "civilization"), for the adult groups whose survival
may depend on these formulas, there is a chance that they will not
"grow up" at all—but remain childlike (in the dominant culture's imagination), or become fugitives or corpses.

The Great Brain: Tom Sawyer Revisited?

If Tom Fitzgerald follows in this liminal tradition of surrogation, we
would expect him similarly to borrow from oral rituals, as well as to
straddle that adolescent space/time in acts of both rebellion and ultimate socialization. The books should, we suspect, produce similar "subversive flickers" in their readers, followed by the comfort and safety of
capitulation.

But perhaps because satire would seem to need a radical kind of
moral innocence and hope to enable it, Fitzgerald's *The Great Brain* re-
sorts instead to irony, disingenuous naïveté, and moral evasion; it is perhaps too late by 1967 for authentic childishness. The autobiographical
narrator J. D., who briefly claims in the opening to be speaking from an
adult perspective, does not emulate either the nostalgia or the superior
understanding (some would say, condescension) of Twain's narrator. Instead, although he seems to be rewriting *Tom Sawyer* from the perspective
of the 1960s, the text primarily adopts the single-consciousness of the
frustrated younger brother. In addition, the communal or liminal gang
ethos of the earlier text is rewritten as a capitalist or liminoid fulfillment

of the American Dream—for children—and there is no Huck Finn figure to mediate the borderland areas of desperate "otherness." Enlightened self-interest replaces seat-of-the-pants survival, and the "trickster" figure metamorphoses into the prototypical entrepreneur-in-the-making: as Tom says (and we and J. D. have no reason to doubt him), "'I'll be a millionaire before I'm old enough to vote'" (ch. 1, 18). Moral commentary is relegated to an occasional half-articulated sentence by the narrator on his brother's questionable ethics; for example, "I could tell from the conniving look on Tom's face during lunch that his great brain was working like sixty to turn this to his financial advantage" (ch. 1, 7). Finally, the language and ritual of boyhood are appropriated and fully controlled by our "hero," who ultimately even performs his own moral mock-transformation.

Tom/The Great Brain, the con artist of language and manipulation, is far from the learned and quixotic Tom Sawyer, though he appears equally reliant on ritual and trickery. Yet even the pretense of a liminoid ritual has vanished: Tom Fitzgerald's rebellion against adult rules may be conscious and post-literate, but it is not transformative of anything beyond his own financial status. Less the trickster than the lawyer or snake oil salesman, Tom uses oral lore and stereotyped ritual to ensure his own dominion over his friends and, indeed, the whole town.

The difference between the Toms is predicted immediately in their different reading lists: while Sawyer has memorized *Robin Hood* and rejected the Bible, and J. D. and their older brother Sweyn "read books like *Black Beauty* and [yes!] *Huckleberry Finn*, Tom read *The World Almanac* and the set of encyclopedias in our bookcase" (ch. 1, 6): learning is not "play" nor an end in itself for Tom, but a means to other goals.

Even more importantly, Tom's own language mimics not the ritual wisdom of the outsider but the white, middle-class adult rhetoric he has heard and learned to use to his advantage. When he and Sweyn teach J. D. to swim, for instance, he threatens J. D. with parental rejection: "'they will never forgive you if you turn out to be a coward.'" J. D. necessarily concludes, in clichés that ironically echo Twain's racism: "I was pretty young to go into the mountains and live like a naked savage. If I ran now, I would be a coward. Better by far to drown than to disgrace our family name" (ch. 3, 48). Despite the humor, the diction confirms Fitzgerald's ideological bent: all the "traditional" American values are celebrated, including civilization (represented by wearing clothes), courage (represented by his willingness to risk drowning), and loyalty to "the family name" (again suggested by his potential martyrdom). J. D. therefore instantly absorbs the value system and takes credit for his triumph, "the proudest moment of my life" (ch. 3, 48), even though he has been threatened and bullied into bravery. Imaginative childhood jingles and African American incantations have been replaced by jingoistic Americanisms—never directly called into question by an adult narrator who signals his ironic reservations only in the most implicit ways; the point of view remains steadfastly that of the child J. D. even though he is writing as an adult.

Race is also less central than in *Tom Sawyer*. In fact, it seems to be more an excuse for, than a defining fact of, this simplified "melting pot"—subsumed into Tom's plots rather than persisting in the margins as a constant reminder of a central and problematic hegemony. Rather than questioning white, middle-class "Americanness," this book reifies it. Thus the Native American is an occasional dinner guest, and the "genuine Indian beaded belt" (ch. 2, 30) has become merely an object of capitalist exchange: first given as a present to J. D., then extorted from him, and ultimately returned at the time of Tom's "conversion." When J. D. mistakenly applies Tom's techniques and gets the mumps on purpose, his brothers give him "the Silent Treatment," modeled on their parents' own bizarre child-rearing practice, and he complains, "'It is worse than Indian torture,'" to which his mother replies, "'Then bear it like an Indian'" (ch. 2, 37). This stereotypical cooptation of Native American behavior later resurfaces in an ironic juxtaposition when the kids mistreat the Greek immigrant Basil, and Papa preaches "'we are all immigrants except the Indians'" (ch. 5, 88). This is closely followed by a graphic scene, which echoes comically the earlier scene in *Tom Sawyer* when Injun Joe describes his intended sadistic torture of the Widow Douglas. The boys "had Basil tied to a tree in the middle of the clearing. They had piled dead brush around Basil as if they were going to burn him at the stake. They were dancing around the tree, letting out Indian war cries as they waved homemade tomahawks in the air" (ch. 5, 89). Unlike Tom Sawyer, who cites firsthand African American sources for his superstitions, Tom Fitzgerald relies on white (mis)perceptions of Native American behavior for his performative scenarios. Although both of them are representing apparently authentic native rituals, filtered through the surrogacy of the children, in the latter case the process has become empty. Moving far beyond Sawyer's own sprightly manipulation of incantations and procedures, the Great Brain in his stereotyping has reduced the rituals to their static and instrumental functions.

Climaxing the Native American motif and, again, curiously ironizing the earnest use of superstition in *Tom Sawyer*, Tom has the boys all swear "an oath on the skull of this dead Indian chief" (ch. 7, 125) not to tell about their plan of revenge against Mr. Standish, the new school teacher. Like Sawyer before him, Tom chooses to break the oath unilaterally and to confess to the despicable scheme, rendering himself a hero but betraying the other boys and terrifying J. D. Of course, Tom reassures him, cavalierly setting himself up as superior in judgment, not desperately conscience-stricken like Sawyer: "'There comes a time in every man's life, . . . when he must break his word to help somebody'" (ch. 7, 136). Besides, he claims, rather cynically: "'There is no such thing as a ghost'" (ch. 7, 137). Unlike Huck, J. D. accepts Tom's disclaimer with relief and goes to sleep (ch. 7, 138). And unlike Tom Sawyer, Tom Fitzgerald doesn't even flirt with the possibility that such rituals may have communal validity; from the beginning, he has viewed them as expedient, merely using them to exact his revenge.

The text's treatment of the itinerant merchant Abie Glassman's death as an exploration of ethnic and racial mistreatment in this chauvinistic Mormon town would seem promising. But this chapter partially domesticates or sentimentalizes death (as the earlier novel did not, with Injun Joe's grisly demise in the cave), using Abie as a stereotypical representation of the honorable Jew. As the ultimate outsider, Glassman becomes the sacrificial lamb that enables Papa's pious pronouncement on Jewish dignity and the town's liberal guilt (ch. 6, 111–112). This insistence on respect for "difference" would be more effective, of course, if the melting-pot mentality did not reassert itself in Papa's subsequent rationalization for Abie's Christian burial. The enemy has also moved indoors because, as Tom confesses to J. D., he has known all along that Abie's cash box was empty and "'I was wrong'" (6, 114) not to tell the adults so that they could save Abie from starvation. In the ethical conflict (Tom's loyalty to his oath and Abie's pride versus a man's life), this could be the one point in the text when the Great Brain makes a life-and-death mistake and admits it. However, instead of analyzing the tragic effects of having "kept his word," according to boyhood ritual, Tom merely goes on to accuse J. D. and the rest of the town of not patronizing Abie's store and therefore causing his death. Tom thereby undermines any moral superiority he may have temporarily earned. The text does at least try to redeem this tragic error by allowing J. D. the "last word": "'I gave my word [not to tell] and kept it until now'" (6, 115). While keeping one's word is clearly valorized in the various Tom episodes, it is also called into question by both Abie's death *and* the narrator's willingness to break his own silence at the time of writing the book. Hence, although the child reader is not led systematically through this moral dilemma, there is at least the suggestion that everyone has erred and that J. D. feels compelled to report, if not to scrutinize, the community's collective responsibility—that is, to seek a higher good than his childish promise to Tom.

In contrast, there is not even implicit complexity in the central chapter on "Americanness," when Tom teaches the Greek immigrant Basil to be a "hundred per cent American kid" (ch. 5)—a phrase that is repeated almost ritualistically throughout the chapter by both Tom and J. D. Instead, the reductive dichotomy—American/foreigner—reveals a fundamental miscomprehension of Twain's exploratory child-world: there is no rebellious flirtation with "otherness" here, only a practical lesson in immigrant survival in an inhospitable land.

As in the earlier text's treatment of the new boy in town, fighting occupies the center of American child culture in this chapter. We have earlier learned from J. D. that the Fitzgeralds had taught the "Mormon kids . . . tolerance" for non-Mormons:

> It was just a question of us all learning how to fight good enough for Sweyn to whip every Mormon kid his age, Tom to whip every Mormon kid his age, and for me to whip every Mormon kid my age in town. After all, there is nothing as tolerant and understanding as a kid you can whip. (ch. 1, 2)

While John D. Fitzgerald's use of blatant irony in this last sentence (one of few exceptions to his general narrative rules) would seem to signal disapproval of his family's boyhood violence, chapter 5 presents the success of Tom's strategy. Bullied by Sammy Leeds and the others, Basil must learn to "whip" them so that they will accept him. The alternative is to look "like a valentine" (ch. 5, 80) and to be "'a cry baby and a Mamma's boy'"—that is, a sissy—which is "unAmerican"; there is no middle ground.

Thus Basil has "'to learn to do his own fighting'" (ch. 5, 91) or be permanently ostracized, beaten up, and defined as "other." "'Basil has got to prove he deserves to be an American,'" (ch. 5, 92) says Tom—thereby overtly conflating nationality with violence. He discovers and reports Greeks' preference for wrestling (another cultural stereotype); then he systematically pretends to be Basil's friend as he teaches him how to beat Sammy Leeds in a "rough and tumble fight" (ch. 5, 98–99). Unlike Sawyer, who asserts his power over the new boy in town with words and flourishes, the Great Brain takes Basil on an a commercial venture, executing what J. D. (to do him justice as both a marginal participant and a narrator) calls a "swindle in pantomime" as he extorts money from Basil and proceeds to get "rid of all his old junk": his agate marbles in an empty tobacco sack, his homemade slingshot, and so on. As J. D. judiciously comments, "I couldn't help thinking he [Mr. Kokovinis] would have saved time by just giving the dollar to Tom" (ch. 5, 85). Also unlike Tom Sawyer's swindle of his friends in the fence-painting scene, the Great Brain's motives are paradoxically both higher (to make Basil a "real American boy") and lower (to continue to make money on the deal). He is, after all, interested in the long term; as J. D. explains, once "Tom had made Basil a genuine American kid like the rest of us, it made the Greek boy fair game for my brother's great brain" (ch. 5, 101). J. D. knows, but does not condemn, Tom's next move, to teach Basil English, and we suspect he is right as he conjectures: "I'll bet Tom is trying to figure out how much to charge Mr. Kokovinis for each new English word he teaches Basil" (ch. 5, 101).

It is impossible to imagine Tom Sawyer's charging his friends for teaching them new Robin Hoodisms or superstitious jingles he has learned from slaves. This individualistic capitalist move certainly constitutes the "Fall" of childhood and communal culture—even as it marks the premature acquisition of so-called adult economic mores in an age of advanced capitalism; in Van Gennep's and Turner's terms, it is *incorporation* with a vengeance; it is also, of course, a valorization of the socially normative value of individualism.[23] In a conflation of crass materialism with a reductionist Utilitarianism ("the greatest good for the greatest number"), J. D. Fitzgerald's book and his "hero" represent the triumph of xenophobic "Americanness" over Twain's deconstructive boyhood.

Conclusions

Nowhere is this degeneration confirmed more graphically than in the two books' conclusions. In Twain's book, Tom Sawyer succeeds in persuading the runaway Huck to rejoin his gang of robbers, as a condition of which he must return to the Widow Douglas's stifling bourgeois household as her "'respectable'" ward. Tempting the recalcitrant Huck with tantalizing initiation rites and activities that promise to be "'a million times bullier than pirating,'" Tom convinces Huck to "'stick to the widder till I rot, Tom'" (ch. 33, 259). It is significant, of course, that Tom reinserts his own somewhat elitist principles into this conversation: "'A robber is more high-toned than what a pirate is'" (ch. 33, 258), but Twain has the good sense to stop the narrative's open-endedness *before* the boys' new adventures actually begin and Huck defects once more—this time to accompany the slave Jim down the river to freedom. Thus the reader must imagine what further childish adventures are possible within this playful economy; as Twain says in the conclusion, "the story could not go much further without becoming the history of a *man*" (260), at which point it would presumably cease to be safely liminal or subversive.

Fitzgerald's book *seems* to promise similar open-endedness but, in fact, constructs its opposite: in an act of implausible self-transformation, the Great Brain first saves Andy-the-amputee from suicide and from being "plumb useless"; then he magnanimously refuses the promised erector set as reward and returns the Indian beaded belt to J. D. This series of acts at first persuades the skeptical J. D. that Tom "expected to die any moment" (ch. 8, 174), but he ultimately becomes convinced of the "miracle" and decides that "Things got mighty dull after The Great Brain decided to give up his crooked ways and to walk the straight and narrow. . . . So dull there is no more to tell" (ch. 8, 175). Too little, too late, we remark if we have been offended by Tom's self-interest all along. But, we begin to wonder, why has J. D. mentioned the "night the schoolhouse burned down," in the penultimate sentence? Perhaps we are being set up for a sequel—one in which Papa will once again be constructed as a dupe and a fool for not "bother[ing] to come upstairs and see if Tom was in bed" that night? Rather than anticipating the delightful adventures of a gang of playful robbers who operate "by the book," we are reduced to imagining the miniaturized financial wizard coming back to swindle his friends and relations—as he, in fact, does in subsequent volumes.

But perhaps Leslie Fiedler was wrong all along, and the quintessential "boys' book" for the twentieth century is *not* "a male fantasy which encourages a flight out of the drawing room, away from mothers and wives, but with another male of a different race or class" (Greiner 16). Although there are no little girls (not even a Becky Thatcher) or substantial adult females (not even an Aunt Polly or a Widow Douglas) to flee from in *The Great Brain,* there are also no deep male companions, nor is there even a fictional or linguistic wilderness. There is only the lone capitalist entrepreneur—now significantly split off from his more "literary" narrator-brother who seldom has the courage to critique the Great Brain's often-reprehensible actions. The result is very funny— and very depressing at the same time. For the half-voiced criticism, far from setting up a rich ethical ambiguity, instead ends up celebrating the hero-brother and his repeated financial successes. Although Tom may be a great "talker," his talk is not constitutive of mythic transcendence or even temporary imaginative flight, never mind being a challenge to social normativity; it is only self-serving, an ultimately pathetic child's version of Michael J. Fox (Alex Keaton on *Family Ties*) or even, alas, of *Death of a Salesman*'s Willy Loman in his younger years. The racial and cultural multiplicity of American children's lore and ritual has been re-duced to the homogeneity of marketplace clichés and selfish individual-ism. This reduction may produce humor—but my laughter, at least, is hollow if I remember that Tom Fitzgerald is the "new" American-in-training, the appropriate forerunner of the 1980's "Me Generation"— and perhaps beyond.

The Great Brain may self-consciously echo the motifs, characters, and ritual structures of *The Adventures of Tom Sawyer,* but it does not achieve the status of a deliberate liminoid production. It cannot responsibly be considered ritualistic at all—but only a paradoxical and parodic replay-ing of form without substance. Parasitical on both the earlier text and on the contexts of American culture without being genuinely intertex-tual or revisionary, *The Great Brain* subverts Twain's vision and con-structs the child as a proto-capitalist and proto-adult, a small surrogate who simply mirrors his culture's hegemonic individualism and melting-pot racism. Perhaps Zora Neale Hurston was wrong, and there *are* cul-tures too "civilized" to produce—or even reproduce—vital forms of folklore.[24]

I would like to thank Larin McLaughlin, Jan Montefiore, Patricia O'Connor, and Lucy Maddox for reading the manuscript at various stages and offering their wise advice. An earlier version of this essay was delivered at the Children's Literature Association Conference on "Children's Literature and the Lore of Childhood" at the University of New Hampshire in June 1995.

NOTES

1. Judith Fetterley has named this figure "the sanctioned rebel." Discussing the "Bad Boy" books popular immediately after the Civil War, she writes: "The Bad Boy is not really bad, only 'mischievous,' and it is clear that when he grows up he will be a pillar of the community. The implications behind this literature is clear: socially useful adults develop only from real boys who have shown some life as children" (125).

2. There are differences, of course, as well, because the world has "fallen" even farther in the hundred years between the time of the two authors' writing; see my conclusion. Thus the genial satire of Twain's third-person narrator has given way to the irony of J. D.'s first-person, innocent portrayal of his beloved older brother Tom; in Fitzgerald's refusal to allow J. D. an adult, corrective perspective on his brother's exploits, he also cynically eschews moral and social growth for the reader except in the most implicit way. J. D. seems permanently awed and bewildered by the Great Brain's cunning.

3. This structure anticipates Perry Nodelman's generic "no-name story" as the basic pattern of children's literature, with its "home-away-home" structure (53, 147–149, and throughout).

4. Csikszentmihalyi and other scholars do admit that play, for those of any age, may occasionally be serious or even dangerous, as both novels make very clear.

5. Scholars after Turner have also begun to deconstruct his dichotomy between oral and literate cultures. Ronald L. Grimes claims that "ritualizing is the action by which we mediate what is given and what is made, what is involuntary and what is chosen" (62). Unlike Turner, he refuses to see (even liminal) rituals as involuntary. Less certain, Richard Schechner claims that "Even to say it in one word, ritual, is asking for trouble. Ritual has been so variously defined—as concept, praxis, process, ideology, yearning, experience, function—that it means very little because it means too much" (228). He also claims, somewhat contradictorily, that the realm of art (our concern here, after all) occurs when the "creative and/or subversive function of ritual dominates, spills over its usually well-defined boundaries" (258). Ritual is thus, since Turner, both well defined and blurry, both different and the same, wherever it appears.

6. The issue for my argument is not whether Twain was or was not a "racist," although, as Shelly Fisher Fishkin has carefully demonstrated, "Twain intermittently played havoc with his culture's categories of 'blackness' and 'whiteness' in fresh and surprising ways" (80).

7. A failure to understand this temporary occupation of liminal space/ time has led critics to fault Twain for his "capitulation" in the construction of

---

Tom's character. See, for example, Wolff: "Thus Tom's final 'self' as we see it in this novel is a tragic capitulation: he has accommodated himself to the oddities of his environment and given over resistance" (158); and Robinson: "After all, Tom is what we would be inclined—in a righteous mood—to call a hypocrite" (177).

8. "In the life of a community, the process of surrogation does not begin or end but continues as actual or perceived vacancies occur in the network of relations that constitutes the social fabric. . . . Because collective memory works selectively, imaginatively, and often perversely, surrogation rarely if ever succeeds. . . . The intended substitute either cannot fulfill expectations, creating a deficit, or actually exceeds them, creating a surplus" (Roach 2).

9. When she and Tom are lost in McDougal's cave, Tom at least maintains the appearance of active resistance to their deaths while Becky cries in his arms and sinks "into a dreary apathy" (ch. 31, 231). Women (and, by extension, girls) apparently cannot resist revealing secrets, are dependent on men's strength to save them, and are so unfailingly "beautiful and rich, and awfully scared" that even robbers "don't kill" them, according to Tom's detailed instructions to Huck about their planned life of collective crime (ch. 33, 244). Women require special rules and certainly do not engage in mythic "deeds." As Leslie Fiedler and others have pointed out, even the early structure of romantic pursuit fails to engage Tom's imagination beyond the episode in the cave; hence Becky cannot be said to provide even the *occasion* for action or plot. Ann Romines states an alternative case, defending the presence of active ritualizing and creativity in women's activities as well: "In much male literature of the nineteenth century, domestic ritual is presented as a paradigm of triviality and limitation, the oppressively 'sivilized' alternative to the wide expanses of the 'territory.' But several other studies of ritual also stress its liberating capacities and art, especially in the 'liminal' stage" (13); she, of course, cites Victor Turner.

10. Green suggests that the "mock" nature of all Twain's adventure books is the result of "the author's eyes [which] meet the reader's in amused complicity over the heads of the protagonists. The characters' adventures [therefore] make them laughable rather than heroes" (133). As should be clear from my argument here, I see this interpretation of Twain's strategies as reductive and monologic.

11. Greiner, citing and complicating R. W. B. Lewis's ideas, claims that women always disrupt that Lewis calls "space" and Carolyn Heilbrun calls "masculine wilderness": "Worse, although Lewis does not say so, domesticity and women mean time. Time is always the enemy of spaciousness for the bonded male in the American novel because, if possible immortality is associated with space. Certain mortality is equated with time. Women mean expulsion from the garden and the ticking of the clock. If men are to fulfill the destiny of America—and it is clear in the classic American novel that women cannot do so—then they must avoid the reality of time for the illusion of space" (13). If

one applies this paradigm to male children, the form necessarily translates into repeated pranks, evasions of maternal authority, and temporary forays to caves, haunted houses, and islands.

12. And girls are subsumed in that unmarked but nonetheless gendered childhood, yet they also signify the fall/ascent into pedestaled Victorian womanhood.

13. Hollindale might explain this internal contradictoriness as a conflict between Twain's "intended surface ideology" and his "unexamined assumptions" (28, 30), but I can't divide the contradiction so neatly.

14. His stereotypical and racist portrayal of Injun Joe as the exaggerated villain of melodrama presents a more egregious slippage; as "pure" evil, Injun Joe comes dangerously close to an essentialist portrayal of innate viciousness, or as the stereotypically good "Welchman" says to Huck, "'When you talked about notching ears and slitting noses I judged that that was your own embellishment, because white men don't take that sort of revenge. But an Injun! That's a different matter, altogether'" (ch. 30, 214). The speech is allowed to stand without narrative correction. In an earlier reference to Native Americans: when the boys are smoking the "pipe of peace" on the islands, the boys "were glad they had gone into savagery," even though the spectre of their homesickness haunts them (ch. 16, 128). The narrator compounds the boys' and his own ambivalence by concluding the chapter with a gratuitous comment on violent Indian practices: "They were prouder and happier in their new acquirement than they would have been in the scalping and skinning of the Six Nations" (ch. 16, 128).

15. As James P. Leary writes, "Anthropologists and folklorists have long noted the cross-cultural existence primarily among males of a ritually framed communicative mode termed the 'joking relationship,'" which includes verbal taunts, horseplay, and "'ritual insults'" (125).

16. In the past, even a so-called objective account of children's behavior could easily link them to other despised populations: "It must, after all, be borne in mind, that the children here under observation are only at the stage of mental development sometimes ascribed to a savage tribe, whom anthropologists are not at all surprised to find dominated by superstition" (Opies 230).

17. And "Honest Injun" becomes the preferred term for making a promise (ch. 2, 15).

18. For the subversive and entertainment functions of lying as a kind of art form among African Americans, see, for example, Zora Neale Hurston, *Mules and Men,* 9–10, 21–22, 60.

19. The speech, of course, foreshadows Huck's denial of white racist religion when he chooses to help Jim in *The Adventures of Huckleberry Finn* and decides to "'go to hell'" rather than betray his black friend. In a reversal of *Tom Sawyer,* Huck's *words* betray him in a way that his *actions* do not.

20. See Zora Neale Hurston's discussion of hoodoo rituals in *Mules and Men*, 193–252; see also Thaddeus Norris, "Negro Superstitions," 134–143: "In my childhood I firmly believed in witches, and it was with some dread that I went out of doors or through a room when it was dark, and frequently dreamed of them after hearing some of the stories told by the servants on long winter evenings" (142); and A. M. Bacon, "Folk-Lore and Ethnology: Conjuring and Conjure Doctors," 284–292.

21. Ironically, the Opies go on to cite an example that would apply precisely to Tom and Huck's situation here: "Bet you anything. Honest Injun./ Cut my throat if I tell a lie" (149).

22. Anne MacLeod calls this unilateral decision "morally ambiguous" (along with his revelation to, and acceptance by, Aunt Polly that he had lied to her about the "dream"). MacLeod claims that "for the objective reader, ethical questions may dim the glory a little. In spite of their pact of silence and although his testimony endangered Huck as much as himself, Tom made his decision without a word to Huck. Twain observes that "Huck's confidence in the human race was well-nigh obliterated' and drops the matter. A boy's most solemn oath must be understood, apparently, as something less than a full commitment" (74). Yes, I would add, when another person's life is at stake and the "oath" has been sworn between intellectual unequals. I see MacLeod's reading of Twain's text as representative of her focus on issues of "morality" throughout; for example, she concludes in this case: "Gone are the moral lessons that justified the very existence of fiction" (74). Although Twain has frequently been accused of condescending to children in his narrative voice, I am suggesting quite the contrary: that his handling of this instance of complex "situation ethics" reveals both his fundamental respect for children and his commitment to a morality that transcends simple loyalty or following the rules. As this essay will, I hope, make clear, it is Fitzgerald's book that can more properly be said to have eclipsed the "moral lessons" of Twain's nineteenth-century satire.

23. As Joyce W. Warren points out, "Americans took the concept of individualism—in Europe, a negative concept connoting selfishness and social anarchy—and transformed it so that it not only came to represent the positive qualities of freedom and self-determination but actually became synonymous with Americanism and the proudly proclaimed 'American way of life'" (4).

24. Hurston writes in "Go Gator": "No country is so primitive that it has no lore, and no country has yet become so civilized that no folklore is being made within its boundaries" (69).

WORKS CITED

Bacon, A. M. "Folk-Lore and Ethnology: Conjuring and Conjure Doctors." In Jackson, ed., 284–292.

Bordelon, Pamela. *Go Gator and Muddy the Water: Writings by Zora Neals Hurston from the Federal Writers' Project.* Edited with a biographical essay by Bordelon. New York: W. W. Norton, 1999.

Cheska, Alyce Taylor, ed. *Play as Context.* 1979 Proceedings of the Association for the Anthropological Study of Play. West Point, NY: Leisure Press, 1981.

Csikszentmihalyi, Mihaly. "Some Paradoxes in the Definition of Play." In Cheska, ed., 14–26.

Fetterley, Judith. "The Sanctioned Rebel." In Scharnhorst, ed., 119–129.

Fiedler, Leslie. *Love and Death in the American Novel.* Rev. ed. New York: Dell, 1966.

Fishkin, Shelley Fisher. *Was Huck Black? Mark Twain and African-American Voices.* New York: Oxford University Press, 1993.

Fitzgerald, John D. *The Great Brain.* Illus. by Mercer Mayer. New York: Dell Yearling, 1967.

Fox, Steven J. "Theoretical Implications for the Study of Interrelationships between Ritual and Play." In Schwartzman, ed., 51–57.

Green, Martin. *The Great American Adventure.* Boston: Beacon Press, 1984.

Greiner, Donald J. *Women Enter the Wilderness: Male Bonding and the American Novel of the 1980's.* Columbia: University of South Carolina Press, 1991.

Grimes, Ronald L. *Beginnings in Ritual Studies.* Rev. ed. Columbia: University of South Carolina Press, 1995.

Hollindale, Peter. "Ideology and the Children's Book." *Signal* 55 (January 1990); rpt. in Peter Hunt, ed. *Literature for Children: Contemporary Criticism,* 19–40. London: Routledge, 1992.

Hurston, Zora Neale. "Go Gator and Muddy the Water." In Bordelon, ed., 68–88.

———. *Mules and Men.* Preface by Franz Boas; intro. by Robert E. Hemenway. 1935; rpt., Bloomington: Indiana University Press, 1978.

Jackson, Bruce. *The Negro and His Folklore in Nineteenth-Century Periodicals.* Ed. with an intro. by Jackson. Published for the American Folklore Society. Austin: University of Texas Press, 1967.

Leary, James P. "White Ritual Insults." In Schwartzman, ed., 125–139.

MacLeod, Anne Scott. *American Childhood: Essays on Children's Literature of the Nineteenth and Twentieth Centuries.* Athens: University of Georgia Press, 1994.

Nodelman, Perry. *The Pleasures of Children's Literature.* 2nd ed. White Plains, NY: Longman, 1996.

Norris, Thaddeus. "Negro Superstitions." In Jackson, ed., 134–143.

Opie, Iona, and Peter Opie. *The Lore and Language of School Children.* 1959; rpt., Frogmore, St. Albans, UK: Paladin, 1977.

Roach, Joseph. *Cities of the Dead: Circum-Atlantic Performance.* New York: Columbia University Press, 1996.

Robinson, Forrest G. "Social Play and Bad Faith in *The Adventures of Tom Sawyer.*" In Scharnhorst, ed., 160–178.

Romines, Ann. *The Home Plot: Women, Writings and Domestic Ritual*. Amherst: Univ. of Massachusetts Press, 1992.

Scharnhorst, Gary, ed. *Critical Essays on "The Adventures of Tom Sawyer."* New York: G. K. Hall, 1993.

Schechner, Richard. *The Future of Ritual: Writings on Culture and Performance*. London: Routledge, 1993.

Schwartzman, Helen B., ed. *Play and Culture*. 1978 Proceedings of the Association for the Anthropological Study of Play. West Point, NY: Leisure Press, 1980.

Smith, Jeanne Rosier. *Writing Tricksters: Mythic Gambols in American Ethnic Literature*. Berkeley: University of California Press, 1997.

Turner, Victor. "Liminal to Liminoid, in Play, Flow, and Ritual: An Essay in Comparative Symbology." In *From Ritual to Theatre: The Human Seriousness of Play*, 20–60. New York: Performing Arts Journal Publications, 1982.

Twain, Mark. *The Adventures of Tom Sawyer*. Foreword and notes by John C. Gerber. Text established by Paul Baender. 1876; rpt., Berkeley: University of California Press, 1982.

Warren, Joyce W. *The American Narcissus: Individualism and Women in Nineteenth-Century American Fiction*. New Brunswick, NJ: Rutgers University Press, 1984.

Wolff, Cynthia Griffin. "*The Adventures of Tom Sawyer:* A Nightmare Vision of American Boyhood." In Scharnhorst, ed., 148–159.

12

The Many Faces of Childhood

Costume as Ritualized Behavior

JAMIE MCMINN and H. ALAN PICKRELL

For most of our nation's juveniles, the ritual of disguising themselves for special celebrations, such as Halloween, other holidays, masquerades, play situations, or drama productions, is one of the more memorable and exciting events of childhood.[1] Disguisings in childhood (literally, of the physical self) become a rite of passage into the adult world, which usually harbors some reluctance at the very thought of "dressing up." Still, early on, children learn the power of the costume. Generally, when a costume is donned, the wearer tends to emulate characteristics associated with the costume (i.e., a monkey costume will cause the wearer to hoot, make monkey noises, jump about, and scratch himself). The costume itself facilitates this behavior. As children mature into adults, they learn to disguise themselves in more subtle and sophisticated ways. Rather than assuming an actual mask, they adapt social conventions that mask their actual thoughts and intentions. Thus, adults adapt the costume and mask that are to be expected in the work place of the social group with whom they identify.

In defining ritual, Oscar Brockett discusses his understanding of the concept of disguisings. He bases his definition on the universal patterns found by social anthropologist Lévi-Strauss. According to both men, ritual, disguise, and magic are inextricably interrelated (Brockett 4). Ritual is a form of knowledge, a way of understanding the universe and its impact on humanity. Rituals are accompanied by disguise because those spirits that constitute the unseen part of the world are evoked by likenesses of themselves. In this way, ritual becomes magic (5). This entire concept is not so very far removed from the Jungian concept of archetypes.

Rituals have played an important role in the routine affairs of all societies throughout history (Driver 12). Given the centrality of rituals in group dynamics, it is necessary to understand what functions rituals play for the people who enact them. Lukes (289–308) proposed three characteristics of ritual: (1) they are rule-governed; (2) they are symbolic; and (3) they focus attention on specific objects of thought and feeling. Thus, rituals may occur only at certain times of the year, or at particular times in a person's life. Rituals often have their own set of rules that displace a group's normative rules—at least temporarily (Driver 164), and they may involve behaviors that reflect the history or significance of the occasion (e.g., dramatic productions, feasts, ceremonies). Rituals often have associated with them such objects as masks, symbolic clothing, and food. Although these objects may be ordinary in the everyday life of a group, they take on special significance in the context of ritual. Those who possess these objects during the ritual also take on special significance.

One of the most important functions of rituals is to communicate information. They provide opportunities to share knowledge between older and newer group members, knowledge that may be critical for such processes as entry into and status change within a group (Levine & Moreland 429). More importantly, rituals communicate information related to survival (Grimes 37) and to significant structural and procedural changes in the group. Rituals are also important socialization agents that proliferate the group's norms, values, and beliefs (Furth & Kane 149–173, Campbell 50–131). Information about relationships (e.g., humanity, group-group, old-new) is similarly expressed through the content of rituals (Mead 89). Thus, rituals can help people in one group to identify more strongly with fellow members or to distinguish themselves from individuals in another group. For example, all the members of a gang or club may wear a particular uniform to identify themselves as belonging to the same group, and their dress will be distinct from that used by other gangs or clubs. In a sense, ritualized behavior can lead to greater cohesiveness and unity among members of a group (Driver 9) by confirming their roles and mitigating intragroup conflict (Gersick & Hackham 71) and by reminding them of their connection to members or events in the group's past (Mead 101).

Carl Jung, like his mentor Sigmund Freud, became interested in the concept of myth as truth. In this vein, he went so far as to propose a collective unconscious, common to all human beings (Jung, "Psychological" 310). This portion of the unconscious is an amalgamation of experiences and predispositions that have occurred in all cultures across all time (Jung, "Instinct" 133–134). Even though specific experiences may be different for different people (which Jung captured in his writings on the personal unconscious), we are nevertheless all endowed with the same collective unconscious (Jung, "Structure" 158).

Jung theorized that the collective unconscious rests at the deepest level of the human psyche, and that it was a repository of "primordial images," or archetypes. Because archetypes are a part of our collective unconscious, they are transmitted from generation to generation through myths, literature, art, dreams, and so on. The evolutionary history of humankind is reflected in these images (Jung, "Significance" 112). According to Jung, these images have tremendous influence on human behavior, and the same archetypes often appear in different and otherwise unrelated cultures. Jung elaborated on many archetypes, only three of which are discussed here: the persona, the shadow, and the anima or animus. Not surprisingly, these are among those primordial images that Jung believed had the most profound and frequently occurring impact on the human psyche (Jung, "Shadow" 8).

The persona is most easily conceptualized as the character that we present to others, or the symbolic masks we wear. Jung described the persona as a "false-self," a creation that emerges from the interaction between an individual and his or her society (Jung, "Persona" 157). As Mattoon notes, "The persona reveals little of what a person is; it is the public face, determined by what one perceives to be acceptable to other people" (28). The persona helps us to relate to other people, allowing us to manage the impressions we make on them. At the same time, the persona enables us to conceal our shadow selves from those with whom we interact (28). We have a potentially infinite number of persona images available to us, but most people probably only incorporate a small number of them into the psyche. For example, a woman may adopt the personae of parent, friend, worker, and sports enthusiast. While the persona rests in the collective unconscious—and we all have the predisposition to experience it—the contents of the persona will vary across individuals. The persona archetype is fully apparent in disguise. Just as roles allow us to display a variety of behaviors, masks enable us to change our faces, to hide our true identity from those around us. Costumes transform us into something we are not—at least not consciously.

Over time, the ego begins to identify with a persona, which can be problematic if an individual is dissatisfied with the persona's contents (Mattoon 29). Likewise, costumes transform the wearer both physically and symbolically (Hopcke 199; Campbell 21). Turner suggests that masking endows an individual with the power of the figure symbolized (172). A Superman costume not only changes the appearance of a young boy, for instance, but it also suggests that he possesses such abstract qualities as truth and justice.[2] Indeed, we create a false self through disguising, and as the ego continues to identify with this self, the persona can easily become a central part of our daily lives.

Disguises born of play encourage a transformation of the literal disguise into the acceptable "social" disguise in which all human behavior becomes a "deception" of sorts. Since this study uses various series books as demonstrations of the concept of disguising, Betsy Caprio's Jungian analysis of fictional Nancy Drew is a starting point for consideration. She notes "That a laugh or a smile is always on Nancy's face, a mask behind which the person who represses and denies reality can hide. Whatever the situation" (59). All children learn this deceptive disguise in denying fright, pain, and hurt, and they project, instead, a nonchalant, socially acceptable poise and insouciance. Nancy's persona is that of a very mature girl who is extraordinarily capable. On the surface, hers is a well-integrated personality that demonstrates intelligence, resourcefulness, control, and single-mindedness. She is a natural leader who can master anything to which she applies her concentration. On the whole, hers is a very positive and strong persona, and she is capable of rationalizing any action if she believes the outcome will be in society's best interests. This is true of most series heroes.

The shadow archetype is closely related to the Freudian notion of id. It is a storehouse of base, uncivilized instincts (Jung, "Shadow" 8). For most people, the shadow is the manifestation of all that makes them uneasy: inadequacy, evil, uncontrollable instincts, and other undesirable traits (Robertson 186). But Jung also suggested that the shadow is the source of human creativity. Without the shadow, the psyche would become lifeless. Thus, the shadow must be expressed in some fashion to maintain optimal psychological health. Disguise is one common way to express the shadow archetype and to integrate its contents into the psyche. The reader might consider the disguise rituals of Halloween, for example, to find myriad shadow-related costumes such as monsters, ghouls, and witches.[3] In general, the shadow figure is always of the same sex as the individual expressing it (Jung, "Shadow" 10). As the examples from juvenile series reflect, children often express their shadow side by dressing as same-sex monsters: girls dress as witches, while boys dress as vampires.

Certainly these Jungian constructs can be illustrated and reinforced from examples of various classic juvenile series books that were designed to present recognizable experiences to an audience of flesh and blood youngsters. Of course, disguise figures heavily in many of these books since much of childhood play centers of role-playing and disguising. These series books were and are immensely popular with young people from the beginning of the twentieth century through the present day. Included, however, are examples drawn from that body of juvenile literature considered to be "classics" by those who study that genre. These books were written for specific age groups of children: the Bobbsey Twins books were for children from six to eight years of age, and the more "mysterious" books were written for children in the eight- to twelve-year-old age group, although there were many cross-overs, and in some cases, these series were read through adulthood. These books, although deplored and ostracized by teachers and librarians, were loved and admired by children. Four of these series, the Bobbsey Twins, the Hardy Boys, Nancy Drew, and the Oz books, have passed into our culture as icons and megamyths. References are made to these books in other works of literature, in films, on TV, in newspapers, in magazines, in cartoons, in speeches, and in passing conversation; these four series permeate our national and social consciousness.

As a literary convention, disguise was a part of the popular mystery fiction that prefigured juvenile mysteries. Dime novels, pulps, and Conan Doyle's Sherlock Holmes presented both detectives and arch criminals as masters of disguise. The Jungian critic might well argue that the criminal and detective are inverse and transferable sides of the same individual: in disguise the criminal might seem kindly and well disposed toward humanity, whereas the detective might mask himself as a nemesis to society or to individual beings. Jung would construe this dichotomy as the struggle between the shadow and the persona. If the shadow is the stronger, then chaos is the result. If, however, the persona assumes control, then the shadow is neutralized and order is restored. In the case of some of the dime novels (Frank Merriwell, for instance), the novels were later reprinted as juvenile series books, so it is of small wonder that characteristics of the one merged into the other. There can be no doubt of the tremendous popularity and impact of these juvenile series books. Caroline Stewart Dyer and Nancy Tillman Romanov's collection of essays, papers, and remembrances from the first Nancy Drew conference demonstrates the popularity of the series by Carolyn Keene. Men and women alike reminisced about the influence that the character had on their lives. Still in publication even today, the Nancy Drew series has reached around 150 titles. The same is true of her masculine counterparts, the Hardy Boys. In 1986, records indicated that eighty million Nancy Drew books had been sold since their inception in 1930 (Billman 100). Sales of the Hardy Boys books, which first appeared in 1927, were behind by approximately ten million (79). The Bobbsey Twins books, first of the Stratemeyer Syndicate series, number in the seventies, and the twins are still making their way merrily to the seashore and Blueberry Island. And before the Oz books were discontinued, the dust jackets carried a boast from the publisher that the Oz books were the most popular children's books ever.

Why were these books so universally embraced by girls and boys? (Incidentally, boys did read the girls' books and vice-versa.) Of course, there were the plot elements of suspense and excitement, but more central was the appeal of character. The heroes of these books are primarily teenagers, young enough for the readers of the books to identify with. These heroes are always extremely independent and seem to act with adult-like assurance and ingenuity, and although only teenagers, they play at being adults by solving mysteries on an amateur basis, often in disguise. Also, by the end of every mystery, they manage to subjugate the shadow portions of themselves to reaffirm the healthy, whole individuals that readers have grown to know and love.

Some specific examples of disguise as play occur in many juvenile mystery series. These same examples also serve as an illustration of the release of the shadow side (or "other") by the individual through the use of disguise. In *The Hidden Harbor Mystery* by Franklin Dixon (a pseudonym of the Edward Stratemeyer Syndicate), Frank Hardy and his brother Joe are the sons of famous detective Fenton Hardy. Frank and Joe enjoy solving cases that come their way by accident or default. They are only amateur sleuths, and as such, solving of mysteries is their hobby and "play." Fenton, the boy's father, is an expert at disguise and has given his sons some instruction in the art. In the books, the boys frequently resort to some kind of disguise. Frank, the older brother, is described as a serious, thoughtful, somewhat cautious young man, in juxtaposition to his impulsive, irrepressible younger brother, Joe. Yet in *The Hidden Harbor Mystery*, Frank Hardy, in disguise, is found doing things that Frank Hardy, undisguised, would never consider doing. In the guise and dress of an elderly Jewish second-hand merchandise dealer, Frank gains access to a private home by misrepresenting himself. Once there, he steals private papers containing secrets pertaining to a prominent family. Admittedly, he does this in order to solve a mystery that threatens this family, but children are taught that theft is wrong in any circumstances. Frank, however, becomes a thief to catch a thief. His shadow side is neutralized when the disguise is discarded, and Frank rather regrets his actions. With the overthrow of "the other," Frank becomes the hero that the audience expects him to be.

The Hardy Boys' female counterpart is Nancy Drew. As with Frank and Joe, her zeal to solve mysteries, protect the innocent, and penalize wrongdoers often unleashes her shadow side, and she is frequently to be found in disguise. Daughter of well-known attorney Carson Drew, Nancy frequently finds herself involved with her father's cases. In *The Password to Larkspur Lane*, Nancy disguises herself as an elderly woman and gives false information in order to gain entrance to a nursing home where she suspects an old family friend is secluded against her will. Lying and misrepresentation are sides of the shadow self, but when Nancy saves the elderly friend from victimization, the "other" is vanquished and Nancy's true persona reasserts itself.

The Bobbsey Twins books, written by the fictional Laura Lee Hope for the Stratemeyer Syndicate, concern the Bobbsey family, which, in addition to parents and employees, contains two sets of twins. Bert and Nan are the older twins, and Freddie and Flossie are the younger. Freddie wants to be a fireman when he grows up, and his favorite toys are a red fireman's hat and a toy engine that can pump water through its hoses. When Freddie dons his fireman's hat, he becomes "Mr. Fireman" and is capable of working all kinds of mischief with the water from the fire truck hoses. In *The Bobbsey Twins at Home*, Freddy manages to squirt water all over Dinah, the cook, as she attempts to remove a pot of burning candy from the range. On removing his hat and putting away his toy engine, he becomes repentant and sorry for the havoc he has created (135–136). Of course, the persona is forgiven for the chaos created by the shadow. All juvenile series books teach this lesson: the persona is responsible for the actions of the shadow.

A further instance of play as shadow can be found in two of the popular series written by Leo Edwards (a pseudonym of Edward Edson Lee). The Poppy Ott and the Jerry Todd series, written in the 1920s and 1930s, show realistic play among boys. The characters and their activities were based on real boys known by the author. In many of the books, an element of disguise is present as a part of the natural play of boyhood. In these books, boys pretend to be cave men, pirates, or Indians and are dressed appropriately. They are threatened by a rival gang dressed as and pretending to be cannibals, Indians, or other pirates. Disguise releases the boys from the inhibitions imposed upon them by parents, churches, teachers, and authority figures. These boys frequently create problems and destruction while in disguise; however, once the disguise is removed, the boys are able to surmount whatever trouble they have made under the influence of shadow.

According to the theories of Brockett and Lévi-Strauss, the impulse toward disguise has existed within the human psyche from the beginnings of time. Within modern times, that impulse exists only at certain legally and socially approved times of the year, consistent with Lukes's initial characteristic of ritual (298–308). Masquerade balls might be held at any time of the year, but they seem to be associated with holidays. Most seem to fall on New Year's Eve or in the Lenten season . . . particularly Fat Tuesday, or Mardi Gras. In New Orleans, few inhibitions dissuade the masked revelers from enjoying themselves to the utmost, and these revelers are usually adults who use disguise as a way to behave in ways that are diametrically opposed to normally accepted behavior.

Examples of adult misbehavior in disguise can be found in juvenile series books as well. In fact, most of the villains and criminals in juvenile series books are adults who are frequently disguised as something other than what they actually are. For example, in *Jerry Todd and the Bob-Tailed Elephant,* Jerry and his pal, Henny, must pass the local haunted house on their way to the civic Halloween party held in the town square. They are waylaid by the headless ghost that haunts the place. The boys are badly frightened until the ghost falls into a well and is revealed to be

Henny's father in disguise. The father, estranged from Henny's mother, has pretended to be a ghost in order to keep folk away from the old house that has been his refuge during the separation. With the removal of the disguise, Henny's mother and father are reconciled, and the shadow father is removed when the real persona is reasserted.

The psychological literature is not naive about this tendency toward misbehavior while one is disguised. As noted earlier, costumes serve a protective function by concealing the identity of the person beneath (Hopcke 193). Consequently, we often feel less inhibited to participate in activities that we would avoid if unmasked. Research has borne out a relationship between anonymity and behavioral disinhibition or misbehavior. Miller and Rowald (422; see also Diener, Fraser, Beaman, & Kelem 181), for example, found that masked children were significantly more likely than unmasked children to disobey an adult directive, by taking more than a specified amount of Halloween candy from a bowl. Presumably, such deviant behavior is connected to the masked children's anonymity. The ritual of Halloween and disguise divert children's attention away from themselves. This tendency toward disobedience decreased as the children's identities were made salient, thus increasing their sense of personal responsibility and self-awareness (see also Beaman, Klentz, Diener, & Svanum 1845). Other studies (e.g., Miller, Jasper, & Hill 196) have found that college students are more likely to consume alcohol while wearing Halloween costumes than those who are not. And a discussion of disguise and disinhibition would be incomplete without mention of the Ku Klux Klan and thieves who often wear hoods or masks when engaging in antisocial behaviors. It would seem, then, that the expectations for misbehavior associated with disguise rituals are developed early in childhood and persist even in adulthood.

These studies are further demonstrated in two other Nancy Drew mysteries. In *The Clue of the Velvet Mask* and *The Haunted Showboat*, teen detective Drew is in full disguise: first, for a masquerade and next for Mardi Gras. In each instance, Nancy, in disguise, performs actions that Nancy, undisguised, would feel some pangs of conscience about doing. She eavesdrops, spies, and accepts confidences meant for another. In her everyday pursuits of justice and tracking down criminals, Nancy frequently performs such actions, but in disguise, she is even more blatant. Still, Nancy regards herself as an upright and moral individual.

Likewise, teen detective Kay Tracy, hero of her own series by the pseudonymous Frances Judd, experiences a similar incident in *The Red*

Scarf Mystery. Kay, like Nancy Drew, considers herself to be the soul of honor and integrity, and decides the interception is justified, since that incident allows her to solve the mystery.

Obviously, the holiday most associated with disguise is Halloween. Many series books do not deal with this holiday, since it was associated with pranks and misdeeds. Series books were supposedly presenting heroes and situations for young people to model themselves upon. In fact, the character of Jerry Todd explains his community's attitude toward Halloween in *The Bob-Tailed Elephant:*

> In Dad's day the boys used to cut up some pretty wild capers on Halloween. Lumber wagons were hung in trees. And small buildings were tipped over. Down our way, though, that kind of fun is a thing of the past. What we do, instead of wrecking stuff, is to dress up in all kinds of ridiculous costumes. A sort of street carnival. Even the old folks turn out with their horns and noisemakers. Everybody has fun, with the horn tooting and the mayor dressed up in the most ridiculous costume of all. Starting at dusk, the carnival frequently lasts until midnight. (20)

In this example, the community entices the young people into one place, and the shadow is overcome. In many communities across the United States, efforts are made to overcome negative energies of the holiday. In some places, no one above the age of twelve may wear disguises on that night. In other communities, there is a curfew, after which no disguises may be worn. Often community parties are held by churches, civic groups, and businesses (such as indoor malls). In so doing, the disruptive forces of the shadow are held in check until the disguises are discarded and harmony is restored.

A further example of this reconciliation theory can be found in *The Happy Hollisters and the Mystery of the Golden Witch,* a book about the celebration of Halloween. The villain of the piece, Mr. Fred Ragay, comes to the Hollisters' party disguised as a tiger. The tiger is usually regarded as a cunning and vicious animal, and Mr. Ragay is as cunning and as vicious as the animal he represents. Still, when unmasked, he is abjectly ashamed of himself and his previous actions. His shadow neutralized, Mr. Ragay becomes apologetic and contrite and regains his true identity. Some further excursions of series books into the Halloween holiday are examined later as illustrative of the Jungian concepts of anima/animus.

The literary examples above have highlighted how the shadow self can manifest itself in immoral behaviors (e.g., stealing) but at the same time fuel creativity (e.g., solving a mystery). Costumes do not, however, always reflect the shadow. Jung recognized that biological and psychological sexuality are continuous variables, rather than dichotomous ones (Jung, "Syzygy" 14). Therefore, he conceived of the female psyche as having a masculine component (i.e., the animus), and the male psyche as having a feminine component (i.e., the anima). An individual's anima/animus was shaped not only by the contents of the collective unconscious, but also by members of the other sex and his or her larger society (Mattoon 84–95). The expression of the animus was achieved when men exercised the emotional components of their psyche; in contrast, the anima was expressed as the woman employed reason and analysis (Jung, "Syzygy" 14–15). Jung argued that the healthy individual is one who can integrate both masculine and feminine components of the psyche. Integration of the contrasexual archetype is not a simple task, however. The anima/animus rests at a lower level of the unconscious than the shadow archetype; consequently integrating the anima/animus into the psyche can require many years, perhaps lasting throughout one's entire life (Robertson 199–204). Because this integration usually occurs in adulthood and the integration is necessary for a whole psyche, children have not yet formed a complete Self.

Although Ogletree, Denton, and Williams were not directly testing the Jungian constructs of anima/animus, their findings on costume preferences among children are enlightening (636). The researchers found that a sample of young children was more likely to prefer traditional gender appropriate, or stereotypic, costumes than an older sample. That is, younger boys preferred masculine costumes, and younger girls preferred feminine costumes. These findings are consistent with Serbin and Sprafkin's assertion that as children form schema about what it means to be male or female, they tend to prefer gender appropriate behavior (1188). Nevertheless, other-sex costumes are common, and they often arouse surprise and amusement. These costumes are expressions of the masculine and feminine within us all, and, arguably, are one way to synthesize the archetypes.

Just as younger children choose disguises to reinforce themselves and their identities, as shown in the Ogletree, Denton, and Williams study, series book characters sometimes choose to do the same thing, choosing costumes to echo their personas. In fact, children's series books go so far as to suggest gender appropriate costumes in most cases. The majority of female characters are garbed in costumes that represent ideals of femininity and beauty, while male characters choose the appropriate masculine costumes to accentuate manly qualities. In *Puzzle in Purple*, Connie Blair decides to attend the Fairy Tale Ball given by her art school as the Snow Queen. This is an appropriate image for the cool, virginal Connie, who is romanced by many but withholds her heart from everyone. Connie, new to the art school and a large, urban environment, could be seen as "younger," naive, and immature. However, it would be possible to argue that there is a shadow present, since Connie's identical twin, Kit, attends the ball also, in a costume identical to Connie's. Still, Connie's literal shadow side (Kit) is banished when Kit returns home the very next day. In this instance, however, the costume is a reinforcer to the persona of both Connie and Kit.

A further example of costume as reinforcer of persona is *The Mardi Gras Mystery*. Nancy Drew's friend, Bess, appears garbed as a southern belle, a costume that reinforces Bess's excessive femininity. Bess is also the least assertive of the trio of girl friends and definitely the most immature, so her choice is in keeping with the findings of the Ogletree study. Nancy and her boyfriend, Ned, are disguised as Marie Antoinette and Louis XVI. The association is obvious: Nancy is the queen of detectives, and Ned, her chosen consort, is king by association. His costume as an ineffectual king reflects his ineffectual role in the mysteries. Since Ned didn't care to choose his costume for himself, Nancy chose it for him and, in doing so, revealed her concepts of both herself and her escort. Nancy's costume could be seen as a reinforcer of her shadow side, because, in that costume, she is as heedless and reckless of danger as was that unhappy queen whose behavior and attitudes helped to touch off the French Revolution.

In yet another Mardi Gras setting, *The Haunted Showboat*, Nancy and her girlfriends, Bess and George, are disguised as winged fairies. These disguises emphasize a Sleeping Beauty aspect to the story, since the girls are the means of bringing their friend, Donna Mae (disguised as a princess), safely through all her tribulations. Nancy, Bess, and George are, in effect, the Fairy Godmothers, who protect and ultimately are responsible for saving the princess.

Within the realms of juvenile series books, there are myriads of examples of the integration of the masculine and the feminine. One of the more surprising literary examples is found in L. Frank Baum's *The Land of Oz*. The protagonist, Tip, is a young boy whose guardian, Mombi, is a wicked witch. In reality, Tip's true identity is that of Princess Ozma of Oz. While she was still an infant, an enchantment changed the baby girl into a baby boy, in order to conceal the identity of the rightful ruler of Oz. With the breaking of the enchantment, the crone (or shadow) Mombi is overcome by the maiden (Ozma). Although Tip protests that he does not want to become a girl prior to the overcoming of the enchantment, once the spell is broken, Ozma is the essence of femininity, even though she retains the masculine residue of a lively intellect, a fierce dedication to justice, and a predilection for adventures. In Ozma, the masculine and feminine unite into a perfect synthesis.

However, Jack Snow (who continues the Oz series with three books) in a little-known short story, "A Murder in Oz," conceived the idea that when Ozma is found dead, the murderer is her animus, Tip. Tired of being repressed, Tip has re-emerged, but since there was only one life between him and Ozma, Tip took it in order to exist. This story is a prime illustration of the Jungian concept that anima and animus must be integrated to produce a well-balanced persona.

Two further series examples illustrate the impact of the Ogletree study, as well as Jung's theory of masculine/feminine. In the final volume of the Dana Girls' series, *The Witch's Omen*, Jean and Louise Dana's Halloween party is crashed by two uninvited guests. Although they are totally disguised from head to foot, the girls feel that the mysterious witch and scarecrow seem to be men. The witch utters a prophetic warning that propels the Dana Girls into an involved and convoluted enigma concerning animal thefts, multiple disguises, and smuggling. Jung discussed three aspects of femininity: the maiden, the matron, and the crone. In this case, the male, disguised as a hag in order to frighten and project malevolence, is neutralized and returned at last to masculinity by the two maidens, whose femininity is confirmed by their choice of unabashedly feminine Halloween costumes.

And in another series with a Halloween party, most of Jung's theories are brought together and confirmed. In the second volume of the Judy Bolton series, Judy gives a Halloween party that is intended to reconcile the disparate social strata in the small town where she resides. Social snob Lorraine Lee decides to give a spite party to rival Judy's. She wants to prove to Judy that the social upper crust of the town are not interested in associating with the "dregs." In spite of Judy's expectations of a social fiasco, her party is well attended. Judy herself is dressed as a witch. Judy's friend Peter, destined to become her husband in future volumes, is dressed as a woman. Judy, as the crone, works her magic on the group, and Peter's costume demonstrates that he is secure enough in his masculinity to appear in public in "drag." In later volumes, we learn that Peter, who holds the extremely masculine position of special agent for the F.B.I., is also capable of being tender and sentimental. He is "in touch with his feminine side."

Eventually, the unmasking occurs, and we learn that Judy's party has fulfilled its purpose. A group of maskers, previously unidentified, reveal themselves to be Lorraine and her clique of friends. Judy's goal of uniting separate social strata is accomplished, and when the shadow masks are removed, the true Judy and the true Lorraine are reconciled. Margaret Sutton, author of the Judy Bolton series, based her plots and characters on actual happenings and people of her youth, and consequently, the removal of the shadow and the reconciliation are truthful and factual: both literary and literal reinforcements of Jung's postulations and study findings.

As these examples from juvenile series demonstrate, unmasking is associated with reconciliation: once the mask is removed, the individual must make amends for misbehavior that he or she enacted while disguised. As a result, the unmasked individual learns even more about his or her culture, gaining knowledge about acceptable behavior and responsibility. That individual stands to become a more "useful" member of the group who will further promulgate the content of ritual. And yet, for children, there is no doubt that the ritual of disguise is one of the more magical, memorable, and liberating experiences involved in growing up. Disguising encourages their imaginations and helps them to assimilate wonder and practicality.

NOTES

1. This statement should be followed by a brief disclaimer, for although this essay deals with the concept of disguising, drama production is a very specialized area of concern that will be omitted from consideration. Instead, the essay concentrates its analysis on the issues of disguising as an area of creative play and holiday observance in the United States. By following the precepts of psychologist Carl Jung, exploring various psychological studies, and using classic juvenile series book as examples, a kind of personal synthesis can be traced as a direct result from the ritual of disguising.

2. Interestingly, research by Miller, Jasper, and Hill suggests that in adults, women are less likely than men to believe that they have been "transformed" by their costumes (807–813).

3. Robertson (186) points out that variations of these beings are also common representations of the shadow in dreams.

WORKS CITED

Allen, Betsey. *Puzzle in Purple.* New York: Grosset & Dunlap, 1948.

Baum, L. Frank. *The Land of Oz.* Chicago: Reilly & Lee, 1903.

Beaman, Arthur L., Bonnel Klentz, Ed Diener, and Soren Svanum. "Self-Awareness and Transgression in Children: Two Field Studies." *Journal of Personality and Social Psychology* 37 (1979): 1835–1846.

Billman, Carol. *The Secret of the Stratemeyer Syndicate: Nancy Drew, the Hardy Boys, and the Million Dollar Fiction Factory.* New York: Ungar, 1986.

Brockett, Oscar. *History of the Theatre.* Boston: Allyn & Bacon, 1977.

Campbell, Joseph. *The Masks of God: Primitive Mythology.* New York: Viking Press, 1959.

Caprio, Betsey. *Girl Sleuth on a Couch: The Mystery of Nancy Drew.* Trabucco Canyon, CA: Source Books, 1992.

Diener, Edward, Scott C. Fraser, Arthur L. Beaman, and Roger T. Kelem. "Effects of Deindividuation Variable on Stealing among Halloween Trick-or-Treaters." *Journal of Personality and Social Psychology* 33 (1976): 178–183.

Dixon, Franklin. *The Hidden Harbor Mystery.* New York: Grosset & Dunlap, 1935.

Driver, Tom F. *Liberating Rights: Understanding the Transformative Power of Ritual.* Boulder, CO: Westview Press, 1998.

Dyer, Caroline Stewart, and Nancy Tillman Romalov. *Rediscovering Nancy Drew.* Iowa City: University of Iowa Press, 1995.

Furth, Hans G., and Steven R. Kane. "Children Constructing Society: A New Perspective on Children at Play." In *Childhood Social Development: Contemporary Perspectives,* ed. Harry McGurk. Hove, UK: Lawrence Erlbaum (1992): 149–173.

Gersick, Connie J. G., and J. Richard Hackman. "Habitual Routines in Task-Performing Groups." *Organizational Behavior and Human Decision Processes* 47 (1990): 65–97.

Grimes, Ronald L. *Beginnings in Ritual Studies.* Lanham, MD: University Press of America, 1990.

Hopcke, Robert H. *Persona and Ritual: The Mask as Archetypal Symbol of Transformation.* Boston, MA: Shambala, 1995.

Judd, Frances. *The Secret of the Red Scarf.* New York: Books,, 1941.

Jung, Carl G. "Instinct and the Unconscious." In *The Collected Works of C. G. Jung,* ed. Herbert Read, Michael Fordham, Gerhard Adler, and William McGuire. Vol. 8, 2nd ed., *The Structure and Dynamics of the Psyche,* 129–138. Princeton, NJ: Princeton Univ. Press, 1969.

———. "The Persona as a Segment of the Collective Psyche." In *The Collected Works of C. G. Jung*, ed. Herbert Read, Michael Forham, Gerhard Adler, and William McGuire. Vol. 7, 2nd ed., *Two Essays on Analytical Psychology*, 156–162. Princeton, NJ: Princeton Univ. Press, 1969.

———. "The Psychological Foundation of Belief in Spirits." In *The Collected Works of C. G. Jung*, ed. Herbert Read, Michael Fordham, Gerhard Adler, and William McGuire. Vol. 8, 2nd ed., *The Structure and Dynamics of the Psyche*, 301–318. Princeton, NJ: Princeton Univ. Press, 1969.

———. "The Shadow." In *The Collected Works of C. G. Jung*, ed. Herbert Read, Michael Fordham, Gerhard Adler, and William McGuire. Vol. 9, part 2, 2nd ed., *Aion*, 8–10. Princeton, NJ: Princeton Univ. Press, 1968.

———. "The Significance of Constitution and Heredity in Psychology." In *The Collected Works of C. G. Jung*, ed. Herbert Read, Michael Fordham, Gerhard Adler, and William McGuire. Vol. 8, 2nd ed., *The Structure and Dynamics of the Psyche*, 107–113. Princeton, NJ: Princeton Univ. Press, 1969.

———. "The Structure of the Psyche." In *The Collected Works of C. G. Jung*, ed. Herbert Read, Michael Fordham, Gerhard Adler, and William McGuire. Vol. 8, 2nd ed., *The Structure and Dynamics of the Psyche*, 139–158. Princeton, NJ: Princeton Univ. Press, 1969.

———. "The Syzygy: Anima and Animus." In *The Collected Works of C. G. Jung*, ed. Herbert Read, Michael Fordham, Gerhard Adler, and William McGuire. Vol. 9, part 2, 2nd ed., *Aion*, 11–22. Princeton, NJ: Princeton Univ. Press, 1968.

Keene, Carolyn. *The Clue of the Velvet Mask*. New York: Grosset & Dunlap, 1959.

———. *The Haunted Showboat*. New York: Grosset & Dunlap, 1957.

———. *The Mardi Gras Mystery*. New York: Minstrel Books, 1988.

———. *The Witch's Omen*. New York: Grosset & Dunlap, 1979.

Levine, John M., and Richard L. Mooreland. "Small Groups." In *The Handbook of Social Psychology*, ed. Daniel Gilbert, Susan Fiske, and George Lindzey. 4th ed., 415–469. Boston, MA: McGraw-Hill, 1998.

Lukes, Steven. "Political Ritual and Social Integration." *Sociology* 9 (1975): 289–308.

Mattoon, Mary Ann. *Jungian Psychology in Perspective*. New York: Free Press, 1981.

Mead, Margaret. "Ritual and Social Crisis." In *The Roots of Ritual*, ed. James D. Shaughnessy, 87–101. Grand Rapids, MI: William B. Eerdmans.

Miller, Franklin G., and Kathleen L. Rowald. "Halloween Masks and Deindividuation." *Psychological Reports* 44 (1979): 422.

Miller, Kimberly A., Cynthia R. Jasper, and Donald R. Hill. "Costume and the Perception of Identity Role." *Perceptual Motor Skills* 72 (1991): 807–813.

———. "Dressing in Costume and the Use of Alcohol, Marijuana, and Other Drugs by College Students." *Adolescence* 28 (1993): 189–198.

Ogletree, Shirley Matile, Larry Denton, and Sue Winkle Williams. "Age and Gender Differences in Children's Halloween Costumes." *Journal of Psychology* 127 (1993): 633–637.

Robertson, Robin. *Jungian Archetypes: Jung, Godel, and the History of Archetypes.* York Beach, ME: Nicholas-Hays, 1995.

Serbin, Lisa A., and Carol Sprafkin. "The Salience of Gender and the Process of Sex Typing in Three- to Seven-Year-Old Children." *Child Development* 57 (1986): 1188–1199.

Snow, Jack. *Spectral Snow.* Bloomfield, NJ: Hungry Tiger Press, 1996.

Sutton, Margaret. *The Haunted Attic.* New York: Grosset & Dunlap, 1932.

Turner, Victor. *The Ritual Process: Structure and Anti-Structure.* Ithaca, NY: Cornell University Press, 1969.

West, Jerry. *The Happy Hollisters and the Mystery of the Golden Witch.* Garden City, NJ: Doubleday, 1996.

PART 7

ELECTRONIC MEDIA

In modern society, children consume electronic mass media in a ritualized way. Beginning in the early decades of the twentieth century, children embraced the movies, typically attending once a week and developing a fondness for particular genres and stars whose behavior they tried to emulate. By the time of the Depression, American children had another obsession, radio, and religiously listened each night to shows such as *Little Orphan Annie* and *The Lone Ranger*, drawn in by their engaging characters and cliff-hanging endings. In the 1950s, television presented another choice in the media menu as advertisers sought to attract a youth audience for a myriad of products. From children's variety shows to Saturday morning cartoons to prime-time sitcoms, children watched, and the shows provided common experiences for them to discuss with their friends. Children began to see the world through the lens of the television set, often adopting its value system, characterized by consumerism, violence, and stereotypical portrayals. Today videocassette recorders, DVD players, video games, the Internet, and computer games provide entertainment opportunities to children, socializing them and transforming traditional modes of play. Increasingly, the mass media play a major role in children's lifestyle patterns.

The two essays that appear here address children's use of mass media and the effects that they have. Ray Merlock shows in "Growing Up with Westerns" how a generation of boys became avid consumers of Western movies and television shows, their ritualized viewing contributing to their later social and political agendas. Jo Ann Oravec, in "From Gigapets to Internet: Childhood Technology Rituals as Commodities," discusses more recent trends: how children's lives, routines, and concept of play have been transformed by computer technologies. The functions

233

previously provided by family and friends are overwhelmingly being usurped by media, with both positive and negative consequences. Both articles emphasize the ways in which media structure children's lives, providing a meaning and rhythm that are indicative of traditional rituals.

13

Growing Up with Westerns

RAY MERLOCK

This exchange occurs in the 1980 film *Bronco Billy:*

ANTOINETTE LILY (Sondra Locke): "You're living in a dream world. There are no more cowboys and Indians. That's in the past."

BRONCO BILLY (Clint Eastwood): "Miss Lily" *(train whistle in background),* "I was raised in a one-room tenement in New Jersey. As a kid, I never even saw a cowboy much less the wide open spaces—except when I could scrounge up a quarter for the picture show. I was a shoe salesman until I was thirty-one years old. Deep down in my heart I always wanted to be a cowboy. One day I laid down my shoehorn and swore I'd never live in the city again. You only live once. You got to give it your best shot."

Many people who grew up in the first half of the twentieth century (sometime between 1916 and the 1950s) could relate to or identify with Bronco Billy's memories—except, instead of a quarter for the picture show, the price of admission was perhaps merely a dime or a nickel. The thrill kids felt at seeing cowboys and Indians on the screen certainly did not end in the early 1950s when numerous neighborhood movie theaters closed down. Cowboy heroes and the wide open spaces were now on television, and the childhood practices of watching Westerns, outfitting

235

one's self with cowhand garb (including guns and holsters), playing cowboys (and cowgirls), and accumulating movie and TV cowboy merchandise continued from the 1920s (with William S. Hart and Tom Mix) until the 1970s (with Matt Dillon, Ben Cartwright and his sons, and a few straggler television Western heroes); most American childhoods were filled with ritualistic weekly experiences involving screen Westerns. For some the experiences and the personalities, aesthetics, and values associated with Westerns are distant, perhaps nearly extinct, memories. For others, the memories are immediate and robust—that long-ago stomping and cheering during a climatic rescue, chase, or ride off into the sunset. Maybe there is still a bit of nostalgic wistfulness recalling the Saturday afternoon crowds at the Bijou or the Majestic—or perhaps the memories involve the figures of Hopalong Cassidy, Gene Autry, and Roy Rogers on the black-and-white console in the living room. There are, on the other hand, those (Jon Tuska, J. Fred MacDonald, Jane Tompkins) who have become critical and suspicious of Western entertainments, of the eras and mindsets that produced them, and of the influences these entertainments may have had on the generations that grew up with them. Current programmers and audiences are apt to argue that despite some obvious, notable connections to the formulas that were the mainstay of the Western, later children's and adolescents' entertainments stand as improvements or, at the very least, fresh artifacts more in keeping with contemporary issues and preoccupations.

Kids growing up with Westerns, however, was a phenomenon that lasted over seventy years, longer than the era of the Old West itself, defined by historians as the post–Civil War Southwestern United States roughly between the late 1860s and 1900. Except for a few vestiges—not the least of which is Woody the cowboy doll from *Toy Story* and *Toy Story 2*—entering the twenty-first century meant that growing up with Westerns was a passé experience that belonged to a time thirty years past. Even preceding that by two or three decades was the era when growing up with Westerns meant Saturdays and all the kids in the neighborhood gathering in the local movie house for the Western movie matinee.

According to Richard deCordova in his study "Ethnography and Exhibition: The Child Audience, the Hays Office, and the Saturday Matinees," "local movements began in the 1910s and '20s to hold children's matinees on Saturday to 'place' the child both symbolically and physically at the movies, to give children a particular way of looking at films that satisfied adult conceptions of childhood innocence" (162).

"Motion Pictures Specifically for Children" in the October 31, 1916, issue of the *Rutland Evening News* addressed concerns with films made primarily for children to be screened at selected times specifically for child audiences. "As one little girl of twelve expressed it: 'We like to see them making love and riding off in automobiles.' And a boy explained, 'There won't be any shooting or dynamiting in those kid pictures. What's the use of seeing them?'" (deCordova 164).

In 1925 the Hays Office, established a few years earlier by the industry to scrutinize and then determine the appropriateness of film content, strongly favored the children's matinee as one solution to the problem of protecting children from more mature celluloid subjects. A drive for Saturday morning movies for children was initiated by the Hays Office with a well-publicized April 25, 1925, program at the Eastman Theatre in Rochester, New York, attended by 2,700 children who paid their dimes to enter (deCordova 163). Although by 1926 the Hays Office, attending to other issues, abandoned the crusade for designated Saturday screenings for children, local organizations and the National Committee for Better Films continued to plan and promote matinees. As deCordova describes their efforts, local organizations used techniques begun after 1910, such as encouraging members to have their children attend the matinees; "some organizations and businesses bought up blocks of tickets to give to poor children or to their employees. Within the theatre, Boy Scouts, Girl Scouts, or college women in caps and gowns served as ushers. . . . . It was quite common to award a five dollar gold piece or a season pass for the best essay written about the film viewed that day. And, in some cities, Public Library tie-ins encouraged children to read books related to the films" (164–165). By the 1930s, Saturday matinees had gained the community's seal of approval.

Of course, what came to dominate Saturday matinee fare was the budget or B-Western. It might be accompanied by a cartoon, a newsreel, perhaps an episode of a twelve- or fifteen-chapter serial, previews of coming attractions, and another B-picture (perhaps a second Western or a comedy or a detective film). The Westerns, however, are what the kids looked forward to all week. When asked to name his favorite Western film, actor Larry Hagman (best known for his role as oil tycoon J. R. Ewing in the 1978–1991 television series *Dallas*) replied, "The Westerns I loved the most were the ones I used to watch every Saturday afternoon at the Pantages Theatre in Hollywood. They made you check your guns at the box office (cap guns, that is), but you got to spend all

day there watching cowboy stars like Tom Mix and Bob Steele. The titles all run together now, but it was always a good time" (Hofstede 155).

Hagman's confession that "the titles all run together now" is under-
standable. The list of Hopalong Cassidy films, for example, includes
*Texas Masquerade, Texas Trail, Three Men from Texas, Three on the Trail,.
Trail Dust, Twilight on the Trail,* and, of course, *Sunset Trail.* Alan "Rocky"
Lane starred in *Vigilantes of Boomtown* and *Vigilante Hideout; Stagecoach to
Monterey* and *Stagecoach to Denver; Sheriff of Wichita* and *Sheriff of Sundown;
Rustlers on Horseback* and *Rustlers of Devil's Canyon; Marshal of Cripple Creek,
Marshal of Cedar Rock,* and *Marshal of Amarillo; Fort Dodge Stampede* and *El
Paso Stampede; Desperadoes Outpost* and *Desperadoes of Dodge City;* plus *Bandits
of the West, Bandits of Dark Canyon,* and *Bandit King of Texas.* Not to belabor
the point, but Johnny Mack Brown's B-Western titles include *Land of
the Lawless, Law and Order, The Law Comes to Gunsight, Law Men, Law of the
Panhandle, Law of the Range, Law of the Valley,* and *Law of the West.* Johnny
Mack Brown also starred in *West of Carson City, West of El Dorado, West of
the Rio Grande, West of Wyoming,* and *Western Renegades.*

Budget Westerns were also known as "shoot-em-ups" or "oaters."
The 1944 Johnny Mack Brown oater, or Western, *Law Men* from Monogram Studio ran fifty-eight minutes and used a familiar plot. Johnny
Mack Brown and his partner and sidekick Sandy Hopkins (played by
Raymond Hatton) are United States marshals who have been dis-
patched to clear up outlaw trouble in a small prairie community. As
they approach on their horses (Brown rides a splendid Palomino), Sandy
suggests, "We'd better split up going into town. Kinda be strangers for
a while." Brown replies, "Same old system." Sandy nods and agrees,
"Same old system." Brown laughs good-naturedly. Of course, Brown
will work on the inside, pretending to be an outlaw so he can become part
of the gang and learn the identity of the duplicitous mastermind planning
the robberies. Sandy will work on the outside learning all he can about
the townspeople, preparing them to assist Brown in the finale. At the
climax, after his henchmen have been vanquished, the suit-and-tie-
wearing brains villain will attempt to escape on horseback. The hero will
ride after him, overtake him, leap from his saddle, and knock the treach-
erous enemy from his mount as both men tumble to the ground. Spring-
ing to his feet and launching one exceptional punch, the handsome hero
will subdue the foe and return him to town to stand trial for his crimes.
This was probably the most often used plot in the budget Westerns.

There could be other variations, all involving disguise and the establishment of one's true identity. A favorite plot in 1930s Westerns involved two boys separated at birth. One grows up with badmen and becomes an outlaw. One grows up with decent folk and becomes a good, caring, heroic person. At the end, when the bad brother discovers who he really is, he reforms and sacrifices himself to aid the good brother and the community.

The mid-1930s brought the singing cowboy: Gene Autry initially and then dozens of others including Tex Ritter and Roy Rogers. Trigger trios—such as the Three Mesquiteers; Hopalong Cassidy with pards Windy and Lucky; or the Rough Riders played by Buck Jones, Tim McCoy, and Raymond Hatton—gained popularity. Several Westerns even used a contemporary 1930s or 1940s or 1950s setting instead of the post–Civil War Southwest, but always there were familiar characters.

There was the hero with his marvelous horse accompanied by his comical sidekick. There was the heroine in danger, often still residing with her aged father. There would be the suave "brains heavy" pretending to be a respectable, professional townsman but actually the instigator of the criminal activity. The boss had his henchmen who were quick to start a fight but incapable of ever defeating the hero in a brawl or in any kind of gunplay. All these characters were played by familiar actors placed in familiar landscapes and settings. The sameness of the fare, the recognizable formulas used and reused, provided a weekly sense of comfort and security to the youngsters at the picture show. At the same time, the kids could reverently support the bashful but well-dressed and well-groomed hero in his attempts to attract the girl. They could laugh at the sidekick's antics (verbal and physical) and as a group cheer and shout at the fights, the stunts, and the chases. Then they would all applaud as the film concluded and "The End" flashed on the screen.

In some ways, going on a regular basis to the Western movie matinee was similar to the ritual of being a major-league baseball fan. The game, the rules, and the playing fields were the same. What could be grand, however, was choosing a favorite player. A youngster could select the son of an Arkansas sharecropper, Dizzy Dean, or the son of an Italian immigrant, "The Yankee Clipper" Joe DiMaggio himself, or the aloof Ted Williams, or the Jewish slugger Hank Greenberg, or, in the Negro Leagues, Josh Gibson, Satchel Paige, or Cool Papa Bell, or, after 1947, Jackie Robinson or Roy Campanella of the Brooklyn Dodgers.

Similarly one could choose a favorite Western hero, which meant praising him and defending him to the other kids during the week. There were many deserving choices: Roy Rogers or Gene Autry, the smallish but always battling Bob Steele, or tall, lanky Wild Bill Elliott; or Whip Wilson in the white hat as opposed to Lash LaRue clad all in black. The Western stars and Western films were, as scholar Steve Tatum has suggested, celebrations of the male body. The Western heroes were uniformly handsome; each was an impeccably costumed male model on the one hand yet also a caring, always-there-to-teach-and-protect big brother on the other. Each was intensively likable, and each had his own powerful, well-taken-care-of horse. For many youngsters the cowboy movie experience involved personal choices connected to some degree of individuality, resulting in a decision in the 1930s to buy a Tim McCoy instead of a Ken Maynard Big Little Book or in the 1950s a Rocky Lane rather than a Rex Allen comic book. Although there could be individual preferences, with Westerns one was still always part of a group; there were the day-to-day personal friends and playmates, plus there were all the other kids from near and far who had come to the theater.

One might spend a good part of a day playing cowboys and Indians or law officers and outlaws. One could pretend to be Buck Jones or Roy Rogers and sometimes even have that name or visage on a toy pistol or on a Dixie Cup lid, a drinking glass, or a cereal bowl. Or one might be out playing baseball and hit right-handed like Ralph Kiner or DiMaggio or left-handed like Williams or Stan Musial or Eddie Mathews and have that name on the bat or on the mitt. And likewise one might find that favorite player's name and face on a penny arcade card, or a baseball trading card, or on a box of cereal. Family and political figures notwithstanding, Western movie stars and major league baseball players were the idols at the center of young lives.

James Horwitz, in a 1976 book titled *They Went Thataway*, remembered his days as the Front Row Kid when he had to "hang up his six-guns, 'Lone Ranger' model .44s with the mock silver bullets" to attend to, at his mother's insistence, his Hopalong Cassidy drinking glass and Gene Autry dinner plate (2). Most vivid of all were the memories from afternoons of the last day of each week:

> The Saturday Matinee. If you were the Front Row Kid, coming up before rock 'n' roll, and you had not yet discovered the fantasy possibilities of baseball and girls, for one thin dime you bought the best of all possible worlds and believed in the Western movies. Life without them

was unimaginable, empty, dull. It was more than an event, those three or four hours in the dark looking up. It was a living daydream. A ritual. An idea. Better than a birthday party. Better than recess. Better even than a 500-pound hamburger and a chocolate sundae as big as your house.

Horwitz further recalls

just to be able to pay your dime at the ticket booth and walk into that lobby at one o'clock on a Saturday afternoon, to slip through the crowd of kids at the refreshment stand and plunk your extra nickel down on the glass-top counter for a Mars Bar or a Coke or a box of popcorn popped before your very eyes and still warm in the box (with plenty of salt and butter) . . . rows of kids from all over town squealing and scuffling, whistling, laughing, bouncing up and down on their springy cushion seats, meeting and greeting each other.

Then came

the last unbearable moments until the time, looking up at the ceiling so high above you covered with mock clouds and stars at night, turning around in your front-row seat to look at the balcony so far above and behind you and watch the candy wrappers and paper airplanes come sailing down until the ushers below, done out in uniforms like the Phillip Morris midget, shine flashlights up towards the garbage-bombers, trying to keep everyone's excitement in check but knowing it is impossible and not trying very hard because there are just too many of us.

And finally "to have the lights go down into darkness like a blanket being draped over our shoulders . . . knowing what is coming next but unable to hold on to our excitement one second longer, we burst, as the red curtain folds away, and the Eagle flies! Republic Pictures Presents . . . Yeeaaahooo! Ride'em cowboy!" (5–6).

Most of the B-Western memories that have been recorded are from a male perspective. Patt Rocks, a Spartanburg, South Carolina, television personality, has similar memories, but hers are from a female perspective. When interviewed, she recalled,

Every Saturday meant the Norwood Theatre in Norwood, Alabama, in the Birmington area. All week each of us would work towards getting ten cents. Sometimes we would find pennies under a cushion in the couch or collect bottles for deposit or help around the house or yard. On Saturday, my friends and I would walk the five or six blocks to the Norwood. And, if you had a quarter, and quarters were hard to come by, you could get into the movies and also buy candy and popcorn and a soft drink. The program would be a serial chapter, previews, a cartoon, and always a Western movie. And afterwards and during the week we would play Western roles. It didn't matter if you were a boy or a girl. The girl could be the hero too. (Rocks interview)

In his introduction to *Focus on the Western*, a 1974 collection of critical essays, Jack Nachbar also muses about the ritualistic quality of Saturday matinees:

It's now a quarter of a century since Westerns took up my whole life. There were, first of all, in those pleasant postwar years in Minnesota, endless summer hours of "playing cowboys." Whenever it rained we read or traded our Western comic books. I remember especially liking Monte Hale and "Rocky" Lane comics because their movies never came to our theater. Three times a week supper was bolted to catch "The Lone Ranger" on the radio. All those activities, of course, were just killing time, trivial warm-ups for Saturdays, when we would gather an hour before the box office opened in front of the Nokomis Theater, only three blocks away, in order to be the first neighborhood bunch to shove our twelve cents at the cashier and have our choices of seats to watch a Western serial, invariably featuring Zorro or the James Brothers, and to see a matinee Western, with Johnny Mack Brown or Sunset Carson, whom we disliked, or Charles Starrett, Whip Wilson, or Hopalong Cassidy, whom we liked, or, on very special days, Roy Rogers, who was always shown with ten extra cartoons and whom every one of us adored. So predictably ritualistic were the gunplay, fistfights, and riding on the screen and so religious was my attendance that once, when I got to the theater a few minutes late and alone . . . , I unthinkingly betrayed my Catholic school upbringing and genuflected by the side of my seat. I saw nothing incongruous about this until a couple of my pals told each other out loud what I'd done and began to giggle. None of this ever struck me as in any way "meaningful." It was simply what I liked to do and what everybody I knew liked to do. It was not until long into my adulthood that it occurred to me that it was because of the very ordinariness of my boyhood cowboymania that Westerns were significant, that the same Saturday ritual experienced by millions of children and adults in thousands of theaters in all parts of the country for three generations hinted at something important about the collective mind of twentieth-century America. (1–2)

The ritualistic, quasi-religious weekly experience youngsters had with Saturday matinees from the 1930s until the early 1950s might be

compared to another ritualistic, quasi-religious weekly cinema experience large numbers of adolescents and college-age students would have
twenty to thirty years later. Again individuals would go to the theater
at the appointed time on the same day. They would meet old friends
as well as new members of a packed theater audience. Many would be
dressed like the figures on the screen. The situation and dialogue to all
present would be extraordinarily familiar. The audience could be noisy
and rowdy yet still enthusiastic. At the end of the screening, the members of the audience, perhaps feeling a bit drained, would file from the
theater almost as if leaving a church service, having enjoyed camaraderie and shared knowledge and information, even the sense of involvement in a speak-along liturgy. Certainly there are obvious differences
between the audiences who attended and the fare that comprised the
Saturday afternoon Western movie matinee and what comprised the
Friday and Saturday midnight showings of *The Rocky Horror Picture Show*.
What the events have in common is the blending of quasi-religious
weekly ritual with hyperactive, "blowing off steam" cheerfulness and
rowdiness. This occurs while engaging in a sustained over-the-years
group dream punctuated by entering and leaving the place of ritual to
return to the day-to-day work or school world.

African American children also had some access to the experience
of growing up with Westerns. Varied booking, admission, and seating
policies meant blacks could attend standard B-Western features. Indeed, in the late 1950s after the production of B-Western films ceased
and many neighborhood theaters closed, B-Westerns continued to be
shown and draw crowds to theaters where audiences were predominantly African American. Earlier "race films" of the 1930s and 1940s
that featured all-black casts and that were made and screened almost
solely for black audiences included four all-black Westerns. A vocalist
for the Duke Ellington Orchestra, Herb Jeffries, was billed as Herb Jeffrey and starred in *Harlem on the Prairie* (1937), *Harlem Rides the Range*
(1939), *The Bronze Buckaroo* (1939), and *Two-Gun Man from Harlem* (1940).
On a Country Music Television (CMT) retrospective on "Singing
Cowboys" Jeffries explained what led him to make those four Western
movies. He had come across a boy crying. When Jeffries asked the
African American child why he was weeping, the boy replied he
wanted to be Tom Mix, but the other kids would not let him play with
them because "there weren't any black cowboys." Despite the films'
low budgets even by B-Western standards, Jeffries hoped to correct that

impression, at least for the audiences who were able to see any of his four Westerns.

Others viewed and enjoyed B-Westerns not during the fabled Saturday matinees but on other days of the week. In larger urban areas, B-Westerns were booked in specific theaters during the week, perhaps Wednesday to Saturday. Other more prestigious movie houses might provide a B-Western at the bottom of a bill following an A-production.

Many post–World War II baby boomers saw B-Westerns not in local neighborhood theaters (most of which had closed by the mid-1950s) but on television. An initial problem facing networks and stations was having sufficient programming to fill airtime. Rerunning B-Westerns on television introduced the films to an entirely new audience of youngsters. Indeed, by buying the rights to his old Hopalong Cassidy theatrical Westerns and making them available in syndication to television, actor Bill Boyd reaffirmed just who Hopalong Cassidy was and paved the way for a Hopalong Cassidy television series. The series consisted of 99 half-hour episodes and ran on NBC from June 29, 1949, to December 23, 1951. The Hopalong Cassidy lunch bucket from that era is a valuable collectible item, the first child's lunch bucket based on a television/film character. *The Lone Ranger* television series based on the radio character premiered on ABC on September 15, 1949, and counted 221 original episodes, not ceasing production until September 4, 1965, and proving successful even afterward in reruns.

Following Bill Boyd's example, several B-Western film stars made or attempted to make the transition to television. Actors familiar to Saturday matinee audiences were now visible on a regular basis in television markets as prints of their old movies had been purchased and were being used to fill airtime. Along with Bill "Hopalong Cassidy" Boyd, Gene Autry and Roy Rogers were, of course, the most successful at making the transition to television. *The Gene Autry Show* consisted of 104 episodes and ran from July 23, 1950, through August 7, 1956. Autry's *Melody Ranch* radio program, which first aired on January 7, 1940, also continued until 1956. *The Roy Rogers Show,* which premiered on December 30, 1951, totaled 104 episodes and ran until June 23, 1957. B-Western leading man Kirby Grant played the title role in *Sky King,* a 1951–1952 series on NBC and 1952–1953 series on ABC, while singing cowboy Rex Allen forsook vocalizing to play the lead in *Frontier Doctor,* which ran for thirty-nine episodes. Both *The Range Rider* (1951–1954) with Jock Mahoney and

Dick Jones and *The Cisco Kid* (1950–1956) with Duncan Renaldo and Leo Carrillo had roots in the B-Western tradition and style.

Autry, for a time, was able to convince movie theater owners that his television series could be used to promote his films, and for a while that was the case. In the 1940s, the United States had over seven thousand single-screen theaters. By the 1950s many were closing. Drive-in theaters, on the other hand, were becoming popular. Although new feature-length Western films and fresh half-hour and hour Western television series continued to appear, by the mid-1950s they were different in tone and direction from the Saturday matinee B-Western movies and were the sponsored-by-cereals, designed-for-kids early Western TV series. The last B-Western film is generally held to be *Two Guns and a Badge* with Wayne Morris, released in 1954. Autry's final B-Western film, *Last of the Pony Riders* (Columbia Pictures), was released in 1953. The last Republic Studio B-Western release came in 1954 with *The Phantom Stallion* starring Rex Allen. At the end of the film, when Allen turns to wave good-bye as he rides away, there is no final "Come back and see us, Rex" appeal from the settlers he has helped. The enchanted afternoons of Republic Western releases had lasted from 1934 to 1954, and now they were over.

Still, the 1950s were boom years for Western hero merchandising. Hopalong Cassidy, Gene Autry, and Roy Rogers items were plentiful. Later as television Western series became more "adult" in subject matter and focus with series such as *The Life and Legend of Wyatt Earp* (September 6, 1955–September 26, 1961), *Cheyenne* (September 13, 1955–August 39, 1963), and the long-running *Gunsmoke* (September 19, 1955–September 1, 1975), merchandising continued to flourish with comic books, lunchboxes, board games, and an assortment of other products filling store shelves. Perhaps the merchandising tie-in campaign of the era hit its peak with Walt Disney's *Davy Crockett, King of the Wild Frontier*, a five-part chronicle airing on television from December 15, 1954, to December 14, 1955. According to Douglas Brode in *The Films of Steven Spielberg*, the Davy Crockett merchandising phenomenon had a lasting effect on young Steven Spielberg:

> He was in third grade when he learned firsthand the impact film and TV could have on the popular psyche. Every kid in school had seen Walt Disney's Davy Crockett; when, on the playground, Spielberg arrived without the requisite coonskin cap, he was tagged the villainous Santa Anna, at which point pint-sized Alamo defenders came at him

with the butts of toy flintlock rifles. He was regularly chased home until he convinced his parents to buy him the proper Disney paraphernalia. He was made aware, early on, of the significance of movie merchandising, an aspect of the film business he and colleague George Lucas would carefully oversee. (14)

The transition of child-oriented Westerns from film to television could, in some instances, lead to fathers and sons sharing Western hero memories and experiences. Perhaps a child could enjoy on the small screen a Hoot Gibson or Ken Maynard movie seen and remembered by a parent (probably the father) twenty or thirty years ago. Enjoying Westerns and having Western heroes in common constituted a form of generational male bonding. In Larry McMurtry's *Horseman, Pass By* (the novel that served as the basis for the film *Hud*), the grandfather and grandson go to town on Saturday night to see a Gene Autry picture. In Ken Kesey's 1964 novel *Sometimes a Great Notion*, rugged logger Hank Stamper finds time each week to watch a new television episode of *Tales of Wells Fargo* with his cousin's young son. Yet by the 1960s, a shared generational enthusiasm for Westerns was beginning to waver.

Screen Westerns—film and television—designed specifically for child and juvenile audiences had been the first to disappear. After the Saturday matinee B-Western movie era ended and after the various Saturday morning cereal-sponsored Western television series ceased production, movie and TV "adult" Westerns did remain popular and, for a period, were available in abundance. "Adult" implied Westerns with broader audience and demographic appeal. On television, juvenile "horse Westerns" gave way to "gun Westerns" as a new breed of heroes was more deeply associated with a powerful and unusual pistol or rifle than with an impressive mount. These "gun Westerns" included *Wyatt Earp, Wanted Dead or Alive, The Rifleman,* and *Johnny Ringo* and were, as critic Ralph Brauer records, replaced with the various "piece of property" Western series. Included in this subgenre were *Bonanza, The Big Valley, The High Chaparral,* and other versions of the civic-minded family defending its massive ranch holdings.

For two decades or so after the end of the Saturday Western matinee, kids were still growing up with Westerns. Instead of carrying a Gene Autry or Roy Rogers lunchbox to school, a child might have a lunchpail depicting Paladin from the 1957–1963 TV series *Have Gun, Will Travel.* Instead of a Hopalong Cassidy drinking glass, a child might have a mug featuring Ben, Hoss, and Little Joe Cartwright from *Bonanza.* Certainly kids still talked about and argued about Westerns; perhaps they watched a Western series episode with siblings or a parent. If the mass experience of the Saturday matinee was gone, Westerns still provided merchandise purchasing opportunities and cultural exchange currency. In school on Monday there would always be Sunday night's *Bonanza* episode to discuss.

As Gary Yoggy recounts in *Riding the Video Range: The Rise and Fall of the Western on Television,* "In 1958, 12 of the top 25 and, indeed, seven of the top ten Nielsen-rated programs were Westerns. In 1959, 32 different Western series filled twenty hours of prime time programming" (1). By 1984, however, the Western, like the buffalo, had all but disappeared. Only one Western series aired in 1984, and only a scant few (*Dr. Quinn, Medicine Woman,* for example) have been accorded any primetime consideration since. By the late 1990s, Westerns on television consisted solely of reruns and an occasional made-for-TV venture on a cable channel.

In movie theaters, Westerns, while not of the Republic B-variety, were still plentiful in the 1950s and 1960s. The 1950s provided at least three classic Western films—*High Noon, Shane,* and *The Searchers.* Filmmakers in the mid-1960s, initially sparked by Sergio Leone's successful Clint Eastwood spaghetti Westerns, were able to inject some new creativity into a resurgent genre. The 1960s ended with three notable Western films, all released in 1969: *Butch Cassidy and the Sundance Kid, True Grit,* and *The Wild Bunch.*

By the 1990s, however, the production of Western films was rare. Two star-driven personal projects, Kevin Costner's *Dances with Wolves* (1990) and Clint Eastwood's *Unforgiven* (1992), won "Best Picture" Academy Awards, with both Costner and Eastwood winning "Best Director" Oscars. If, however, a child or a juvenile did venture to see a Western theatrical release in a mall Cineplex, it would obviously be an isolated rather than a weekly experience. The phenomenon of growing up with Westerns now belonged to an earlier generation.

Numerous theories and suppositions have been presented concerning why the popularity of the Western dwindled in the last quarter of the twentieth century. Comic actor Pat Buttram once speculated at a film festival that "in the 1930s and '40s Westerns were so popular because kids all dreamed of owning a horse; then they didn't want a horse anymore. Every kid just wanted to own a car." Others like John Cawelti speculated the formulas simply wore out, that perhaps a more difficult question is why the Western genre, the B-Western in particular, with those all-too-typical programmer plots, did as well as it did for as long as it did. Obviously, during and after the Vietnam War, sentiments were being modified about the style and type of violence to be found in entertainment media. Also being questioned were suspect or flawed depictions of the lone white male heroic champion, the role or roles of women, and the historical experiences of minorities. Certainly in the last twenty years of the twentieth century, movie series such as, beginning in the 1960s, the Secret Agent 007 James Bond films or, beginning in the 1970s, the dedicated-but-hampered-by-bureaucracy police investigator "Dirty Harry" Callahan pictures seemed, for a time, more relevant and fresh. On television, following the success of *The Cosby Show* in the 1980s, the situation comedy dominated prime time programming. Dramatic series with law enforcement, legal, or medical center settings, such as *Hill Street Blues*, *LA Law*, and later *E.R.*, also seemed modern and contemporary in ways Westerns did not. With their large multicultural casts including fallible white males and strong, sympathetic female and minority characters, these cop, lawyer, or doctor programs joined with sitcoms to render Westerns or, for that matter, variety shows emblematic of a much earlier time and sensibility.

That did not mean all the Saturday afternoon Front Row Kids or the children who, with their cap pistols, shot back at the television screen desperadoes completely forgot or dismissed their years of growing up with Westerns. Beginning in the early 1970s in Memphis, Western film festivals proved popular, allowing fans to meet with aging stars, see the movies and television series episodes they enjoyed as children, and spend time in dealers' rooms bargaining for and buying decades-old movie posters or cowboy hero memorabilia. As of the year 2005 Western film festivals in Memphis, Tennessee, Williamsburg, Virginia, and Charlotte and Asheville, North Carolina, are still scheduled annually, although few performers from the B-Western movie era remain, and when the fans return for the three-day event each year, they seem grayer and less spry.

It should be realized that although white females and African Americans of either gender had some access to and empathy with B-Western movies and early Western television series, the appeal of the form was primarily to young white males watching on the screen what they hoped would be older facsimiles of themselves. Although in the 1940s and 1950s, girls may have had crushes on Roy Rogers or Hugh "Wyatt Earp" O'Brien or their counterparts, the individuals today who best remember the era of horse operas and who deem themselves most influenced by those experiences are white males who can recall Westerns and even define themselves as growing up with Westerns. Film historian Leonard Maltin is one example. In an article by Jeff Hildebrandt titled "Hopalong Cassidy's Mesquite Mystique," Maltin is quoted as saying: "I like to think I'm a moral person. I like to think I have some sense of right and wrong and I can't help but think that some of it came from watching those Westerns where those values were driven home every single time" (33). J. G. O'Boyle's article "Be Sure You're Right, Then Go Ahead: The Early Disney Westerns" examines various Disney Western characters of the 1950s (Davy Crockett, Spin and Marty, Elfego Baca, Texas John Slaughter, the frontier family that owned Old Yeller, the Sioux who fought the megalomaniac Custer in *Tonya*) and states, "Actress Dorothy McGuire's strong portrayal of the frontier wife and mother" in *Old Yeller* "is based on the casual assumption that she could handle anything that came along, and that proves true. . . . It is arguable that many similar 1990s values took root from the seeds of Disney's embedded anti-authoritarian, egalitarian, antiwar, and ecologically minded messages" (79). The 1974 song "Hoppy, Gene, and Me" written by "Snuff" Garrett, Stephen Dorff, and Milton L. Brown and sung by Roy Rogers included the line "We taught you how to shoot straight—Hoppy, Gene, and Me." The meaning is not that the three leading heroes of B-Westerns and early television assisted youngsters in being better pistol shots or marksmen but that they instilled in their fans a sense of honesty and fair play.

Of course, it could be argued persuasively that for some people watching Westerns may have proved harmful. Westerns can be seen as promoting gunplay and fistfights—violence—as suitable responses to aggressiveness. After the assassination of President Kennedy, Western star Rex Allen expressed regret at his early image and vowed he would never again appear in public wearing a gun. In the television Western series *Gunsmoke*, Matt Dillon, instead of shooting the criminals, came simply to yell "Hold it!" and the villains, for the most part, would drop their guns and raise their hands.

Violence in Westerns is only one issue. Sexism, racism, and the support of imperialism are additional charges that, perhaps not altogether inappropriately, have been leveled against the preponderance of Western fare that filled movie and television screens in those long ago decades.

Whatever the long-term or short-term effect of the genre on the American personality, the Western provided one of the earliest, most easily documented, systematical, and sustained childhood electronic media rituals throughout almost the entirety of the twentieth century. Although this particular form of entertainment has, for the most part, vanished from the electronic and cinematic landscape, no longer providing weekly childhood or adolescent memory experiences, other popular media entertainments designated primarily for that age group serve similar purposes and provide similar bonding and value-bestowing capabilities. Power Rangers, Ninja Turtles, He-Men, and varied recycled characters in summer movie sequels and series have replaced the courageous Westerner wearing his iconic Stetson, embroidered shirt and pants, and leather holster with ivory-handled guns and riding a gallant horse. Hopefully, later generations will gain as many rich memories and as much clapping and cheering enjoyment from whomever or whatever their current fictional media heroes—and heroines—might be as did kids from 1915 through the 1970s growing up with Westerns.

WORKS CITED

Brauer, Ralph with Donna Brauer. *The Horse, the Gun, the Piece of Property: The Television Wester.* Bowling Green OH: Bowling Green Popular Press, 1975.

Brode, Douglas. *The Films of Steven Spielberg.* New York: Citadel Press, 1995.

Bronco Billy. Dir. Clint Eastwood. With Clint Eastwood, Sondra Locke, and Scatman Crothers. Warner Brothers / Malpaso, 1980.

deCordova, Richard. "Ethnography and Exhibition: The Child Audience, the Hays Office, and Saturday Matinees." In *Moviegoing in America,* ed. Gregory A. Waller, 159–169. Oxford, UK: Blackwell, 2002.

Hildebrandt, Jeff. "Hopalong Cassidy's Mesquite Mystique." *American West Magazine,* Winter 2002: 32–34.

Hofstede, David. "The 100 Best Westerns Ever Made," *Cowboys and Indians,* January 2002: 144–156.

Horwitz, James. *They Went Thataway.* New York: Ballantine Books, 1976.

Law Men. Dir. Lambert Hillyer. With Johnny Mack Brown, Raymond Hatton, and Jan Wiley. Monogram, 1944.

Nachbar, Jack. Introduction to *Focus on the Western,* ed. Jack Nachbar, 2–8. Englewood Cliffs, NJ, 1974.

O'Boyle, J. G. "'Be Sure You're Right, Then Go Ahead.' The Early Disney Westerns." *Journal of Popular Film and Television* 24 (Summer 1996): 69–80.

Rocks, Patt. Personal Interview. February 7, 2002.

Yoggy, Gary A. *Riding the Video Range: The Rise and Fall of the Western on Television.* Jefferson, NC: McFarland, 1995.

14

From Gigapets to Internet

Childhood Technology Rituals as Commodities

JO ANN ORAVEC

Rituals help to shape and guide a child's passage to adulthood. Family, school, and religious rituals serve to influence children's behavior and affect the way they interpret their places in relation to various institutions (Neville 151; Fiese 633; McCadden). Such familiar rituals as nightly bathing and tooth brushing structure children's time and help them make sense of everyday life. Adults check their e-mail, Internet horoscopes, and online weather forecasts with ritualistic fervor and may soon be establishing automated households with even more opportunities for technology ritual. Computing technologies play major roles in childhood as well as adult rituals. In many of these rituals, the technologies serve as not just ritual "props" but as ritual participants, providing forms of feedback and control in the ritual context. Commodification plays an assortment of roles in these ritual contexts, including the acquisition, display, and discarding of particular sets of items.

It may seem odd to link modern computing technology with ritual, for the latter has connotations of the ancient and sacred. But Ronald Grimes claims in his book *Ritual Criticism* that the ritual formation process is dynamic and creative, and it integrates new technologies as well as more traditional objects. Thomas Driver argues that rituals can introduce an "economy" into behavior, establishing routines that become part of a whole repertoire of societal activities (134). Family rituals include celebrations, traditions, and daily patterned routines, according to Dennis Rook (251–252). Rituals can serve to provide meaning and cohesion to the family unit. Various props and objects are often important aspects of rituals; childhood rituals increasingly incorporate technology, including such rites of passage as learning how to "tell time" with a digital clock, being entrusted with a pager or cell phone, and obtaining a driver's license. Many children appear to adapt readily and enjoy participating in a wide range of technology rituals, even when they are required to learn intricate routines and arcane technological functions. However, there are some important questions as to whether adults should foster the ritual use of technology by children or use it in strategic ways to support various educational and family goals.

Lessons Children Learn through Technology Ritual

The societal values we place upon technologies are tightly coupled with these ritual contexts. As information technology becomes a larger and more highly valued part of our everyday lives, the realms of childhood ritual are incorporating interaction with computers in increasingly complex ways. According to Sherry Turkle, children obtain some levels of self-efficacy and learn about their future roles in society through their encounters with computer technology. Through interactivity, they also gain experience in dealing with the ritualistic and symbolic aspects of exchanges with machines as they are expressed in their culture. Just as spinning a prayer wheel in some cultures is intended to manifest and connect with certain religious values, interaction with computers can be seen as linking computer users to the larger society. Computer-based rituals are becoming commodified; for example, the acquisition and maintenance of computer devices can themselves serve ritual functions, just as rings serve ritual functions in weddings (Otnes & Scott 35–38) and various food items do in Thanksgiving Day celebrations in the United States (Wallendorf & Arnould 13–20). Computer devices can in many ways provide direct feedback as to their correct usage in rituals; however, unlike engagement rings, many of the virtual pets that children play with will simply cease functioning if they are not attended to properly.

Children often learn about technology rituals by observing adults, although (as described later in the essay) some technology rituals are largely linked to peer interaction. Many adults begin their daily home and work routines with rituals involving computer technology, such as the morning practice of checking electronic mail, programming a microwave or coffeepot, and scanning online news services. In similar ways, even some preteens are incorporating interactive tools and toys into their everyday rituals. For example, some children consult electronic organizers for their schedules and interact with electronic playthings during recess; the electronic organizer Dear Diary by Tiger Electronics is specially designed for use by children.

The direct utilitarian value of these child and adult interactions with computer technology is often unclear; generally, our schedules or electronic mailboxes need not be checked as often as we check them, and many of us obtain the time or weather report more often than required to stay punctual or keep dry. The ritual aspects of the behavior—the periodic activities of establishing contact with an electronic device in a patterned manner—are often the most salient aspects of the encounter. The reassurance that the activity of interacting with a computer apparently provides can be fulfilling and affirming to its participants, manifesting a form of control not often obtainable in everyday life. Whether or not children receive responses from their parents, teachers, or peers, they can receive them from their interactive toys and other gear. For children, this reassurance may be especially important, particularly when encouragement and comfort by adults are lacking or when school environments are otherwise unsettling. However, technology rituals can thus displace efforts to establish or participate in more human-centered rituals, rituals that involve higher levels of human response and permit more spontaneity, playfulness, and even magic.

School officials and parents are encountering issues of children interacting with computers. As many educators plan for increased use of technological gear in schools, the ritualistic aspects of children's encounters with computing technology should be considered with special care; the rituals can encourage the noncritical adoption of technologies and the placement of human value in nonsentient objects (Oravec, "Interactive"). For instance, in classroom settings, children's use of calculators is more than just a means for adding numbers; it is also a way of integrating technology into an everyday process. Adding numbers by hand can be uncertain and frustrating. However, with the calculator, the process becomes patterned in a manner that is shaped by the technology; many students' insistence that the calculator is always "right" and their refusal to check the results with commonsense estimates reflect the calculator's symbolic value in the ritual context. Writing is also changed in form and focus as pen-and-paper encounters are displaced by a series of interactions with machines. Children are encouraged to adopt routines to "save" their work periodically in their word-processing efforts and to create back-ups on a regular basis in case of technical problems. Intellectual activities thus become linked with specific technological routines.

The childhood computer technology rituals explored in the following pages are undergoing rapid changes, as are the technologies themselves: the characters of these rituals are evolving as people become more knowledgeable about computer technology and as it becomes more of a consumer item. Computer-based rituals can be readily commodified in ways not feasible with non-computer-based rituals; routines (along with instructions for human response) can be literally programmed into the microchips of various items, such as virtual pets and electronic organizers. Children's computer rituals are also changing as parents learn more about computing and assume a stronger role in shaping and reinforcing the rituals, as well as integrating them into everyday family life. Not long ago, many children served as their family's "computer ambassadors," distinguishing themselves by being more comfortable and capable with computer technology than their elders. However, children who felt they were differentiating themselves from parents and other family members merely through their acquaintance with computer technology will have to work harder to display their computer savvy as technology becomes more widely used by everyone and more tightly integrated into everyday life. These rituals are also changing as the computer technologies that are involved in the rituals become more complex and permit more "intelligent" and responsible interaction with their users.

The question of whether childhood rituals incorporating computer technology are something that should be reinforced or discouraged is extraordinarily complex, as I outline in the following three cases: (1) virtual and interactive pet rituals, (2) family technology rituals, and (3) childhood rites of passage. I conclude by arguing that computer-centered rituals can indeed be comforting and often harmless and yet foster an approach toward technology that is uncritical and automatic. Commercialism is also a major and often dysfunctional aspect of many of today's technology rituals, as reinforced by many advertising and educational efforts. Many everyday consumer items are being infused with symbolic value, in a process that can be construed as part of the "aestheticisation of everyday life" (Featherstone 67). Computer technology has received especially high levels of symbolic value, often being linked with progress, education, and opportunity. Teachers and parents who attempt to use technology rituals in a strategic way to reinforce certain childhood behaviors should thus be wary. Rather than participating in technology rituals noncritically, children should be encouraged by parents and teachers to consider how and why they are infusing technology into their daily lives. This stance will help them acquire the kind of critical distance that will allow them to make creative and conscientious decisions about technology adoption and use.

Virtual Pets in Children's Everyday Rituals

An example of how computer technology rituals can emerge involves the "virtual" or "interactive" pets that flooded store shelves in many industrialized nations since the mid-1990s, which have included egg-shaped Gigapets, fuzzy Furbys, and talkative Interactive Poohs. Gigapets (from Tiger Electronics), along with Tamagotchi (from Bandai) and Nano (from Playmates), were originally introduced in Japanese markets—where they caught on very quickly (Thompson 15). Many children apparently formed close bonds with Gigapets: reports of how difficult it was to sever children from the pets were common ("Should Virtual" 31). Many adults as well have brought virtual pets into their workplaces for companionship and diversion (Oravec, "Working" 78).

In comparison with many software packages and programming languages, Gigapets are relatively simple to interact with and require a minimum level of computer expertise. The pets still provide a kind of exposure to computer concepts, which may have increased the willingness of parents to purchase them for their children and put up with their annoyances (which include various noises). However, some educators have deemed Gigapets and comparable toys a distraction from a child's educational efforts, and a number of schools have banned them from the premises during school hours ("Should Virtual" 31). A technological fix for the problems schoolchildren face in leaving their Gigapets at home during school hours was subsequently devised: pets with "sleep modes" were developed so that the electronic critters could hibernate while their owners were studying or playing with friends.

Children can engage in a number of personally involving and time-consuming rituals in relation to the pets. Many of the pets require daily if not hourly attention, thus drawing children into periodic patterns of contact with technology. Some of these contact rituals have forms similar to those of interpersonal rituals established with friends or family. In their rituals, participants exhibit habits and mannerisms and react to those of each other in patterned ways (Bruess & Pearson 25–27). Virtual pets provide some, albeit limited, dimensions of this interpersonal interaction, signaling their "needs" to their owners through various sounds as well as reflecting their programmed characteristics (or "personalities") through pictures on their fairly tiny screens. The owners, if diligent, monitor their pets and respond in appropriate fashion to variations in their behavior. Pets that do not receive adequate interaction become "unhappy" or even "die." The pets cannot yet respond to variations in their owners' moods. One would suspect that initiatives will soon be underway to remedy this deficiency, however, since research on how computers can detect and possibly reflect the moods of their users is being conducted (Picard).

Many families have supported virtual pet interaction by reinforcing the successful raising of pets, with "success" being constituted by the sustained life of the pets; peer groups are also apparently supporters of these efforts. The fact that one's Gigapet is alive over time thus demonstrates sustained attention and loyalties to the family's or peer group's values and interests. By managing their Gigapets, children also learn lessons about technology that are considered valuable in today's society, lessons that prepare them for jobs and home life that are permeated with automated equipment. For example, children learn that by responding promptly and appropriately to the demands of technologies, they themselves can gain value in the eyes of their family and peers. Children also learn through advertisements and peer interactions that virtual pets are incomplete by themselves, and that they must purchase other items such as training manuals or T-shirts in order to participate properly in the rituals; thus an assortment of aspects of consumption is involved in the rituals.

Gigapets and similar virtual toys open a number of important questions concerning the value of technology rituals and the dangers of dependence on information technology. The status of many of these computer-based toys as "fads" with a rapidly rising and subsequently fading popular appeal may indeed make these issues seem less critical. However, even as the popularity of some of the toys fades, other interactive toys are emerging in prominence. Furbys (by Tiger Electronics) are small stuffed animals with microprocessors that allow them to generate and respond to various speech patterns (Pereira B-1). Interactive Pooh (by Mattel Media) is equipped with a CD-ROM through which his interaction with children can be personalized (the child's own name can be used, for instance). Some virtual pets and interactive toys reside entirely on computer screens: for example, the "dancing baby" is an image that moves around one's computer screen when it is clicked on; it was portrayed on several news and entertainment television shows in 1997 and 1998 (Seligmann 46). Virtual Puppies are also widely available on the Internet. The Website www.virtualpuppy.com equips potential pet owners with playful online puppies and related puppy activities. The puppies' behaviors are occasionally out of the control of their owners, adding adventure to the interactive experience. Those who are looking for a challenge in raising virtual pets can play the game *Creatures* (by Mindscape Corporation). It gives one the means to raise Norns, which are fluffy, big-eyed entities; one is given six Norn eggs to start.

Real-life pets provide some sense of daily routine (they need to be given water and food and to be walked regularly); on the other hand, they offer substantial variation within the confines of that routine. Interactive pets can reinforce household practices, requiring regular attention and interaction; they can also be programmed to provide some of the kinds of fortuitous entertainment and stimulation that real-life pets provide. However, virtual pets can encourage the formation of personal attachments to an inanimate object and the siphoning of attention into something that is nonsentient. These attachments and the rituals that accompany them are supported by peers and often by families and are buttressed with the high value our society places on computer technology.

The healthiness of close attachments to technology is indeed questionable, even at the adult level: some computer users have complained of disabling levels of "computer dependence" in which their relationship with their machinery has become dysfunctional, and they are not able to engage in and enjoy everyday interaction with other persons (Oravec, *Virtual Individuals*). It may appear bizarre that individuals would become attached to small, egg-shaped entities. However, as the toys become infused into daily routines, personal attachments apparently develop. Virtual pets can indeed supplement other forms of socialization but raise real moral questions if they are used to displace interaction with real-life people and animals. Contact with these pets may indeed provide some forms of reassurance (as many kinds of ritual encounters do), but it could divert children from putting effort into understanding how to obtain human comfort and support. The effort to collect and maintain virtual pets could thus displace more creative and sustaining forms of human interaction. Parents and teachers should engage children in critical discussions of the value and functions of these virtual pets in order to encourage their thoughtful yet playful adoption.

From the "Children's Machine" to the Family Hearth: Commodifying Family Technology Rituals

A common lament among parents is that children understand computers far better than the parents do. Computing pioneer Seymour Papert labels the computer as the "children's machine," reflecting the ease with which many children accept computing devices in their activities. Many of the children Papert describes were either hobbyists working with friends or students who spent a great deal of time in a structured educational environment; these children developed creative programs and other technological applications that they subsequently shared among each other. In the era when programming skills were required to use computers, far fewer children had access to computers than today; at that time access to computers, when available, was often provided in computer clubs or after-school activities. Some children are still spending time programming, but their efforts often seem futile in relation to the sophisticated, graphics-laden products of Disney or Microsoft. Computers are moving into a different kind of environment, that of everyday family settings, and the computing technologies involved are becoming readily available consumer products, not hard-to-program machines. Many living rooms have temporarily been turned into video parlors through the use of PlayStation, Nintendo, and various computer games: everyday family interactions are increasingly becoming the sites for involvement in even more advanced computing systems, and parents are playing a stronger role in activities involving technology.

Rather than computers being hobbyist gear that is limited to the technologically skilled, a wide range of kinds of computer devices is becoming available on the market for purchase by families, along with "user-friendly" instructions for parents and other adults. A number of the technology rituals that children participate in have thus undergone a subtle shift: they have changed from being largely centered either on school or peer interaction to incorporating more intense family (generally parental) involvement and direction. Parents are becoming more knowledgeable about their children's interaction with computers and more directly involved for a variety of reasons. Paramount among these concerns is the safety of some Internet activities. Evening newscasts have warned parents about the predators who have lured children through conversing with them in chat rooms, as well as about the pornography that children can easily find on the Internet.

Parental involvement in children's computer activity is bringing with it increased levels of monetary power, and often a greater emphasis on the purchase and collection of computer items rather than the exercise of skill in developing programs for them or in otherwise using them creatively. Consumption rituals involve investment of symbolic value into inanimate objects, which are integrated into particular practices of public or personal significance, according to Grant McCracken. In many contexts, children are construed as performing computer technology rituals satisfactorily if they simply acquire and collect the technologies involved (for example, through Christmas or birthday gifts) and display a minimal level of proficiency at using them. Many CD-ROMs, for example, are more objects of collection and display than vehicles for skill development; the primary activity for children is to select the most appropriate CD-ROM to suit their personal interests and peer relations and to convince their parents to acquire it for them. A child can load a CD-ROM, engage in "educational" interaction with a character on the screen, and then unload the CD-ROM, all with a minimal level of computer skill or direct creative input.

Consumption-related rituals can be complex, however, and teach other kinds of lessons besides computer programming: children often collect software that has direct connections with their other media consumption activities, and consequently they learn that the same narratives can be delivered via different media modalities. For example, Barbie and Disney character CD-ROMs are becoming popular choices for children who want to coordinate their toy purchases or film or television viewing with the interactive software packages with which they play. In contrast, in some of the technology rituals of the 1970s and 1980s, children were deemed "successful" if they could perform the task of using a programming language (such as BASIC or LOGO) to develop a creative product and then exchanging those products with other children.

Consumption rituals can serve to reinforce various societal roles and reproduce social structures just as other kinds of rituals do. Through these consumption rituals, children learn that technology is a consumer item, and that the purpose of human interaction with computers is to collect various devices and then follow the programmed instructions, experimenting within their affordances and constraints. Families can work to de-emphasize consumption rituals, and can increase reflective engagement with computers, by stressing and rewarding children's creative interaction with computers as well as their conscious decisions not to use them. For example, adults can stimulate children to discuss and analyze their online experiences, helping them to create description and explanatory narratives about their activities.

The Internet: A New Realm for Childhood Rites of Passage

As just described, many families have already integrated Internet usage into their pastimes as well as their health and home maintenance efforts. Some children are "surfing the Internet" for other purposes, however. A great amount of concern about how children are using the Internet centers on the status rituals performed with computer networks. Apparently, some children access the Internet to conduct such rites of passage as obtaining bomb-making information as well as "adult" information and graphics and subsequently sharing this material with their peers (Oravec, "Countering"); other children establish relationships with mature-appearing individuals via chat rooms. Rites of passage signal transitions between various developmental stages (Gennep 30). The technical feat of assessing the Internet can itself establish that a young person is capable of reaching beyond the home to make contact with stores, libraries, and other organizations. However, the location and capture of graphics and information that are forbidden in some way are especially effective in demonstrating that the child has acquired adult capabilities and tastes as well as the means of manifesting them. In a similar manner, establishing relationships with mature-appearing individuals via the Internet can apparently be used by children to signify that they have value to others outside the home. Technology-related status rituals are often similar to those found in noncomputer contexts—for example, the "pornography magazine" exchanges common among some teens or the alcohol consumption rituals of some teen peer groups described by Ellen Butler (48). The Internet adds new complexities and dangers to these rituals, as those who prey upon children can take advantage of the anonymity possible in computer network communications.

Widespread concern about this use of the Internet by children has resulted in the development and sale of a bevy of software packages that attempt to "filter" material deemed inappropriate, thus thwarting the effects of children who want to express themselves—and demonstrate their impending adulthood—by obtaining pornographic images or other materials forbidden by society. In effect, parental control mechanisms are also being commodified. Efforts to design and implement these filters should take into account the needs of many children to display their increasingly sophisticated abilities and distinguish themselves from other family members (especially younger siblings) through status rituals. Those who are blocked from certain sites can be steered toward other sites that are interesting and challenging though less offensive (sites that portray sports heroes or adventure situations, for instance). The groups that children form through computer network interaction can also be monitored so that they do not include adults who wish to take advantage of children; for example, with some commercial software packages, adults can monitor what electronic mail messages children send.

The forms of rites of passage that young people will undertake with computers are still emerging; the rites of passage just described are peer-centered, but status rituals that are more rooted in the family or other institutions, such as rituals that are comparable to graduations or baptisms, are also likely to develop. New ways for individuals to obtain status and signal life changes will emerge as computing technology becomes more ubiquitous.

Strategic Use of Technological Ritual in the Home and Classroom

A number of teachers have explored the strategic use of ritual to increase students' compliance with school standards and policies. For instance, Brian McCadden describes the use of ritual as a means of helping children make the transition between their everyday family roles and the role of student. Teachers, as well as many other kinds of employees, engage in their own workplace rituals, as the structure of routine faculty meetings reinforces school structures as well as the roles of various participants (Cameron 57–58; Riehl 91). Even the standard handwriting methods of the past were instilled with strong ritualistic elements designed to reinforce such values as conformity and attention to detail (Boyd 436–437). Some rituals can be designed to be attractive to youth who are uninterested in other kinds of school activities. For example, many schools have utilized sports, music, and theater programs in part as ways to foster the compliance of children with specific sets of rules and procedures. Many students who are reluctant to follow school rules willingly comply with the rituals and routines imposed by baseball or soccer.

In the advent of readily available computer technology, educators have new means for creating classroom rituals. These rituals are buttressed not just with the teacher's own charisma or the force of school regulation but also with the high value our society places on computing. Merely by going through the specific steps needed to start up a personal computer, students learn that technologies will generally not work unless certain basic sequences are followed. Even if these sequences are boring and time-consuming to administer, they are supposedly required for the operation of the computer. Often, the line between routines that are required for computer operation and those that are specified by the teacher in order to establish daily routine is thin. For example, a number of teachers begin and end the school day by having their students perform superfluous computer operations such as start-up and shutdown procedures for the PCs in their classrooms—even though some experts advise that leaving a computer on overnight is less damaging. By starting the day with a booting up of a computer—rather than less precise but more human morning rituals—children learn to associate computing with certain everyday educational routines.

Other classroom technology rituals may involve information collection and analysis routines of the kinds that are often found in workplaces (Feldman & March 171–172). Just as many employees collect and process massive quantities of information that will probably never be directly used in decision making, students strive to gain skill in gathering and massaging data in the classroom. Teachers who choose to use technological rituals should be aware of how these rituals can disempower students from using information technology more creatively and conscientiously, as well as from learning when to apply nontechnological means for addressing problems. Many educators consider the introduction of computer technology in the schools as a "moral imperative" and are working for its widespread adoption (Shields 27–30)—so the drawbacks as well as benefits of computer technology rituals should be scrutinized carefully.

A number of psychologists as well as writers in the popular press have focused on the role of parents in creating psychologically "healthy" and rewarding family rituals (Fintushel; Bria). Parents who wish to structure household rituals with the use of computer technology will face a number of problems. The frustrations of dealing with technology (such as those just portrayed) make stable and predictable routines less likely. Many children are still more competent than their parents in dealing with some aspects of computers and networking. Parents engage in power struggles when they attempt to construct a stable mealtime ritual (Grieshaber 649–652); efforts that involve something as complex as computing technology in general bode even larger difficulties. Computing and information-related rituals can indeed play an important role in family existence, however, merging powerful cognitive and affective elements. For instance, the evening ritual of watching the television news together is still a part of many families' lives (Selberg 3–10), linking the comforting routine of shared meals with banter about current issues. The dimensions that computer technology rituals will take as interactivity becomes an increasingly salient part of everyday life will provide challenges as well as opportunities for families.

Some Conclusions and Reflections

Many years ago, Henry David Thoreau characterized individuals as being heavily influenced if not owned by their possessions (5–14); in a comparable way, technologies such as virtual pets and electronic schedulers can capture their owners' attention and draw them into elaborate technology rituals. These rituals can bring comfort and a sense of meaning into daily life, whatever their direct utilitarian value. According to Seymour Papert, many children are apparently highly motivated to learn how to work with computers, however intricate the details of such activities. However, the dystopian vision of children who are controlled and pacified by a computer-based companion or overseer can also emerge from this analysis. Theodore Roszak writes, "It would surely be a sad mistake to intrude some small number of pedestrian computer skills upon the education of the young in ways that blocked out the inventive powers that created this astonishing technology in the first place" (244). Children may indeed master dozens and perhaps hundreds of computer commands and routines in their roles in computer rituals, but at the same time they are becoming shaped by the process of engaging in these rituals. They are learning to associate "education" and "interaction" with sets of computer routines and procedures.

A number of recent technology rituals, both at the childhood and adult levels, emphasize the purchase and use of particular items, as wide ranges of sophisticated technological products become available to the everyday consumer. To assert that these rituals are best viewed as consumption rituals is not to diminish their complexity or importance, however. The "state of the art" in terms of technology changes quickly, and the very effort to comprehend these changes can be a struggle. Consumption is a complex activity that involves a myriad of interactions with particular objects, along with the basic cultural symbols and concepts with which they are linked. Consumption rituals involving fashion apparel, for example, incorporate a series of activities involving the acquisition and display of various articles of clothing, each of which is associated with leisure, commerce, traditional ceremonies, or other realms. Learning how to engage in consumption rituals in ways that are in synch with societal norms and values yet somewhat expressive of individual tastes is a lifelong activity. Consuming computer technology is a very special kind of consumption, involving the ability to both interpret and respond in appropriate ways to a particular device's constraints and affordances.

Through their use of computing, children today, along with their parents, are becoming increasingly savvy consumers of information and interactivity. Rituals involving such consumption often involve the collection and use of readily available consumer items—but they can also draw participants to seek out and examine other stimulating commodities and related activities. For example, in their efforts to partake of the full range of Barbie doll–related activities, children and their parents may explore various CD-ROMs and Internet sites and perhaps soon engage in virtual reality; the influences of the corporations involved in the production and distribution of Barbie-related paraphernalia expand in the process. Through their absorption in these rituals, children display their sensitivity to particular societal values.

Children are entering a world in which they will be responding in their everyday activities to machines as well as to people, with the distinction between the two types of response becoming increasingly hazy. Children learn very early in their lives to talk to machines—such as answering machines and pagers—as if they were addressing human beings. Through playing with such toys as Gigapets, Tamagotchis, and Furbys, they are becoming prepared to understand some aspects of person-machine interaction as well as the speeded-up time frames of computer-assisted life. Through computer rituals, they also learn about societal consumption patterns concerning technologies (such as the rapidity of technological obsolescence). Fads fade quickly, and the virtual toys of the future are likely to replace quickly those of the recent past. Although many of today's children are involved with technology rituals through purchase and collection of technology gear rather than through computer programming, some major—and often painful—lessons are nonetheless being imparted about the rigors of engaging with machines. For example, if one does not tend to one's Gigapet properly (with the suitable input at the appropriate time), it will die. Many children are also learning at an early age about the unrelenting demands involved in updating electronic schedulers and performing backups for computer systems, lessons that prepare them for participation in various institutions. They learn how control systems can permeate everyday household life and subsequently draw individuals into particular technology rituals.

An understanding of how children become involved in computer technology rituals in peer and family circles can help in our efforts to educate them in constructive and creative uses of technology. As an increasing number of households attempt to integrate computing into their everyday home activities, we will also see new kinds of family rituals—including those that are linked to interactive toys and to traditional holidays and ceremonies, or perhaps those that explore new ground. As computer technology innovations such as new kinds of virtual reality and voice recognition devices are introduced in the marketplace, they will most likely provide yet another set of artifacts with which to enact childhood—and adult—rituals.

WORKS CITED

Boyd, Richard. "Mechanical Correctness and Ritual in the Late Nineteenth-Century Composition Classroom." *Rhetoric Review* 11.2 (1998): 436–455.

Bria, Gina. "The Power of Rituals." *Working Mother* 18.12 (1995): 28.

Bruess, Carol, and Judy Pearson. "Interpersonal Rituals in Marriage and Adult Friendship." *Communication Monographs* 64.1 (1997): 25–47.

Butler, Ellen. "Alcohol Use by College Students: A Rites of Passage Ritual." *NASPA Journal* 31.1 (1993): 48–55.

Cameron, Katherine. "Workplace Rituals Enhance Productivity." *HR Magazine* 43.2 (1998): 57–61.

Driver, Thomas. *The Magic of Ritual.* New York: Harper Collins, 1991.

Featherstone, Michael. *Consumer Culture and Postmodernism.* London: Sage, 1991.

Feldman, Martha, and James March. "Information in Organizations as Signal and Symbol." *Administrative Science Quarterly* 26 (1981): 171–186.

Fiese, Barbara. "Family Rituals in the Early Stages of Parenting." *Journal of Marriage and the Family* 55.3 (1993): 633–642.

Fintushel, Noelle. "Everyday Rituals." *Parents* 72.8 (1997): 112.

Gennep, Arnold van. *The Rites of Passage.* Trans. Monika B. Vizedom and Gabrielle L. Caffe. Chicago: University of Chicago Press, 1960.

Grieshaber, Susan. "Mealtime Rituals: Power and Resistance in the Construction of Mealtime Rules." *British Journal of Sociology* 48.4 (1997): 649–667.

Grimes, Ronald. *Ritual Criticism: Case Studies in Its Practice, Essays on Its Theory.* Columbia: University of South Carolina Press, 1990.

McCadden, Brian. *Let's Get Our Houses in Order: The Role of Transitional Rituals in Constructing Moral Kindergartners.* ERIC Document Reproduction Service, 1996. ED405096.

McCracken, Grant. *The Culture of Consumption.* Bloomington: Indiana University Press, 1991.

Neville, Gwen. "Learning Culture through Ritual: The Family Reunion." *Anthropology and Education Quarterly* 15.2 (1984): 151–166.

Oravec, Jo Ann. "Countering Violent and Hate-Related Materials on the Internet: Strategies for Classrooms and Communities." *Teacher Education,* 35.3 (2000): 34–45.

———. "Interactive Toys and Children's Education: Strategies for Educators and Parents." *Childhood Education,* 77.2 (2000/2001): 81–85.

———. *Virtual Individuals, Virtual Groups: Human Dimensions of Groupware and Computer Networking.* New York: Cambridge University Press, 1996.

———. "Working Hard and Playing Hard: Constructive Recreation in the Workplace." *Journal of General Management* 24.3 (1999): 1–12.

Otnes, Cele, and Linda Scott. "Something Old, Something New: Exploring the Interaction between Ritual and Advertising." *Journal of Advertising* 25.1 (1996): 33–51.

Papert, Seymour. *The Children's Machine.* New York: Basic Books, 1993.

Pereira, Joseph. "Shutting Up Furby: Talkative Toy Meets 'Deep Sleep.'" *Wall Street Journal,* March 12, 1999: B1.

Picard, Rosalind. *Affective Computing.* Cambridge, MA: MIT Press, 1997.

Riehl, Carolyn. "We Gather Together: Work, Discourse, and Constitutive Social Action in Elementary School Faculty Meetings." *Educational Administration Quarterly* 34.1 (1998): 91–126.

Rook, Dennis. "The Ritual Dimension of Consumer Behavior." *Journal of Consumer Research* 12 (1985): 251–264.

Roszak, Theodore. *The Cult of Information.* Berkeley: University of California Press, 1994.

Selberg, Torunn. "Television and the Ritualization of Everyday Life." *Journal of Popular Culture* 26.4 (1993): 3–10.

Seligmann, Jean. "This Baby's Ready for Prime-Time." *Newsweek,* January 19, 131.3 (1998): 46.

Shields, Jean. "Educational Technology: A Moral Imperative." *Technology & Learning* 18.8 (1998): 27–30.

"Should Virtual Pets Die?" *Family PC* 4.10 (1997): 31.

Thompson, Michael. "Is There Life beyond Tamagotchi?" *Japan Times Weekly International Edition* 37.30 (1997): 15.

Thoreau, Henry. *Walden; or, Life in the Woods.* New York: Houghton Mifflin, 1906.

Turkle, Sherry. *The Second Self: Computers and the Human Spirit.* New York: Simon and Schuster, 1984.

Wallendorf, Melanie, and Eric Arnould. "'We Gather Together.' Consumption Rituals of Thanksgiving Day." *Journal of Consumer Research* 18 (1991): 3–31.

CONTRIBUTORS

VINCENT DIGIROLAMO is Assistant Professor of History at Baruch College, City University of New York. He has a doctorate in Newsboyology from Princeton University.

LEONA W. FISHER is Associate Professor and former Chair of the English Department at Georgetown University and co-founder and former Director of the Women's Studies Program. She has published on Victorian theatre, children's literature, and feminist topics and is currently working on two book-length projects: one on Nancy Drew, the Girl Scouts, and constructions of American girlhood from the 1930s to the 1980s; the other, a study of genre and narrative voice in American children's books of the last two centuries.

KATHY MERLOCK JACKSON is Batten Professor of Communications at Virginia Wesleyan College, where she teaches courses in media studies and coordinates the communications program. She received her B.A. from West Virginia University and her M.A. from Ohio State University, both in English, and her Ph.D. from Bowling Green State University in American culture. She is the author of two books, *Images of Children in American Film: A Socio-Cultural Analysis* and *Walt Disney: A Bio-Bibliography*, as well as several articles and reviews. Her main areas of interest are children's media and culture and animation, and she has completed editing a book of Walt Disney's interviews, which will be published by the University Press of Mississippi. She also edits *The Journal of American Culture* and writes a monthly column on television for *Port Folio Weekly*, a local lifestyle magazine.

JYOTSNA (JOSI) M. KALAVAR is Associate Professor at Penn State New Kensington. Her recent book, *The Asian Indian Elderly in America: An Examination of Values, Family, and Life Satisfaction*, is a portrayal of the relocation experience in late life for Asian Indians. Her substantive areas of interest are acculturation

269

and cross-cultural experiences, intergenerational relations, rural aging, and ethnogerontology.

ELLEN J. NAROTZKY KENNEDY is a professor at the University of St. Thomas in St. Paul, Minnesota, where she teaches both in business and sociology. Her research interests include Jewish studies, immigration, and cross-cultural business ethics. She has published articles in a variety of areas including business, marketing, education, immigration, and ethics. She has taught in Australia, China, Poland, Ukraine, Sweden, and Russia and has studied Jewish communities in various parts of the world. She has given many talks on Jews of the Diaspora and is very interested in issues affecting Jewish continuity.

BARBARA MARTINSON is the Buckman Professor of Design Education in the Department of Design, Housing, and Apparel at the University of Minnesota, Twin Cities. Her research interests include design education, design and cognition, design history, and usability issues with designed objects. She actively exhibits design and art work nationally. Her B.A. is in English literature from Bethel College, and her M.A. and Ph.D. are in design from the University of Minnesota.

JAMIE MCMINN holds a Ph.D. from the University of Pittsburgh and is Assistant Professor of Psychology at Westminster College. His specific interests are in group processes and dynamics, especially as they relate to the perception of groups as entities. His research has focused on how personality differences affect people's perceptions of and behaviors toward groups, and how groups can manipulate how "real" they seem to others.

RAY MERLOCK holds a Ph.D. and MA from Ohio University. He is a Professor of Mass Communications at the University of South Carolina Upstate, where he teaches media history, theory, and production courses and coordinates internships. He has served as a weekly television, radio, and newspaper reviewer rating current film releases and has published in academic journals on *Casablanca* and on various aspects of the Western. A longtime member of the Popular Culture and American Culture Associations, he currently serves on the advisory board of *The Journal of American Culture*.

JO ANN ORAVEC is an associate professor in the College of Business and Economics at the University of Wisconsin–Whitewater. She received her M.B.A., M.A., M.S., and Ph.D. degrees from the University of Wisconsin–Madison. She has taught computer information systems and public policy at Baruch College of the City University of New York and also taught in the School of Business and the Computer Sciences Department at UW–Madison. In the 1990s, she chaired the Privacy Council of the State of Wisconsin, the nation's first state-level council dealing with information technology and privacy issues. She has written several books (including *Virtual Individuals, Virtual Groups: Human Dimensions of Groupware and Computer Networking*) and dozens of articles on computing technology and social issues. She has worked for public television and developed software along with her academic ventures.

H. ALAN PICKRELL is Professor Emeritus at Emory & Henry College and has published numerous articles on juvenile series books in *Yellowback Library*, *Dime Novel Roundup*, and *Newsboy*. In 1995, he was a presenter at the Library of Congress–sponsored symposium on series, dime novels, and pulp books. His paper, "From Immorality to Immortality: Character Transplant from Victorian Romances to the Oz series," appears in both published works of the proceedings: *Pioneers, Passionate Ladies* and *Private Eyes and Primary Sources and Original Works*. He has written numerous work-for-hire articles on drama and playwrights for such reference books as *Masterplots* and *Cyclopedia of World Authors*. He has acted in and directed more than five hundred community, educational, professional, and semi-professional productions in his native Nashville, in Bristol, Tennessee, and Virginia, and at Emory & Henry College. A frequent speaker at inservice meetings and meetings of civic groups, he is the former Chair of the Dime Novel, Pulps, and Series area of the Popular Culture Association. Comments concerning this article should be addressed to H. Alan Pickrell, 223 King Street, Abingdon, VA 24210 (alanpckrll@yahoo.com).

SALLY SUGARMAN teaches childhood studies at Bennington College. Her research and teaching focus on children's culture, media studies, and children's literature. She was formerly Chair of the Vermont State Board of Education and Director of the Bennington College Early Childhood Center. She co-edited *Sherlock Holmes: Victorian Sleuth to Modern Hero*. She regularly reviews for *CHOICE* magazine and for *Deadly Pleasure*.

SABRINA THOMAS received her bachelor's degree in psychology from Tuskegee University, her master's degree from the University of Rochester in early childhood education, and her doctorate from the University of North Carolina–Greensboro in the area of human development and family studies. She has studied Spanish language and culture at the University of Salamanca in Salamanca, Spain. Her current research interests relate to children's early development of racial knowledge. She has several articles currently under review that examine the significance of doll play and the early racial knowledge of women born between 1896 and 1950. Other research interests are the area of family policy, and in 2002 she studied China's One-Child Policy while participating in a Faculty Fulbright to China summer program. She serves as

Vice President of the Durham Chapter of the National Black Child Development Institute, is Second Vice-President of the North Carolina–American Association of Family, and is currently the Coordinator of the Child Development and Family Relations area in the Department of Human Sciences at North Carolina Central University. The research for her chapter was made possible by an American Association of University Women (AAUW) Educational Grant.

ANNE TUOMINEN received her Ph.D. in sociology from the University of Washington. She is currently a part-time lecturer there, in both sociology and the Distance Learning Division. Her research interests include multilingualism, immigrant culture, sociology of family, ethnic tourism, and the Baltic region. While she passes down the ethnic family rituals of her Finnish-American childhood to her young twin sons, she is working on a project based on memoirs of bicultural and bilingual childhoods. Comments on her chapter may be sent to atuominen@mindspring.com.

LUISE VAN KEUREN is Assistant Professor of English at California University of Pennsylvania. She received her Ph.D. in English from the University of Delaware with a specialty in Early American Studies. Her research collecting hundreds of sampler verses reflects her interests in American girls and women and the role of poetry in American life. She recently authored a contribution on samplers in *Girlhood in America*.

MARK I. WEST is Professor of English at the University of North Carolina at Charlotte, where he teaches courses on children's literature and serves as the Associate Dean for General Education. He has written or edited a dozen books that deal with various aspects of children's literature, including *Children, Culture, and Controversy; Trust Your Children: Voices against Censorship in Children's Literature; Roald Dahl; Wellsprings of Imagination: The Homes of Children's Authors; Everyone's Guide to Children's Literature;* and *Psychoanalytic Responses to Children's Literature* co-authored with Lucy Rollin. He is also the editor of *The Five Owls* and the book review editor of the *Children's Literature Association Quarterly*.

INDEX

Ackerman, Diane, 143
Adorno, Theodor, 94
adults: ceremonies *vs.* rituals of childhood, 126–27; childhood innocence
as concept of, 236–37; as childlike
in contemporary U.S., 136–37; depictions of in children's literature,
192; disguise and misbehavior by,
222–23; forms of play for, 124; nostalgia for childhood, 127–28, 136;
social "disguises" employed by, 215,
217–18; virtual pets used by, 256.
See also parents
The Adventures of Tom Sawyer (Clemens),
189; audience for, 201; as "boys'
book," 207–8; children as outsiders
in, 201; female characters in, 195,
207–8; gender in, 210nn9–11; Indians in, 211n14; liminality and
marginality in, 194–95; literature
as source of ritual in, 195–98;
other in, 196; performance rituals
in, 195–96; race in, 192, 194, 196,
198, 209n6; reintegration of the
liminal or subversive in, 207; "surrogation" in, 194, 209–10n8; word
play in, 195, 196
advertising: for dolls, 112–13; marketing
to children, 261, 265–66; media
and merchandising of toys, 236,
240, 245–47, 261–62, 265–66
agon (competition or contest), 125

Ainsworth and Mahler, 3–4
alea (chance), 125, 130, 131
Allen, Rex, 244, 249
The Ambiguity of Play (Sutton-Smith),133
America: "American" values in *The
Great Brain* (Fitzgerald), 202–3; as
child-centered society, 10, 15; edu-
cation as value in, 108; individual-
ism as ideal in, 212n23; westerns in
culture of, 235–36
American Children's Folklore (Bronner), 9
Ames, Chris, 146
anima/animus, 224–25, 227
archetypes, 95; shadow archetype, 218–
19, 222, 224–25, 226
Aries, Philippe, 5–6
Army games, 133, 134, 135
Autry, Gene, 244–45

bar and *bat mitzvot:* as affirmation of
child's success, 63–64, 69; "chain
of tradition" custom during, 69;
education as value and, 61–64, 66;
as "end of childhood," 60; girls
and celebration of *bat mitzvot*, 60,
72, 75n1; Hebrew literacy as central to, 58, 70; integrative function
of, 67–71; intergenerational continuity and, 69, 70, 72, 73; parties as
celebrations of, 71, 73–74; preparation for, 61–64; as professional
preparation, 66; among Reform

273

transmission of children's games or
rituals and, 7
Oravec, Jo Ann, 233–34; article by, 252–
66; contributor's note, 270–71
Ortel, William Henry "Dutch Hiney"
(newsboy), 174–75
other: in *The Adventures of Tom Sawyer*,
196; play as assuming role of, 193;
race and the, 194

Pandey, Raj, 42
Papert, Seymour, 259, 264–65
parents: *bar* or *bat mitzvot* and experiences of, 64–65, 68, 73; as children, 35–36; depictions in illustrations, 102; emotional expression
by, 37–38; in ethnic families, 28–
29; gender stereotypes in depictions of, 97; literary rituals and, 34–
38, 50; moral or values education
and, 89–90; perpetuation of ethnic
rituals by, 28; play and roles of, 125;
role of, 3–4; *samskāras*, roles in, 44,
46, 47, 49, 50, 51; supervision of
children's interaction with technology, 260, 261–62, 264
patterns: of daily events (time), 8–9;
economy of behavior and routine,
253; as foundation for social relationships, 3–4; pet care routines,
258–59; repetition and education,
79; in rituals, 126; rituals as customary behaviors, 95; *vs.* spontaneity in games and play, 133; technology and routine behaviors, 255;
westerns as formulaic or ritualistic,
242
Peck, George W., 178
Perkins, Myla, 112–13
persona, as defined by Jung, 217–18, 222
pets, 258–59
Piaget, Jean, 125, 134
Pickrell, H. Alan, 189–90; article by, 215–
28; contributor's note, 271
play: Caillois's categories of, 125; computer technologies and, 233; dirty

play, 135–36; disguises and, 222; *vs.*
exploration, 125; gender identity
and, 8; group identity formation
and, 129; magical thinking and,
126; reconciliation of opposites,
125; as ritual form or ritual work,
193; as sacred activity, 125, 130, 131;
as socialization, 126; as stylized,
128; as subversive, 124–25, 126, 129,
135–36; theories of, 193–95, 199; as
work, 193–94
poetry, about newsboys, 172
Poltarnees, Welleran, 8–9
Pope, Alexander, 88
Poppy Ott (fictional character in book
series), 222
popular culture: advertisements for toys,
112–13; back-to school as iconic
image in, 79, 93–108, *96, 98, 99,
101, 103, 104, 105, 107;* as "easy" to
access by the uncritical, 94; magazine illustrations as public art, 94;
weddings in, 145–47. *See also* media
Postman, Neil, 6, 136
potter's field, 178, 180, 181–82
poverty, 160, 174
Powell-Hopson, Darlene, 113
power: children as powerless, 136;
games linked to, 110; during play,
126; play as exercise of power by
children, 131
pranks or tricks, 37, 135–36
pregnancy, rituals related to, 43
Preston, Sam, 148
Prince, William Meade, illustrations
by, *101*
promises. *See* oaths and promises
psychology: Jung, theories of, 189, 217–
19, 224–25; theories of play, 125
public mourning, 176–77
Puritans, 6

Quindlan, Anna, 4

race: in *The Adventures of Tom Sawyer*,
192, 194, 196, 198, 209n6; African

A RAY AND PAT BROWNE BOOK

Murder on the Reservation: American Indian Crime Fiction
Ray B. Browne

Profiles of Popular Culture: A Reader
Edited by Ray B. Browne

Goddesses and Monsters: Women, Myth, Power, and Popular Culture
Jane Caputi

Mystery, Violence, and Popular Culture
John G. Cawelti

Baseball and Country Music
Don Cusic

Popular Witchcraft: Straight from the Witch's Mouth, 2nd edition
Jack Fritscher

The Essential Guide to Werewolf Literature
Brian J. Frost

Popular Culture Theory and Methodology: A Basic Introduction
Edited by Harold E. Hinds, Jr., Marilyn F. Motz and Angela M. S. Nelson

Rituals and Patterns in Children's Lives
Edited by Kathy Merlock Jackson

Images of the Corpse: From the Renaissance to Cyberspace
Edited by Elizabeth Klaver

Walking Shadows: Orson Welles, William Randolph Hearst, and Citizen Kane
John Evangelist Walsh

Spectral America: Phantoms and the National Imagination
Edited by Jeffrey Andrew Weinstock

King of the Cowboys, Queen of the West: Roy Rogers and Dale Evans
Raymond E. White